Sedation at the End-of-life: An Interdisciplinary Approach

Philosophy and Medicine

VOLUME 116

Founding Co-Editor
Stuart F. Spicker

Senior Editor

H. Tristram Engelhardt, Jr., *Department of Philosophy, Rice University, and Baylor College of Medicine, Houston, Texas*

Associate Editor

Lisa M. Rasmussen, *Department of Philosophy, University of North Carolina at Charlotte, North Carolina*

CATHOLIC STUDIES IN BIOETHICS

For further volumes:
http://www.springer.com/series/6414

Paulina Taboada

Editor

Sedation at the End-of-life:
An Interdisciplinary Approach

 Springer

Editor
Paulina Taboada
Center for Bioethics and Department of Internal Medicine, Faculty of Medicine
Pontificia Universidad Católica de Chile
Santiago, Chile

ISSN 0376-7418   ISSN 2215-0080 (electronic)
ISBN 978-94-017-9105-2   ISBN 978-94-017-9106-9 (eBook)
DOI 10.1007/978-94-017-9106-9
Springer Dordrecht Heidelberg New York London

Library of Congress Control Number: 2014946068

Printed on acid-free paper

Springer is part of Springer Science+Business Media (www.springer.com)

Preface

The purpose of this book is to analyze several clinical, ethical and legal questions related to the use of sedation at the end-of-life. Indeed, it focuses mainly on seven ethically relevant questions related to palliative sedation (PS). These questions are addressed by an interdisciplinary team of internationally renowned specialists in the fields of bioethics and palliative medicine. Each of the contributors analyses a particular question or dimension of the general topic from the perspective of his/her respective discipline (palliative medicine, bioethics, law, philosophy and theology). Thus, the book as a whole offers helpful clinical, ethical and legal criteria to provide guidance to health care professionals, patients and their relatives in the adequate use of PS. Among them are, for instance, the specific goals of care at the end-of-life; the inviolability of human life; the respect for the dignity of the dying; the ethical principles of therapeutic proportionality, double effect, participation in decision-making, etc.

The book's content is the result of the contributions presented at an International Seminar held at the Pontificia Universidad Católica de Chile (August 2011). During this event, each of the contributors received comments and suggestions from the other experts to improve the final draft of their text. This mutual feedback enabled not only the elaboration of a revised version of each chapter, but also the possibility of bringing the experts into a collaborative dialogue. The improved versions of the chapters were in turn submitted to external peer review. Taking into account the reviewers comments, each author produced the final version of his/her text, which is the one included in this book.

This fruitful international academic collaboration took place in the context of research projects, funded by the Chilean Government's National Funds for the Development of Science and Technology (FONDECYT: Fondo Nacional de Desarrollo Científico y Tecnológico, Project No. 1110721) and the Pontificia Universidad Católica de Chile (Projects No. DGP08-120A002 and DGP09-PADH016), as well as by the Manuel Velasco-Suárez Award for Excellence in Bioethics 2010 (granted to the Editor by the Pan American Health and Education Foundation (PAHEF), the Pan American Health Organization (PAHO) and the

Mexican Government). Hence, the book represents a tribute of gratitude from the Editor for the generous funding received from these institutions.

Sedation has been widely used in medicine since a long time, for instance to alleviate pain and discomfort associated with invasive procedures and surgery, as well as to treat extremely agitated psychiatric patients. Nevertheless, its use for symptom-control in advanced stages of incurable diseases was first published in 1990 and it was not until 2000 that the term 'palliative sedation' (PS) was coined. Since then, sedation has been progressively accepted as a therapeutic tool in the care for dying patients (palliative medicine).

'Palliative sedation' is currently considered to be a last resort therapeutic tool for the management of severe, refractory symptoms at the end-of-life. Indeed, the use of sedatives to alleviate the suffering caused by severe symptoms that have not responded to the usual therapeutic interventions seems to be clinically prudent and ethically correct. Nevertheless, in spite of the improvement of medical knowledge related to the use of palliative sedation during the last decade, available empirical evidence is still limited and important points of controversy persist. Indeed, a review of the medical literature suggests that the prevalence and the spectrum of the indications of sedation in the terminally-ill has been progressively expanding over the past years, including nowadays its more frequent use for the management of psycho-spiritual symptoms (e.g. 'existential suffering'). Moreover, the use of sedatives is associated with some adverse side-effects and/or risks, such as respiratory depression and low blood pressure. Although the literature shows that these risks and adverse effects do not occur when sedatives are used by professionals in an appropriate way, they may indeed occur when using sedatives in inappropriately high doses and/or when the dose is increased too rapidly. In this context, some authors have expressed their concerns about the occurrence of imprudent uses, sub-standard applications and actual abuses of sedation at the end-of-life, which may represent a form of 'slow euthanasia' or 'euthanasia in disguise'.

Hence, available empirical evidence about the current use of sedation at the end-of-life raises a number of interesting and controversial clinical, ethical and legal questions. This book focuses mainly on seven ethically relevant questions, which represent its very *leitmotiv*. These questions are:

1. Whether there is an ethically sound difference between PS and euthanasia and physician-assisted suicide.
2. Whether the principle of double effect can be appropriately applied to justify the use of sedation in some cases at the end-of-life.
3. Whether PS might be ethically acceptable in the case of patients that are not imminently dying (agony).
4. Whether decisions to limit medically assisted nutrition and hydration are essentially linked to PS or whether they should be regarded as independent issues.
5. Whether sedation is an adequate response to 'existential suffering'.
6. Whether sedation could ever be used in the case of patients who are not able to give their informed consent (e.g. patients with cognitive impairment of diverse origins, etc.).

7. Whether clinical guidelines for the use of PS are desirable to orient health care professionals, patients and relatives in the adequate use of sedation at the end-of-life.

Actually, these are the questions that the different contributors address, analyzing the points in which a certain consensus about the adequate use of sedation at the end-of-life has already been reached, but also critically reflecting on aspects where important controversy still persists.

Introducing the reader to the current state of the debate, Taboada (Chap. 1) describes the clinical scenarios, the different terms/definitions and some of the existing guidelines for 'palliative sedation'. It becomes evident that the current debate includes a variety of aspects such as: (1) the definition and terminology (e.g. palliative, terminal, deep continuous sedation, palliative sedation to unconsciousness, etc.); (2) the types of sedation that are included under these expressions (intermittent vs. continuous, mild vs. deep); (3) the clinical indications (physical symptoms vs. existential suffering); (4) the concomitant administration vs. withdrawal of medically assisted nutrition and hydration; and (5) the ethical foundations of its clinical applications and its difference with euthanasia and physician-assisted suicide.

Referring to the framework provided by the European Association for Palliative Care (EAPC), Taboada alerts the reader about the existence of inadequate uses, substandard applications and abuses of 'palliative sedation' in terminally-ill patients. A critical analysis of some of the existing guidelines suggests the need for re-thinking the clinical, ethical and theological foundations of this therapeutic intervention at the end-of-life, a task that is successively undertaken by other contributors.

Sullivan (Chap. 2) analyses the role of sedation in the context of the broader 'goals of care' at the end-of-life. Based on a reflection on the anthropological and ethical foundations of the practice of medicine as such, Sullivan proposes to shift the focus of the ethical discussions about 'palliative sedation' to a deeper analysis of 'goals of care' at the end-of-life. He suggests that this shift can help to clarify the distinction between ethically appropriate and inappropriate applications of palliative sedation.

This author argues that 'palliative sedation' should share certain features with ethically appropriate 'goals of care' in palliative care generally. And since these goals preclude intentionally hastening death, he states that the ethical distinction between palliative care and euthanasia is important, and that appropriate 'palliative sedation' – as a set of practices distinct from euthanasia – is clinically achievable. In order to achieve this in practice, the author urges that beyond the development of clinical guidelines, there is also the distinct but equally important task of developing clinical tools and educational resources that teach clinicians how to formulate 'goals of care' regarding 'palliative sedation'.

The concrete way in which 'palliative sedation' is actually performed in clinical practice is addressed by Walker (Chap. 3). In fact, the author gives the reader a bed-side perspective on palliative sedation for the treatment of refractory symptoms, most notably agitated delirium and dyspnoea, which are the primary symptoms requiring palliative sedation.

This author also describes the practices used at one of the world's leading cancer centres (namely the University of Texas' MD Anderson Cancer Center). He provides in this way an insight into the benefits and risks related to this clinical intervention and also a sense of the aspects that need to be carefully monitored when performing, in a responsible and prudent way, sedation at the end-of-life.

Although palliative sedation is most often used to relieve physical symptoms at the end-of-life, many guidelines for palliative sedation specify that 'existential suffering' is also a legitimate indication for this intervention. This is perhaps one of its most controversial indications. In fact, most of the chapters of this book deal with this issue in one way or the other. So, Rodin et al. (Chap. 4) focus specifically on 'existential suffering' as an indication for palliative sedation, with a consideration of the clinical and ethical questions and controversies which this practice may raise. These authors suggest that the validity of existential suffering as a criterion for palliative sedation is undermined by the ambiguity in its definition and by the practical difficulties in its assessment. Indeed, this term has been used by some to include virtually all psychological symptoms. The suggestion to limit this term to mortality-related concerns may not improve specificity in its usage, since mortality is inevitably a context that shapes all psychological concerns near the end-of-life.

It is interesting to note that Rodin et al. regard 'existential suffering' as a symptom that arises not exclusively 'within the patient', but also from the social context. Hence, they suggest that mobilizing support of the family, any others who may matter, and the multi-disciplinary palliative care team at the end-of-life may all help to diminish or alleviate existential suffering at the end-of-life. They even state that the occurrence of intolerable suffering at the end-of-life may be secondary to the failure to institute appropriate interventions earlier in the course of the disease. Thus, Rodin et al. consider that the use of deep continuous sedation until death to treat 'existential suffering' raises a number of ethical questions, for instance, that it may be regarded as a form of euthanasia in that it causes a 'social death' and the permanent loss of awareness at a crucial moment of a person's life. Moreover, they suggest that the use of deep continuous sedation can also become a covert form of 'slow euthanasia', particularly when the criteria of refractoriness and unresponsiveness to other interventions, including temporary sedation, have not been met. Hence, they conclude that the justification of palliative sedation for existential distress will require greater uniformity and clarification regarding the definitions of existential distress, the criteria for intolerability and refractoriness to treatment, and an early routine referral to mental health experts for the evaluation and treatment of existential distress.

In Chap. 5, Boyle shows how the ethical principle of double effect can help to clarify the moral issues surrounding palliative sedation, specifically by drawing the distinction between hastening a patient's death intentionally or as a consequence of the unintended side effects of sedatives. Aware of the fact that this traditional ethical principle has been frequently misunderstood or misapplied, before developing its application to palliative sedation, Boyle gives an accurate account of its origins and essential content. This author argues that in its application to end-of-life care, double effect states that it can be morally good to shorten a patient's life as a foreseen and accepted but unintended side effect of an action undertaken for a good reason, even if it is agreed that intentionally killing the patient or shortening the patient's life is wrong. Nevertheless, certain conditions need to be fulfilled. Following Anscombe, Boyle reformulates the conditions of double effect as follows: that the action having the bad side effect be good in itself (that is, independent of the bad side effect), that it be done for a good purpose, that the action causing the bad side effect be proportionate to the evil caused, and most importantly the intentional condition – that the bad effect not be a means to the good effect.

It is interesting to remark that, when dealing with the specific question about the moral justification of the use of sedation at the end-of-life, Boyle analyses separately two problems: the suppression of consciousness as such on the one hand and the risk of shortening life on the other. He thinks that the application of double effect proceeds in the latter, but not in the former. Nevertheless, in the case of the intentional suppression of consciousness, the author introduces a further interesting distinction. He states that, although the principle of double effect does not usually prove to be necessary for justifying the ethical permissibility of suppressing a patient's consciousness in the context of the management of refractory symptoms, its application is actually relevant to those cases in which sedation might prevent the patient from executing important moral and religious duties at the end-of-life. So, Boyle remarks that in such cases the prevention of the opportunity for executing moral duties should occur only as an unintended side effect of the treatment, if there is a proportionately serious reason for doing so. This distinction is relevant to cases of 'existential suffering', which is an issue that the author also explores in this chapter.

With regards to the problem of shortening a patient's life through the use of sedatives at the end-of-life, Boyle emphasizes the importance of the distinction between intending and foreseeing. He specifies that although the medical literature suggests that the risk of actually hastening a patient's death through the use of sedatives is not the rule, but rather the exception, double effect can indeed be applied to justify its use, but only if the expected shortening of life caused by the sedation is a side effect and not an intended result.

So, Boyle's conclusion is that "double effect is an important tool both clinically and in public debate for situating end-of-life treatments, and for getting clear about whether or not actions that look like intentional killing really are that. In the light of that clarification, the acceptance of terminal sedation as a part of palliative care for the dying is not precedent for euthanasia, although some questionable uses of terminal sedation may in fact be intentional killing."

Similar questions connected to the precise content, extension and applicability of the principle of double effect to the case of sedation at the end-of-life are further explored by Miranda (Chap. 6). In agreement with Boyle, this author emphasizes that the principle of double effect has been frequently misinterpreted and misapplied, due to a lack of a proper understanding of its philosophical foundations and specific content. Hence, he accurately examines the type of actions that need to be justified by this principle, stating that only those acts that cause effects or a state of affairs that would be never lawful to directly intend – either as an end or as a means – fall under the field of application of double effect. In doing so, the author stresses the importance of both the distinction between intended and foreseen effects and the idea that this principle presupposes the existence of intrinsically bad actions, which would be always morally wrong to pursue.

Miranda reviews the interpretation of the principle offered by contemporary authors within the Natural Law tradition (such as Grisez, Finnis and Boyle) and takes into account two different types of criticisms that have been made to their position: Aulisio's criticism, stating that double effect can be also applied outside an 'absolutist' tradition, and Anderson's objection, suggesting that even within an 'absolutist' context, double effect does also apply to the sort of harms that it would be lawful to directly intend. The analysis of these criticisms gives him the opportunity to clarify important points concerning the precise content and proper field of application of the principle.

After making these important clarifications, the author analyses in depth the question of whether the administration of drugs that reduce a person's awareness are the type of actions that need to be justified by the principle of double effect. His accurate analysis of the scope of application of this principle leads him to the conclusion that palliative sedation does not need to be justified by double effect reasoning, but rather by the principle of totality and proportionality in medical care. In other words, he suggests that in order to justify the act of reducing a patient's level of consciousness – which might be considered as a bad effect – it is sufficient to have proportionately serious reason. Like Boyle, Miranda does not see a serious reason to hold that reduction of consciousness as such is an effect that would be always wrong to directly intend as a means for a proportionately serious clinical necessity. Nevertheless, he specifies that if sedation would hasten a patient's death, the application of the principle of double effect would be necessary to justify this bad effect, as it corresponds to the type of effects that would be always wrong to directly intend. Similarly this occurs with the total and permanent abolition of a patient's consciousness, which also corresponds to a state of affairs which would never be lawful to directly intend.

In Chap. 7, Keown offers an overview of some basic concepts central to a legal and ethical analysis of palliative sedation. In particular, this author deals with the concepts of 'sanctity of life', 'best interests' and 'autonomy' which are key to understanding when palliative sedation is legally and ethically defensible. The author suggests that only after these basic concepts have been soundly understood is it possible to address specific questions such as, for example, whether it is ethical and lawful to administer sedatives with intention to shorten a patient's life, or when the patient is not 'terminally ill', or as a response to 'existential suffering', etc.

Keown's proposal is that the most important concept underlying the ethical and legal analysis of palliative sedation is the 'inviolability of life'. Indeed, he argues that respect for the patient's autonomy – in spite of its evident importance – ought to be always subordinated to the respect due to basic human goods, among which human life is the first. In fact, it is a necessary condition for exercising freedom.

An interesting clarification in the context of the current debate about sedation at the end-of-life is Keown's distinction between medical judgments based on the benefits related to a patient's 'quality of life' and judgments about what can be considered as a 'beneficial quality of life'. According to this author, the former can have a place in medical decision-making, while the latter may result in arbitrary discrimination against certain types of patients and an eventual lack of respect for the inviolability of their lives.

In the context of drawing the ethical and legal difference between palliative sedation and euthanasia, Keown stresses the importance of distinguishing between 'direct' and 'oblique' intentions of our actions, a distinction that had been already addressed both by Boyle and Miranda in the previous chapters, as the difference between 'intended' and 'foreseen' effects of human actions. In accordance to his previous affirmation of the inviolability of human life as the most fundamental criterion to judge the ethical and legal justification of the use of sedatives at the end-of-life, Keown strongly rejects acts that directly intend to hasten a patient's death.

Given the fact that legal regulations vary from country to country and since the International Seminar that led to the preparation of this book was held in Chile, an analysis of the legal situation regarding palliative sedation in Chile was necessary. This task was undertaken by Vivanco (Chap. 8), who focused her analysis mainly on three questions: (1) whether palliative sedation is legally justifiable in the context of contemporary medicine, (2) whether it can be conceived as a patient's right, and (3) whether it can be distinguished from other legally non-admissible acts, such as euthanasia or medically assisted suicide (which are actually illegal in most countries).

This author argues that although in Chile there is no explicit legal regulation regarding either palliative sedation or euthanasia, the former can be considered as a part of the patient's right to adequate palliative care, while the latter would be considered illegal, as it is contrary to the Chilean Constitution. In order to draw such a clear-cut distinction between palliative sedation and euthanasia, the author analyses the differences between both according to: (1) the agent's intention, (2) the content of the informed consent, (3) the procedure, and (4) the expected result.

The interest of this chapter in the context of the overall aim of the book rests precisely in the fact that it provides an insight about the situation in Latin-American countries (exemplified in Chile), where little has been published about this subject. And it is certainly interesting to be aware of some cultural differences regarding these controversial issues.

An accurate exploration of the contextual history of end-of-life care is provided by Henry in Chap. 9, particularly as it relates to the contentious advent of sedation as a therapy of choice for the palliation of a subset of terminally-ill patients. This historical account enables both a better understanding of the need and potential use of clinical guidelines for sedation of terminally-ill patients and recommendations for future research in the field.

The author compares the practical orientations proposed by the main clinical guidelines, focusing his attention especially on the statements that relate to the seven ethically relevant questions that constitute the book's *leitmotiv*. It is interesting to note that there are actually some significant differences in the solutions proposed in different countries.

Henry suggests that the published literature to-date regarding the use of palliative sedation continues to identify inconsistencies and variances in application with regard to its prevalence in current practice, the overall effect (outcome) of sedation on the patient, the family and health care team, the practice and impact of providing (or not) hydration and nutrition in the dying process when sedation is employed, and the decision-making processes in place when this therapy is being used.

The author concludes that clinical tools (namely clinical protocols and pathways) derived from well established guidelines can improve the consistency and quality of care. In fact, he suggests that the main usefulness of guidelines, consensus statements and frameworks on palliative sedation is to help mitigate unnecessary and inappropriate uses of this therapy.

Henry's conclusion is strongly criticized by Scott (Chap. 10), who sustains a very critical standpoint on the publication of clinical guidelines, suggesting that they can have quite negative effects on judicious medical decision-making. Hence, the author insists on the need for education, to train medical personnel in the habit of making prudent clinical judgments in each particular situation. He states that although guidelines may have a role in clinical practice, they entail the risk of being used in a mechanical way that might end up substituting the individual's clinical and ethical reasoning when faced with difficult situations. Hence, the publication of PS guidelines cannot replace the need for a permanent education of health care professionals, patients and family members on sound criteria for appropriate decision-making regarding sedation at the end-of-life.

The chapter concludes by suggesting the current need for re-thinking the clinical, ethical and theological foundations of an adequate use of sedation in the context of the specific goals of end-of-life care.   .

The book's main contribution is doubtless its interdisciplinary approach to a topic that might seem to be quite narrow, but has actually the particularity of opening up a broad spectrum of very profound questions connected to the 'meaning of life' and the value of a 'good death'. What is truly at stake here is the way in which our societies understand the right of terminally-ill patients to receive a professionally competent, integral and humane care at the end-of-life, a care that enables a peaceful and dignified death, always respecting the 'inviolability of human life'.

The World Health Organization's definition states that palliative care affirms life and regards dying as a normal process, neither hastening nor postponing death. According to this definition, the so-called 'right to die with dignity' cannot be conceived simply as a right to self-determination with regards to death, but rather as a right to live one's life to the end and to be assisted by others in the dying process. Under this perspective, the dying process is understood to pose special ethical challenges to medical professionals as well as to society as such.

The experience with palliative care patients shows that each patient is unique and cannot be replaced. In spite of the similarities of clinical conditions, each individual has a specific constellation of symptoms, which in turn present themselves with different degrees of intensity in each case. Moreover, the personal experience with the disease, with the medical profession, with the family, with the friends and with society differs as well, generating dissimilar psychological reactions among terminally ill patients. Also the spiritual resources and the coping mechanisms vary according to their respective religious and cultural background. Dying persons have the right to receive integral and competent assistance at the end-of-life, addressing the different sources of suffering of the dying person and their relatives ('total pain'). Palliative medicine was originally conceived as an active and competent answer to these ethical demands. This is precisely the framework in which the adequate use of palliative sedation can find its foundations.

Dying persons correspond doubtless to one of the most vulnerable groups in our societies. Hence, their life and dignity deserve our special attention and protection. If we accept the premise that a person's moral quality is shown mainly in the way in which he/she treats the most vulnerable people, then we may argue that future generations will be able to judge the moral quality of contemporary societies by the way in which we treat the most vulnerable, among which the dying are an important group. Hence, the care for the dying offers a privileged context to test our most fundamental moral attitudes. Indeed, not only the truth of our unconditional respect for human life and dignity are put to trial, but also the meaning and value we attribute to pertaining to the human family.

Santiago, Chile   Paulina Taboada

Contents

Contributors

Joseph Boyle St. Michael's College, University of Toronto, Toronto, Canada

Blair Henry Ethics Centre, Sunnybrook Health Sciences Centre, Toronto, ON, Canada

Joint Center for Bioethics, University of Toronto, Toronto, ON, Canada

John Keown Kennedy Institute of Ethics, Georgetown University, Washington, DC, USA

Alejandro Miranda Faculty of Law, Universidad de los Andes, Santiago, Chile

Aron Portnoy Department of Psychosocial Oncology and Palliative Care, Princess Margaret Cancer Centre, University Health Network, Toronto, Canada

Faculty of Medicine, University of Toronto, Toronto, Canada

Punam Rana Department of Psychosocial Oncology and Palliative Care, Princess Margaret Cancer Centre, University Health Network, Toronto, Canada

Faculty of Medicine, University of Toronto, Toronto, Canada

Gary Rodin Department of Psychosocial Oncology and Palliative Care, Princess Margaret Cancer Centre, University Health Network, Toronto, Canada

Faculty of Medicine, University of Toronto, Toronto, Canada

John F. Scott Division of Palliative Medicine, University of Ottawa, Ottawa, ON, Canada

Supportive and Palliative Care Program, The Ottawa Hospital, Ottawa, ON, Canada

William F. Sullivan St. Michael's Hospital Family Practice Unit, Department of Family and Community Medicine, Faculty of Medicine, University of Toronto, Toronto, Canada

Surrey Place Center, Toronto, ON, Canada

Paulina Taboada Center for Bioethics and Department of Internal Medicine, Faculty of Medicine, Pontificia Universidad Católica de Chile, Santiago, Chile

Angela Vivanco Faculty of Law, Pontificia Universidad Católica de Chile, Santiago, Chile

Universidad Santo Tomás, Chile, Santiago, Chile

Paul W. Walker Palliative Care and Rehabilitation Medicine, MD Anderson Cancer Center, Houston, TX, USA

Camilla Zimmermann Department of Psychosocial Oncology and Palliative Care, Princess Margaret Cancer Centre, University Health Network, Toronto, Canada

Faculty of Medicine, University of Toronto, Toronto, Canada

Chapter 1
Sedation at the End of Life. Clinical Realities, Trends and Current Debate

Paulina Taboada

1.1 Introduction

The use of sedation is not new in medicine. In fact, sedation is widely used to allevi-ate pain and discomfort associated with both invasive procedures such as surgery, as well as severe burns (Claessens et al. 2008; Cherny and Radbruch 2009). Similarly, in Psychiatry it is used in extremely agitated patients, or in those suffering from severe panic attacks. Still, the first descriptions of the use of sedation for symptom-control in advanced stages of incurable diseases were published in 1990–1991, and it was not until 2000 that the term 'palliative sedation' (PS) was coined (Claessens et al. 2008). Since then, sedation has been progressively accepted as a therapeutic tool in the care for dying patients (Palliative Medicine) (Claessens et al. 2008; Cherny and Radbruch 2009; Cherny 2006; Krakauer 2009).

During the last decade, medical knowledge about PS has significantly increased. Several clinical studies (Ventafridda et al. 1990; Fainsinger et al. 2000; Muller-Busch et al. 2003; Morita et al. 2002), systematic reviews (Engstrom et al. 2006; Cowan and Walsh 2001; Royal Dutch Medical Association Committee on National Guideline for Palliative Sedation 2009), and clinical guidelines (Cherny and Radbruch 2009; Verkerk et al. 2007; Braun et al. 2003; Morita et al. 2005; Morita 2004a; Beel et al. 2002; Jackson 2002; Cowan and Walsh 2001; Quill and Byock 2000; Quill et al. 1997; Pomerantz et al. 2004; Veterans Health Administration National Ethics Committee 2006; Cassell and Rich 2010; Jansen and Sulmasy 2002) have been published. However, the available empirical evidence is still limited, and the debate continues. Diverse studies show an enormous variation in the preva-lence of PS in different centers, which fluctuates between 10 % to more than 50 % of the patients (Cherny and Radbruch 2009; Ventafridda et al. 1990; Fainsinger

P. Taboada (✉)
Center for Bioethics and Department of Internal Medicine, Faculty of Medicine,
Pontificia Universidad Católica de Chile, Alameda 340, Santiago, Chile
e-mail: ptaboada@med.puc.cl

P. Taboada (ed.), *Sedation at the End-of-life: An Interdisciplinary Approach*,
Philosophy and Medicine 116, DOI 10.1007/978-94-017-9106-9_1,
© Springer Science+Business Media Dordrecht 2015

et al. 2000; Muller-Busch et al. 2003; Morita et al. 2002; Engstrom et al. 2006; Cowan and Walsh 2001; Royal Dutch Medical Association Committee on National Guideline for Palliative Sedation 2009; Verkerk et al. 2007; Braun et al. 2003; Morita et al. 2005; Morita 2004a). These data suggest a lack of uniformity in the clinical criteria applied for its use (Morita 2004a). In fact, this is precisely one of the several aspects that are under debate today. Other controversial points are: the concepts, definitions and terminology ('palliative sedation' vs. 'terminal sedation'); (Beel et al. 2002; Jackson 2002; Cowan and Walsh 2001) the types of sedation that are included under the concept (intermittent vs. continuous; superficial vs. deep); the clinical indications (physical symptoms vs. existential suffering); the concomitant administration of vs. the withdrawal of medically assisted nutrition and hydration and other life-prolonging medical interventions (Claessens et al. 2008; Royal Dutch Medical Association Committee on National Guideline for Palliative Sedation 2009; Quill and Byock 2000; Quill et al. 1997); etc. However, the most debated issues are connected with the ethical foundations of PS and its conceptual difference with euthanasia and physician-assisted-suicide.

In the following, I shall start with the description of two real clinical cases, to introduce some aspects of the current debate on the concepts and definitions of 'palliative sedation', as well as the controversies related to its clinical applications. A critical analysis of the content of some of the guidelines for the use of PS that have been proposed in different parts of the world suggests a current need for re-thinking the clinical, ethical and theological foundations of this therapeutic intervention at the end-of-life. Although I will refer to some of the ethically relevant questions connected to the use of PS, I will not enter into a deep analysis of these issues here, as this will be the task of the following chapters.

1.2   Clinical Settings: Examples of Real Cases

Case 1

29 years-old woman with an end-stage brain tumor (glioblastoma). She has had a very low intake of fluids and nourishment for several months and is currently cachectic and bed-bounded. The tumor's mass effect has been causing her mild headache and confusion over the past weeks, for which she is currently under treatment with steroids and opioids, with a partial response.

Due to tumor involvement at the level of the brain stem, she developed shortness of breath and was admitted to an Acute Symptom Management Unit. Attempts to relieve her dyspnoea with oxygen and with increasing doses of opioids has failed.

As the patient did not have the capacity to participate actively in medical decision-making (due to her mental confusion), the use of sedation was proposed to the parents and fiancé as a last resort therapy to relieve her respiratory distress. They hesitated, as they understood that inducing a state of unconsciousness would prevent them from the possibility to communicate with her during her last days of life. But after witnessing her increasing respiratory distress, they ended up accepting the treatment. Before starting sedation, they requested a priest to come and give her Holy Communion and the Blessing of the Sick, as they were all practicing Catholics.

Sedation was efficiently induced with low doses of Midazolam i.v. and the moderately sedated patient did not look distressed anymore. She died peaceful 4 days later, in the company of her parents and fiancé.

In such a case, one can assume that death was caused by respiratory arrest due to tumour compression at the level of the brain stem and not by the use of sedatives.

Case 2

59 years-old lady with an invasive ductal breast carcinoma and a scamous carcinoma of the vagina. In spite of the intense radio- and chemotherapy, the disease is now widely disseminated. In fact, she has multiple lung, pleural, hiliar, brain and subcutaneous metastases. Her symptom assessment reveals an appropriate control of physical symptoms, but a persistent state of enormous anguish.

She is married to a supportive husband, who visits her daily at the Acute Symptom Management Unit were she has been recently admitted. They never had children, as they got married rather late. The source of her current anguish seems to be related to a deep questioning of some important life-decisions and the overall meaning of her existence. Her emotional state might be labeled as 'existential suffering'.

The patient requests her attending Palliative Care Physician "to be put asleep, as she cannot bare this horrible anguish anymore." The husband agrees with the patient's request. The attending physician hesitates whether this is a case for palliative sedation and decides to consult with other colleagues.

In the mean time, each time the doctor enters the patient's room, she inquires: "Why am I not asleep yet? I have already told you that I cannot stand this anguish anymore!" The patient's strong insistence provokes a distress reaction in the doctor, who decides to initiate a continuous i.v. infusion of Midazolam.

Nevertheless, mild sedation does not seem to work well for the patient. In fact, every time the doctor enters the patient's room, she keeps asking why she is not asleep yet. Hence, the doctor decides to increase the doses of Midazolam after each visit. Since this strategy does not work, the physician decides to add Phenobarbital. After 3 days, a state of unconsciousness is finally reached and the patient dies.

According to the advanced stage of her cancer, the estimated prognosis of this patient was less than 2 month. Nevertheless, she actually died in a few days, probably due to respiratory arrest caused by the rapid increase of sedatives, combining the use of benzodiazepines and barbiturates.

These two cases confront us with questions related to the distinction between 'palliative sedation' and euthanasia. In order to draw this distinction, we first need to clarify the concepts.

1.3 The Debate on Terms, Concepts and Definitions

A review of the medical and bioethical literature reveals that not all the authors understand the same thing when referring to sedation as a useful therapeutic tool in Palliative Medicine. In fact, several definitions have been proposed in the literature (Claessens et al. 2008; Cherny and Radbruch 2009; Cherny 2006; Krakauer 2009; Beel et al. 2002; Jackson 2002; Cowan and Walsh 2001). Strictly speaking, definitions come in various sorts: operational, descriptive and conceptual definitions. Therefore, when liming a concept, one tries to give an 'conceptual definitions' of it (e.g. knowledge is justified true belief). Thus, grasping the essential elements of the subject under study is a first necessary step to provide a good 'conceptual definition'.

In regard to specific 'conceptual definitions', one has to be careful to define the term taking into account what it actually is. And PS is fundamentally an action type. Hence, it should be defined in a way apropos for action types, for example, it should note the object, the intention of the agent and the circumstances. From this perspective, 'palliative sedation' could be defined as the medical act of administering sedatives with the deliberate intention of reducing the level of consciousness of a terminally ill patient as much as needed to achieve a proportionate good therapeutic goal, as is the relieve of severe and refractory symptoms at the end of life. Boyle (Chap. 5), Miranda (Chap. 6) and Keown (Chap. 7) provide good examples of this sort of action-type definition of PS when undertaking an accurate analysis of the problem as to whether the administration of drugs that have the effect of deprivation of consciousness in the patient, is or is not an action that could (or should) be justified by the application of the so called 'principle of the double effect' (PDE).

Indeed, the common idea underlying the various definitions of PS used in the current bioethical and medical literature is that it is "the intentional administration of sedative drugs in dosages and combinations required to reduce the consciousness of a terminal patient as much as necessary to adequately relieve one or more refractory symptoms." (Claessens et al. 2008)

Nevertheless, one can find also important differences among the various definitions of PS used in the literature. The differences refer mainly to:

1. The inclusion – or not – of the requirement to limit PS exclusively for patients during agony (i.e. during the last hours or days of life only) (Claessens et al. 2008; Cherny and Radbruch 2009; Cherny 2006; Krakauer 2009; Royal Dutch Medical Association Committee on National Guideline for Palliative Sedation 2009; Verkerk et al. 2007; Braun et al. 2003; Morita et al. 2005).
2. The level of unconsciousness to be reached (i.e. mild, moderate or deep sedation) (Claessens et al. 2008; Cherny and Radbruch 2009; Cherny 2006; Krakauer 2009; Royal Dutch Medical Association Committee on National Guideline for Palliative Sedation 2009; Verkerk et al. 2007; Braun et al. 2003; Morita et al. 2005);
3. The foreseeable reversibility vs. irreversibility of the intervention ('palliative' vs. 'terminal sedation' or 'continuous deep sedation to death') (Claessens et al.

2008; Cherny and Radbruch 2009; Cherny 2006; Krakauer 2009; Royal Dutch Medical Association Committee on National Guideline for Palliative Sedation 2009; Verkerk et al. 2007; Braun et al. 2003; Morita et al. 2005);
4. The inclusion – or not – of psycho-spiritual symptoms (e.g. 'existential suffering') among its clinical indications (Royal Dutch Medical Association Committee on National Guideline for Palliative Sedation 2009; Morita et al. 2000; Morita 2004b; Breitbart et al. 2000; Cherny 1998; Rousseau 2005; Taylor and McCann 2005).

So, for example, in relation to the foreseeable reversibility or irreversibility of the induced sedation, the Sociedad Española de Cuidados Paliativos (SECPAL) proposed in 2003 a conceptual distinction between 'palliative' and 'terminal' sedation (Fundacio Víctor Grífols i Lucas 2003). Even though not all the authors acknowledge this conceptual distinction, nor accept the use of this terminology nowadays, the idea of stressing the irreversibility of the intervention in the case of so-called 'terminal sedation' seems to point to a clinically and ethically relevant aspect of the medical decision-making. Indeed, the tendency among the experts today is to replace the expression 'terminal sedation' by the expressions 'continuous deep sedation' to death (CDS) or 'palliative sedation to unconsciousness' (PSU) to refer to the pharmacological induction of a deep coma which is predictably going to be maintained until the patient's death (Cherny and Radbruch 2009; Royal Dutch Medical Association Committee on National Guideline for Palliative Sedation 2009; Berger 2010).

Another controversial aspect concerning terms and definitions of PS stresses the present need for clarifying the underlying concept. This is the question regarding the relationship between PS and medically-assisted nutrition and hydration (MANH). When a patient has been sedated, he or she loses the spontaneous ability to take fluids and nourishment. The extent of this effect will obviously depend on the level of sedation. In this context, some authors – like Quill and Rietjens – have proposed that discontinuing hydration and nutrition is a *typical component* of sedation at the end-of-life (Quill and Byock 2000; Quill et al. 1997). Accordingly, they suggest to introduce this idea in the very definition of 'terminal sedation', which is defined as "the administration of drugs to keep the patient in deep sedation or coma until death, without giving artificial nutrition or hydration." (Rietjens et al. 2008) Although these authors' proposal has not found wide acceptance among palliative care specialists, it has certainly motivated a broad debate that points to the need of a serious reflection on the very concept of PS and its medical, ethical and theological foundations.

If we agree that PS should be best analyzed as a type of action, then the intentional *omission* of artificial nutrition and hidration (ANH) is (or could be) conceived as a separate act from the administration of PS. The theoretical and practical importance of this distinction shall become more evident along the different chapters of this book. Indeed, what is actually controversial is not so much the meaning of the terms, but rather whether these two separate types of actions to which these terms refer are morally permissible or not. There seems to be general agreement on the ethical justification of the act of administering sedation temporarily to address refractory physical symptoms. Conversely, many have problems with administering sedation continuously, paired with an omission of ANH (when informed by an intention to dehydrate the patient.)

Coming back to the issue of defining PS, Cherny and Radbruch (2009) made an interesting contribution by listing the different categories of clinical settings in which sedatives are used in Palliative Medicine:

– Transient sedation for noxious procedures;
– Sedation as part of burn care;
– Sedation used in end-of-life weaning from ventilator support;
– *Sedation in refractory symptom management at the end-of- life*;
– Emergency sedation;
– Respite sedation;
– Sedation for psychological or existential suffering.

These authors suggest that *only* "sedation in refractory symptom management at the end of life" corresponds to the concept of 'palliative sedation'. Accordingly, the European Association for Palliative Medicine (EAPC) states that "therapeutic (or palliative) sedation in the context of palliative medicine is the monitored use of medication intended to induce a state of decreased or absent awareness (unconsciousness) in order to relief the burden of otherwise intractable suffering in a manner that is ethically acceptable to the patient, family, and the health-care providers." (Cherny and Radbruch 2009) This concept of PS is in harmony with the goals of Palliative Medicine, as defined by Cherny: "1. To optimize physical and psychospiritual comfort; 2. To optimize functional capacity (when possible) and 3. To respect the patient's 'natural death'." (Cherny 2006)

1.4 The Debate Concerning Clinical Applications

1.4.1 Clinical Indications

In Palliative Medicine a distinction is usually made between 'difficult' and 'refractory' symptoms (Cherny and Radbruch 2009; Cherny 2006; Krakauer 2009). 'Difficult symptoms' represent an important challenge for clinicians. However, despite the difficulties in their management, these symptoms respond – at least potentially – to interventions (invasive or non-invasive), within a reasonable frame of time. On the other hand, 'refractory symptoms' are those symptoms that cannot be controlled in spite of aggressive therapeutic efforts or they fail to respond to treatment within a reasonable time frame.

This distinction becomes relevant when it comes to analyze the available data on the prevalence of PS in diverse centers. Differences in technical knowledge, clinical experience and/or availability of medications might lead to labeling symptoms as

Table 1.1 Frequency of symptoms treated with sedation

Symptom	Claessens et al. (Multicentric)	Ventafrida et al.	Fainsinger et al. (Multicentric)	Porta
Delirium/agitation	12–60 %	11 %	9–23 %	44 %
Dyspnea	12–63 %	33 %	0–13 %	35 %
Pain	10–51 %	31 %	1–4 %	19 %
Psychological distress	1–27 %	–	–	6 %
Nausea/vomiting	6–10 %	5 %	0–6 %	–
Others	3–67 %	–	1–11 %	–

'refractory' when they are actually not. Indeed, to define a symptom as 'refractory' it is required that: (1) No conventional treatment has been effective or available; (2) The expected effect cannot be achieved fast enough; (3) The conventional interventions have had unacceptable adverse effects in the individual case (Cherny and Radbruch 2009; Cherny 2006; Krakauer 2009) Cherny and Radbruch (2009) summarize these criteria stating that "sedation would be potentially indicated in patients with intolerable distress due to physical symptoms, when there is a lack of other methods of palliation within an acceptable time frame and without unacceptable adverse effects (refractoriness)".

A review of the medical literature reveals that the symptoms that most frequently behave as 'refractory', requiring the use of sedation at the end of life are: agitation, delirium, shortness of breath, pain, severe and uncontrollable nausea and vomiting, myoclonus, etc. (Cf. Table 1.1) (Claessens et al. 2008; Cherny and Radbruch 2009; Cherny 2006; Krakauer 2009; Ventafridda et al. 1990; Fainsinger et al. 2000; Muller-Busch et al. 2003; Morita et al. 2002; Engstrom et al. 2006; Cowan and Walsh 2001; Royal Dutch Medical Association Committee on National Guideline for Palliative Sedation 2009; Verkerk et al. 2007; Braun et al. 2003; Morita et al. 2005; Morita 2004a). Some Palliativists state that psycho-spiritual symptoms (including so-called 'existential suffering') should also be included among the indications of palliative sedation (Morita et al. 2000; Morita 2004b; Breitbart et al. 2000; Cherny 1998; Rousseau 2005; Taylor and McCann 2005). This indication is obviously controversial and has not been universally accepted so far.

Hence, another reason that may explain the enormous dispersion in the prevalence of PS in different centers could be the lack of uniformity in its clinical indications. While some groups may limit the use of PS exclusively for the management of refractory *physical symptoms*, others may include also *psycho-spiritual symptoms* among their common indications. Indeed, the literature shows that the use of palliative sedation for the management of psycho-existential suffering is on the rise (Morita et al. 2000; Morita 2004b; Breitbart et al. 2000; Cherny 1998; Rousseau 2005; Taylor and McCann 2005).

Moreover, authors – like Berger (2010) – have recently questioned the use of PS as a 'last resort' intervention for the management of 'refractory' symptoms only, suggesting that this requirement reduces the patient's autonomy to choose PS among the various therapeutic options at the end-of-life. Hence, Berger proposes to use PS in a more liberal way, which for this author means every time a patient (or his surrogate) requests this intervention. Nevertheless, such a proposal does not correspond to the standards of 'good clinical practices' recommended by Palliativist nowadays (Cherny and Radbruch 2009; Verkerk et al. 2007; Braun et al. 2003; Morita 2004a; Morita et al. 2005; Beel et al. 2002; Jackson 2002; Cowan and Walsh 2001; Quill and Byock 2000; Quill et al. 1997; Pomerantz et al. 2004; Veterans Health Administration National Ethics Committee 2006; Cassell and Rich 2010; Jansen and Sulmasy 2002).

1.4.2   Methods

For the purposes of this chapter, it is not necessary to enter into a detailed analysis of the different PS' techniques used by specialists today, but rather to stress the fact that the main therapeutic goal of PS is to reduce the level of a patient's awareness as much as needed to alleviate one or more severe and refractory symptoms. In this context, the most commonly used drugs are benzodiazepines, antipsychotics and barbiturates (Claessens et al. 2008; Cherny and Radbruch 2009; Cherny 2006; Krakauer 2009; Royal Dutch Medical Association Committee on National Guideline for Palliative Sedation 2009; Verkerk et al. 2007; Braun et al. 2003; Morita et al. 2005). Since the opioids – known for their strong analgesic power – are not good sedatives, their use is not recommended for this purpose (Claessens et al. 2008; Cherny and Radbruch 2009; Cherny 2006; Krakauer 2009; Royal Dutch Medical Association Committee on National Guideline for Palliative Sedation 2009; Verkerk et al. 2007; Braun et al. 2003; Morita et al. 2005).

The different ways of implementing PS may vary with regards to its *depth* and its *continuity* in time (Claessens et al. 2008; Cherny and Radbruch 2009; Cherny 2006; Krakauer 2009; Royal Dutch Medical Association Committee on National Guideline for Palliative Sedation 2009; Verkerk et al. 2007; Braun et al. 2003; Morita et al. 2005). Thus, according to its depth, sedation can be classified as *mild, moderate, and deep* (Cherny and Radbruch 2009). According to its temporality, sedation is classified as *continuous, transient, or intermittent* (Cherny and Radbruch 2009). The most controversial clinical practice today is *deep continuous sedation (DCS)*, in which it is foreseen that the patient will die after having spent his/her last days in a deep coma. This delicate context explains why this type of sedation has important ethical, anthropological and theological implications. Different studies have shown that the indication of sedation at the end-of-life may raise ethical concerns both among health care professionals, as well as among patients and their relatives (Cherny and Radbruch 2009; Pomerantz et al. 2004; Veterans Health Administration National Ethics Committee 2006; Cassell and Rich 2010; Jansen and Sulmasy 2002; Jansen 2010; Boyle 2004; Porta-Sales et al. 2002). Such concerns are usually connected with the fear of adverse effects and other important risks related to the use of sedatives.

Indeed, an important adverse effect of sedation at the end of life is that the patient looses the capacity to exercise the so-called 'mental properties', including rational reasoning, free decision-making and communication with other fellows. To lessen the impact of this problem it is usually recommended to use the lowest level of sedation needed to adequately alleviate symptoms (Claessens et al. 2008; Cherny and Radbruch 2009; Cherny 2006; Krakauer 2009; Royal Dutch Medical Association Committee on National Guideline for Palliative Sedation 2009; Verkerk et al. 2007; Braun et al. 2003; Morita et al. 2005).

Among the potential risks of sedation are paradoxical agitation and the eventual hasting of death (Cherny and Radbruch 2009; Cherny 2006; Krakauer 2009). Nonetheless, available data suggest that palliative sedation does not accelerate death in terminal patients, if one considers the overall numbers (Claessens et al. 2008; Cherny and Radbruch 2009). However, in individual cases there might be a small risk of hastening death, due to respiratory depression, aspiration or low blood pressure (Cherny and Radbruch 2009; Cherny 2006; Krakauer 2009). Hence, whenever the use of sedation is considered, one would need to accurately balance its benefits and risks. And the relative weight of these risks will probably vary in the context of agonizing patients as compared to patients with a longer life expectancy.

Precisely because of the adverse effects and risks associated to the use of sedatives, standard clinical practices suggest an accurate, permanent monitoring of respiratory rate and blood pressure, as well as the availability of antidotes. Thus, in those cases in which the implementation of these precautionary measures is not possible, the use of sedation is not recommended (Cherny and Radbruch 2009; Cherny 2006; Krakauer 2009).

1.4.3 Inadequate Uses, Imprudent Applications and Abuses

Published data reveal the existence of inadequate uses, substandard applications and abuses of PS in terminal patients (Cherny and Radbruch 2009; Pomerantz et al. 2004; Veterans Health Administration National Ethics Committee 2006; Cassell and Rich 2010; Jansen and Sulmasy 2002; Jansen 2010; Boyle 2004; Mounjt 1996; Brody 1996; Broekaert 2000; Levy and Cohen 2005). Nevertheless, little is known about the real prevalence of these situations (Cherny and Radbruch 2009).

– *Inadequate uses* of palliative sedation occur when sedatives are administered to a patient with the intention to alleviate symptoms, but in clinically inappropriate circumstances. For example, in cases in which the symptom-assessment has not been carefully done and the symptoms are labeled as 'refractory' when they are actually not; or in situations in which reversible factors that could have been corrected to alleviate symptoms have not been considered.

 In addition, inadequate use of sedation has been reported in the case of physicians experiencing the burned-out syndrome in the care of extremely complex or very demanding patients (Cherny and Radbruch 2009).

- *Inadequate omissions* of PS have bee also reported (Cherny and Radbruch 2009). This might be the case of physicians who unnecessarily delay the decision to start PS due to the fear of eventual adverse effects or risks; or when health professionals prefer not to implement sedation to avoid the time-consuming decision-making process that would be necessary to implement this therapy (Cherny and Radbruch 2009).
- *Substandard applications* occur when the indication of PS is adequate (considered in itself), but does not comply with the standards recommended for 'good clinical practices' (Higgins and Altilio 2007; Levy and Cohen 2005; Broekaert 2000). For instance, in cases in which the information provided to patients and relatives has been insufficient; when the process of informed consent has not been adequately conducted; when inappropriate drugs (e.g. opioids) have been used; or when the monitoring of hemodynamic parameters and respiratory rate have not been adequately done.
- *Abuses* of sedation occur when a physician uses sedative drugs with the *primary intention* of hastening death (Cherny and Radbruch 2009; Pomerantz et al. 2004; Veterans Health Administration National Ethics Committee 2006; Cassell and Rich 2010; Jansen and Sulmasy 2002; Jansen 2010; Boyle 2004; Mounjt 1996; Brody 1996; Broekaert 2000; Levy and Cohen 2005). In fact, it is well known that among the risks of using high doses of sedatives are respiratory depression and hemodynamic collapse, which may lead to the patient's death. Thus, a physician can actually abuse sedation by indicating doses of sedatives that are significantly higher than those needed to control the symptoms adequately, with the covert intention of accelerating the patient's death; or by using deep sedation in patients who do not have refractory symptoms, with the intention to provoke death as a means to alleviate a severe suffering (Cherny and Radbruch 2009; Pomerantz et al. 2004; Veterans Health Administration National Ethics Committee 2006; Cassell and Rich 2010; Jansen and Sulmasy 2002; Jansen 2010; Boyle 2004; Mounjt 1996; Brody 1996; Broekaert 2000; Levy and Cohen 2005).

These types of abuses of PS have been called 'slow euthanasia' or 'euthanasia in disguise' (Cherny and Radbruch 2009; Mounjt 1996; Brody 1996). The expression refers to an ethically unacceptable clinical practice, that is also illegal in most countries of the world. Nonetheless, the literature suggests that these forms of abuses of sedation tend to be more frequent precisely in those countries in which euthanasia or medically-assisted suicide have been legalized (Cherny and Radbruch 2009; Mounjt 1996; Brody 1996).

An eventual explanation for this apparently paradoxical phenomenon might be the fact that the use of sedation as a means to hasten a patient's death seems to be socially more acceptable than the current euthanasia-techniques used in those countries nowadays. In addition, the use of sedation as a method to perform euthanasia may allow the physicians to bypass the formalities required by the different legislations that are in force today (i.e. Holland, Belgium and Luxembourg) (Claessens et al. 2008; Cherny and Radbruch 2009; Mounjt 1996; Brody 1996).

Hence, the use of sedation at the end-of-life raises several important ethical issues not only among palliativists and bioethicists, but also among patients and relatives (Taboada 2006; Tulsky 2006; Moyano et al. 2008; Hospice and Palliative Care Federation of Massachusetts 2004; de Graeff and Dean 2007).

1.5 Some Ethical Issues Related to PS

Among the ethically relevant questions connected to the use of PS are:

1. Whether there is an ethically sound difference between PS and euthanasia and physician-assisted-suicide;
2. Whether the principle of double effect can be appropriately applied to justify the use of sedation in some cases at the end-of-life.
3. Whether PS might be ethically acceptable in the case of patients that are not imminently dying (agony);
4. Whether decisions to limit medically assisted nutrition and hydration are essentially linked to PS or whether they should be regarded as independent issues;
5. Whether sedation is an adequate response to 'existential suffering';
6. Whether sedation could be ever used in the case of patients who are not able to give their informed consent (e.g. patients with cognitive impairment of diverse origins, etc.).
7. Whether clinical guidelines for the use of PS are desirable to orient health care professionals, patients and relatives in the adequate use of sedation at the end of life.

The following chapters of this book address these and other relevant questions related to the current practice of PS from the perspective of different disciplines, such as Palliative Medicine, Philosophy, Law and Theology.

1.6 Concluding Remarks

The critical analysis of the clinical realities, current trends and existing guidelines for the use of PS leads to the conclusion that sedation can be considered as a useful therapeutic tool in the care of terminally ill patients. Nevertheless, due to its adverse effects and inherent risks, sedation should be used under accurate monitoring and as a last-resort intervention, reserved exclusively for the management of severe, refractory symptoms at the end-of-life.

A review of the medical literature suggests that the spectrum of the indications of sedation in the terminally ill has been progressively expanding over the past years, including now more frequently the management of psycho-spiritual symptoms (e.g. 'existential suffering'). Some authors have reported an increase in imprudent uses, sub-standard applications and actual abuses of sedation at the end-of-life, the later being called 'slow euthanasia' or 'euthanasia in disguise'. These facts should motivate a serious reflection on the clinical, ethical and theological criteria that ought to be used by health care professionals, patients and family members for the adequate use of sedation at the end of life.

Currently, there is a trend to promulgate clinical guidelines for the use of PS in different parts of the word, as has been accurately described and discussed by Henry and Scott (Chaps. 9 and 10). Although these guidelines can have a positive role in promoting 'good medical practices' and orienting medical decision-makings, they may also entail the risk of being used in a mechanical way that might end up substituting the person's clinical and ethical reasoning in difficult situations, as Scott suggests (Chap. 10). Hence, the promulgation of PS guidelines cannot replace the need for a ongoing education of health care professionals, patients and family members in sound criteria for appropriate decison-making regarding sedation at the end-of-life, as Sullivan proposes (Chap. 2).

Moreover, since there are important differences in the content of the various PS guidelines proposed in different parts of the world, a critical analysis suggests the current need for re-thinking the clinical, ethical and theological foundations of the use of sedation at the end of life. This is precisely the task that has been undertaken by several experts in the following chapters of this book.

References

Beel, A., S.E. McClement, and M. Harlos. 2002. Palliative sedation therapy: A review of definitions and usages. *International Journal of Palliative Nursing* 8: 190–199.

Berger, J. 2010. Rethinking guidelines for the use of palliative sedation. *Hastings Center Report* 40(3): 32–48.

Boyle, J. 2004. Medical ethics and double effect: A case of terminal sedation. *Theoretical Medicine and Bioethics* 25: 52–60.

Braun, T.C., N.A. Hagen, and T. Clark. 2003. Development of a clinical practice guideline for palliative sedation. *Journal of Palliative Medicine* 6: 345–350.

Breitbart, W., B. Rosenfeld, H. Pessin, et al. 2000. Depression, hopelessness, and desire for hastened death in terminally ill patients with cancer. *JAMA* 284: 2907–2911.

Brody, H. 1996. Commentary on Billings and Block's "Slow Euthanasia". *Journal of Palliative Care* 12(4): 38–41.

Broekaert, B. 2000. Palliative sedation defined or why and when terminal sedation is not euthanasia. *Journal of Pain and Symptom Management* 20(6): S58.

Cassell, E.J., and B.A. Rich. 2010. Intractable end-of-life suffering and the ethics of palliative sedation. *Pain Medicine* 11: 435–438.

Cherny, N.I. 1998. Commentary: Sedation in response to refractory existential distress: Walking the fine line. *Journal of Pain and Symptom Management* 16: 404–406.

Cherny, N. 2006. Palliative sedation. In *Textbook of palliative medicine*, ed. E. Bruera, I. Higginson, C. Ripamonti, and C. von Gunten, 976–987. London: Hodder Arnold.

Cherny, N., and L. Radbruch. 2009. European Association for Palliative Care (EAPC) recommended framework for the use of sedation in palliative care. *Palliative Medicine* 23(7): 581–593.

Claessens, P., J. Menten, P. Schotsmans, and B. Broeckaert. 2008. Palliative sedation: A review of the research literature. *Journal of Pain and Symptom Management* 36: 310–333.

Cowan, J.D., and D. Walsh. 2001. Terminal sedation in palliative medicine – Definition and review of the literature. *Support Care Cancer* 9: 403–407.

de Graeff, A., and M. Dean. 2007. Palliative sedation therapy in the last weeks of life: A literature review and recommendations for standards. *Journal of Palliative Medicine* 10: 67–85.

Engstrom, J., E. Bruno, B. Holm, and O. Hellzen. 2006. Palliative sedation at end of life – A systematic literature review. *European Journal of Oncology Nursing* 11: 26–35.

Fainsinger, R., A. Waller, M. Bercovici, et al. 2000. A multicentre international study of sedation for uncontrolled symptoms in terminally ill patients. *Palliative Medicine* 14: 257–265.

Fundacio Víctor Grífols i Lucas. 2003. Ética y sedación al final de la vida. Cuadernos de la Fundacio Víctor Grífols i Lucas (no 9), Barcelona.

Higgins, P.C., and T. Altilio. 2007. Palliative sedation: An essential place for clinical excellence. *Journal of Social Work in End-of-Life & Palliative Care* 3: 3–30.

Hospice and Palliative Care Federation of Massachusetts. 2004. *Palliative sedation protocol: A report of the Standards and Best Practices Committee*. Norwood: Hospice and Palliative Care Federation of Massachusetts.

Jackson, W.C. 2002. Palliative sedation vs. terminal sedation: What's in a name? *The American Journal of Hospice & Palliative Care* 19: 81–82.

Jansen, L.A. 2010. Intractable end-of-life suffering and the ethics of palliative sedation: A commentary on Cassell and Rich. *Pain Medicine* 11: 440–441.

Jansen, L.A., and D.P. Sulmasy. 2002. Sedation, alimentation; hydration, and equivocation: Careful conversation about care at the end of life. *Annals of Internal Medicine* 136: 845–849.

Krakauer, E.L. 2009. Sedation in palliative medicine. In *Oxford textbook of palliative medicine*, 4th ed, ed. G. Hanks, N. Cherny, N.A. Christakis, M. Fallon, S. Kaasa, and R.K. Portenoy. Oxford: Oxford University Press.

Levy, M.H., and S.D. Cohen. 2005. Sedation for the relief of refractory symptoms in the imminently dying: A fine intentional line. *Seminars in Oncology* 32: 237–246.

Morita, T. 2004a. Differences in physician-reported practice in palliative sedation therapy. *Support Care Cancer* 12: 584–592.

Morita, T. 2004b. Palliative sedation to relieve psycho-existential suffering of terminally ill cancer patients. *Journal of Pain and Symptom Management* 28: 445–450.

Morita, T., J. Tsunoda, S. Inoue, and S. Chihara. 2000. Terminal sedation for existential distress. *The American Journal of Hospice & Palliative Care* 17: 189–195.

Morita, T., S. Tsuneto, and Y. Shima. 2002. Definition of sedation for symptom relief: A systematic literature review and a proposal of operational criteria. *Journal of Pain and Symptom Management* 24: 447–453.

Morita, T., S. Bito, Y. Kurihara, and Y. Uchitomi. 2005. Development of a clinical guideline for palliative sedation therapy using the Delphi method. *Journal of Palliative Medicine* 8: 716–729.

Mounjt, B. 1996. Morphyn drips, terminal sedation, and slow euthanasia: Definitions and facts, not anecdotes. *Journal of Palliative Care* 12(4): 31–37.

Moyano, J., S. Zambrano, C. Ceballos, C.M. Santacruz, and C. Guerrero. 2008. Palliative sedation in Latin America: Survey on practices and attitudes. *Support Care Cancer* 16: 431–435.

Muller-Busch, H.C., I. Andres, and T. Jehser. 2003. Sedation in palliative care – A critical analysis of 7 years experience. *BMC Palliative Care* 2: 2.

Pomerantz, S.C., H. Bhatt, N.L. Brodsky, D. Lurie, J. Ciesielski, and T.A. Cavalieri. 2004. Physicians' practices related to the use of terminal sedation: Moral and ethical concerns. *Palliative & Supportive Care* 2: 15–21.

Porta-Sales, J., J.M. Nuñez-Olarte, R. Altisent-Trota, et al. 2002. Aspectos éticos de la sedación en Cuidados Paliativos: Trabajos del Comité de Ética de la SECPAL. *Palliative Medicine (Madrid)* 9: 41–46.

Quill, T.E., and I.R. Byock. 2000. Responding to intractable terminal suffering: The role of terminal sedation and voluntary refusal of food and fluids. ACP-ASIM End-of-Life Care Consensus

Panel. American College of Physicians-American Society of Internal Medicine. *Annals of Internal Medicine* 123: 408–414.

Quill, T.E., B. Lo, and D.W. Broca. 1997. Palliative options of last resort: A comparison of voluntary stopping eating and drinking, terminal sedation, physician assisted suicide, and voluntary active euthanasia. *JAMA* 278: 2099–2104.

Rietjens, J.A., L. van Zuylen, H. van Veluw, L. van der Wijk, A. van der Heide, and C.C. van der Rijt. 2008. Palliative sedation in a specialized unit for acute palliative care in a cancer hospital: Comparing patients dying with and without palliative sedation. *Journal of Pain and Symptom Management* 36: 228–234.

Rousseau, P. 2005. Existential distress and palliative sedation. *Anesthesia and Analgesia* 101: 611–612.

Royal Dutch Medical Association Committee on National Guideline for Palliative Sedation. 2009. *Guideline for palliative sedation 2009*. Utrecht: Royal Dutch Medical Association (KNMG).

Taboada, P. 2006. Principles of bioethics in palliative care. In *Textbook of palliative medicine*, ed. E. Bruera, I. Higginson, C. Ripamonti, and C. von Gunten, 85–91. London: Hodder Arnold.

Taylor, B.R., and R.M. McCann. 2005. Controlled sedation for physical and existential suffering? *Journal of Palliative Medicine* 8: 144–147.

Tulsky, J. 2006. Ethics in the practice of palliative care. In *Textbook of palliative medicine*, ed. E. Bruera, I. Higginson, C. Ripamonti, and C. von Gunten, 92–99. London: Hodder Arnold.

Ventafridda, V., C. Ripamonti, F. De Conno, et al. 1990. Symptom prevalence and control during cancer patient's last days of life. *Journal of Palliative Care* 6: 7–11.

Verkerk, M., E. van Wijlick, J. Legemaate, and A. de Graeff. 2007. A national guideline for palliative sedation in the Netherlands. *Journal of Pain and Symptom Management* 34: 666–670.

Veterans Health Administration National Ethics Committee. 2006. The ethics of palliative sedation as a therapy of last resort. *The American Journal of Hospice & Palliative Care* 23: 483–491.

Chapter 2
Palliative Sedation and the Goals of Care at the End of Life

William F. Sullivan

2.1 Introduction

The term *palliative sedation* covers a range of current practices. Some have argued that the ethical boundary distinguishing palliative sedation from euthanasia is becoming blurred in a number of these practices (Ten Have and Welie 2014; Hauser and Walsh 2009). Recent policy frameworks and guidelines that have been developed by health care institutions or groups of clinicians in different countries are not consistent in terminology or the medical and ethical guidance that they provide (Taboada 2011; Claessens et al. 2008).

A shared understanding of goals of care among health care professionals, patients, their family and other caregivers is an important guide for clinical and ethical decision making regarding interventions at the end of life and an essential component of person-centred and holistic palliative care (Haberle et al. 2011). This chapter addresses various ethical controversies surrounding palliative sedation in relation to goals of care. The central argument is that, by maintaining the focus in decision making on appropriate goals of care that are informed by well-established principles of good palliative care and ethics, the distinction between palliative sedation and euthanasia can be clarified in practice and the overall good of the patient promoted. Two extremes in palliative sedation may be averted by considering and discussing goals of care: sedating inappropriately when the intention is to hasten the patient's death; not sedating appropriately or proportionately to address the patient's goals, such as to relieve or manage distressing symptoms or to prepare for death.

W.F. Sullivan (✉)
St. Michael's Hospital Family Practice Unit, Department of Family and Community Medicine, Faculty of Medicine, University of Toronto, Toronto, Canada

Surrey Place Center, 2 Surrey Place, Toronto, ON M5S 2C2, Canada
e-mail: bill.sullivan@surreyplace.on.ca

P. Taboada (ed.), *Sedation at the End-of-life: An Interdisciplinary Approach*,
Philosophy and Medicine 116, DOI 10.1007/978-94-017-9106-9_2,
© Springer Science+Business Media Dordrecht 2015

My argument proceeds in three steps:

1. Appropriate goals of care are ones that are informed by well-established principles of good palliative care and ethics. Here I draw upon the definition of palliative care of the World Health Organization (WHO), canons of good health care implicit in the nature and meaning of health care, and the components of the patient's good. Examples of appropriate goals of care in decisions regarding palliative sedation are provided. Other goals of care that have generated ethical controversy are also discussed.
2. Discussing goals of care in decision making regarding palliative sedation serves to clarify the intention of health care professionals, to promote communication and a shared understanding among health care professionals, patients, family and other caregivers of the overall good of the patient, and to provide guidance for a plan of care that can be assessed and reviewed according to whether it meets the needs and goals of patients, their family and other caregivers.
3. I urge the development of education, tools and other resources for health care professionals, patients, family and other caregivers to help them understand and reflect upon appropriate goals of care at the end of life, and to facilitate communication and discussion of these goals.

2.2   Principles of Good Palliative Care

A consensus exists among providers of palliative care that "at the heart of palliative care is the affirmation of life, not the choosing of death." (Scott 1991) Good palliative care has, as its fundamental concern, respecting the inherent dignity and worth of the person who is seriously ill or dying, and this is manifested through efforts to enhance what remains of his or her life. In euthanasia, by contrast, the emphasis is placed on the patient's death and on 'getting it over with'. On this view, the patient's remaining life is held no longer to have much meaning or value.

The World Health Organization (WHO) has defined palliative care as care that, among other things:

- provides relief from pain and other distressing symptoms;
- affirms life and regards dying as a normal process;
- intends neither to hasten nor postpone death;
- integrates the psychological and spiritual aspects of patient care;
- offers a support system to help patients live as actively as possible until death;
- offers a support system to help the family cope during the patient's illness and in their own bereavement;
- uses a team approach to address the needs of patients and their families, including bereavement counseling, if indicated;
- will enhance quality of life, and may also positively influence the course of illness;
- is applicable early in the course of illness… (World Health Organization 2011).

These well-established principles of good palliative care are consistent with the nature and meaning of health care as a healing and comforting profession. They imply certain canons of good health care that Daniel P. Sulmasy has helpfully identified, and which I have reformulated in relation to palliative care as follows:

Restoration: Interventions should aim to restore a patient as much as possible to a state of functioning, well-being and comfort.

Proportionality: Interventions should be appropriate to the goals of care being sought, such as to extend life, restore or maintain function, relieve or manage distressing symptoms, as well as take into account the relation of expected likely benefits and risks of harm and burdens for the patient.

Parsimony: Only as much of an intervention as is needed to achieve the desired response in the patient should be used.

Totality: Decisions regarding interventions should aim at the overall good of the patient rather than only a part.

Discretion: Clinicians should recognize and observe both the limits of their own expertise and the limits of medical interventions (Sulmasy 2011).

The WHO definition of palliative care also stresses that such care "integrates the psychological and spiritual aspects of patient care." In other words, it is holistic care and promotes the overall good of the patient.

Edmund D. Pellegrino has distinguished among four components of the overall good of the patient (Pellegrino 2006). There is the *medical good* or what the intervention of health care professionals hopes to accomplish through interventions to address a biological and/or psychological issue and to bring about as much restoration of a patient's functioning, well-being and comfort as possible. There is also the *patient's perception of the good*. This might include the medical good. It might also differ from the medical good depending on the patient's beliefs, plans for life, values, and level of tolerance of interventions. Beyond the medical good and the patient's perception of the good, there is also what Pellegrino calls the *human good*. This is the set of basic goods that all human beings require in order to live and thrive as human beings. Finally, and ultimately for Pellegrino, there is the *spiritual good* of the patient or those deep and inspiring principles that characterize the patient's seeking of transcendent beauty, truth, goodness and authentic relationships. Good palliative care is care that aims for the overall good of the patient by taking into consideration all components of the patient's good.

2.3 Appropriate Goals of Care in Relation to Palliative Sedation

There is a dialogue in Lewis Carroll's *Alice's Adventures in Wonderland* between Alice and the Cheshire Cat that is insightful:

'Would you tell me, please, which way I ought to go from here?'
'That depends a good deal on where you want to get to,' said the Cat.

'I don't much care where —' said Alice.
'Then it doesn't matter which way you go,' said the Cat (Carroll and Green 1998).

Without goals, there would be no direction for decisions regarding alternatives for treatment and care. Some authors consider goals of care only in relation to promoting patient autonomy. Although the patient's perspective is fundamental to person-centred palliative care, appropriate goal-setting cannot only depend upon the patient's input but should involve their family and other caregivers and health care professionals. The patient depends upon family, other caregivers, who also are affected by decisions regarding treatment and care. Formulating appropriate goals of care is contingent upon understanding the patient's diagnosis, prognosis, the availability and limits of treatments, and the principles of good palliative care, towards which health care professionals can contribute. The practice that works best in palliative care, therefore, is communication and discussion among patients, their family, other caregivers, and health care professionals leading to a shared understanding of goals of care.

Appropriate goals of care in palliative care are those informed by well-established principles of good palliative care, such as the ones elaborated above. This point has several implications for palliative sedation. First, the distinction that is maintained in the WHO's definition of palliative care between such care and hastening death is clear and robust, and it should hold also for palliative sedation. The hastening of death is not an appropriate goal of palliative sedation. Likewise, if we consider the canons of good health care and the components of the patient's good elaborated above, the hastening of death restores nothing to the patient but rather aims to end the patient's life.

Second, the WHO definition of palliative care emphasizes holistic care that addresses the overall good of the person who is seriously ill or dying. The implication of this for palliative sedation is that the relief or management of distressing symptoms might not be the only appropriate goal of care. Considering the good for the patient or the spiritual good might entail that the patient and his or her family or other caregivers have the goal of maintaining consciousness, lucidity of thinking and communication for as long as possible in order to complete plans or prepare for death. Even when relief or management of distressing symptoms is the only or primary goal of care for the patient, decisions regarding palliative sedation must take into account the canon of proportionality, i.e., whether sedation is an appropriate measure for addressing the sort of distress experienced by the patient, and that its benefit is proportionate to the reduction or loss of the capacity for consciousness in the patient, which is a human good.

Third, the WHO definition of palliative care stresses that such care is applicable early in the course of a serious illness. Discussions of goals of care should also be held early on, but they could, and typically do, change over time for the patient, his or her family and other caregivers. Examples of ethically appropriate goals of palliative care are to conserve the function and resilience of the patient, to relieve or manage distressing symptoms temporarily until alternative interventions become available, or to provide respite for family and other caregivers. If sedatives are used, reversibility is a key consideration in relation to these goals of care.

There are, however, two other goals of care cited in the literature on palliative sedation that have generated some controversy among ethicists. I wish to review and comment on what I take to be the principal objections to them.

The first has been described by Greene and Davis as the goal to "dissociate the patient's consciousness from the symptoms" (Greene and Davis 1991). Daniel P. Sulmasy claims that this goal of care is different from that of trying to relieve or manage the symptom itself and can generally be determined by the type and dose of sedative that is used (Sulmasy 2011). He reasons that, when the goal of palliative sedation is to dissociate the patient's consciousness from the distressing symptoms, a continuous state of unconsciousness is not merely foreseen as a side effect but rather what is intended. According to Sulmasy, suppressing the capacity for consciousness, which is a human good, is an act that does not meet one of the conditions for the application of the Principle (or Rule, as Sulmasy prefers to call it) of Double Effect, namely that the act be neutral or good.

It could be argued, however, that, in aiming to dissociate the patient from awareness of the distressing symptom, the health care professional might not have started out intending unconsciousness. This is the argument that Timothy E. Quill et al. have recently put forward in the practice they call 'proportionate palliative sedation' or PPS, in which the depth of sedation is progressively increased to achieve relief of suffering (Quill et al. 2009). Sulmasy maintains that this still does not get around the requirement of the Principle of Double Effect. In PPS, the heath care professional intends reducing the patient's capacity for consciousness to dissociate the patient from his or her suffering continuously until death, only the health care professional does so by intending incremental reductions. These are not two distinct effects that follow from the same act of palliative sedation but "two degrees of the same effect."

Sulmasy's reasoning implies that only the goal of relieving or managing intractable and intolerable symptoms is ethically appropriate for palliative sedation, and the use of a sedative is proportionate when it is capable of doing something to relieve those *particular* symptoms, and not merely to reduce consciousness. It is *not* justified ethically for the sole goal of alleviating the distress that might arise from a patient's *awareness* of those symptoms, such as in the experience of terminal dread.

I would argue that, although the *capacity* for consciousness is a human good, the *content* of consciousness, e.g., the distress that the patient is aware of, might not be. In that case, the health care professional may ethically intend to suppress this distress (i.e., act for the reason of alleviating something that is humanly not good). Moreover the *degree* to which a patient's awareness and responsiveness is reduced (the degree to which dissociation of awareness of a distressing symptom is required in order for the patient to tolerate the symptom) is a relevant ethical factor in the analysis. Mild reductions in the patient's level of consciousness, even if continuous, might actually enable patients to tolerate their symptoms better or, if time-limited, to carry out functions and activities that are humanly good (such as conversing or praying) when they are resilient. Thus dissociating the patient's consciousness from the symptom could sometimes be an appropriate goal of palliative sedation.

Another practice of palliative sedation that has generated ethical controversy regards the goal of relieving or managing a patient's so-called 'existential suffering' (Boston et al. 2011). Part of the controversy has to do with the non-specific meaning of 'existential suffering' that has resulted in a wide range of definitions. Perhaps it would be better to clarify this term by distinction, as the Ancient and Mediaeval philosophers were accustomed to do. Existential suffering is *not* reducible to a particular 'symptom' that is due to some psychosomatic disturbance (e.g., dyspnea or delirium), although it might be influenced by and have an effect on the experience of such symptoms. Nor is existential suffering *simply* the awareness of an aversive symptom such as severe pain (such as might be prompted by a nurse asking the patient to rate pain on a scale of 1–10). It is, rather, the patient's understanding and judgment that such a symptom amounts to *a limitation or a loss* for that person in realizing his or her values, hopes, and relationships, which has a deleterious effect on the patient's overall good. Such suffering is manifested by feelings, for example, of low self-esteem, lack of purpose or meaning in life, guilt, regret, doubt, despair, loneliness, and alienation. Note that this experience is different than what might be classified as psychological symptoms or psychiatric disorders. This existential suffering relates to the patient's negative self-assessment or judgment regarding the meaning and value of his or her continued existence and future, and the meaning of death. In this sense, such suffering is a human issue that has a philosophical and spiritual origin.

The relevant ethical question here, it seems to me, is not whether the goal of relieving or managing existential suffering, as defined, is ethically appropriate within palliative care (it can be, in my opinion), but whether the use of sedatives to address it is a proportionate measure. It would not be a means that is proportionate to this goal as there is nothing in the sedative medications used that is specific to attaining that goal. Pharmacological and technical solutions are not fitting solutions for what are essentially human issues of a philosophical or spiritual nature. Holistic measures such as counselling, social support or pastoral care are better suited and have shown to be effective (Chochinov et al. 2005). I should note, however, that holistic care is not possible in every circumstance, e.g., in response to a crisis, when patients are reluctant or resistant, or when resources are not readily available. Mild to moderate levels of sedation might be ethically justified by the Principle of Double Effect, as explained above, in those instances when the patient's existential and spiritual distress is refractory. Mild to moderate palliative sedation could also play a secondary role in enabling holistic interventions for some patients (International Association of Catholic Bioethicists 2011).

2.4 Clinical and Ethical Benefits of Goals of Care Discussions

Discussing goals of care in decision making regarding palliative sedation serves to clarify the intention of health care professionals, to promote communication and a shared understanding among health care professionals, patients, family and other caregivers of the overall good of the patient, and to provide guidance for a plan of care that can be assessed and reviewed according to whether it meets the needs and goals of patients, their family and other caregivers.

2.4.1 Clarifying the Intentions of Health Care Professionals

Goals of care discussions are one practical way to maintain the ethical distinction between appropriate palliative sedation and euthanasia because it requires health care professionals to reflect upon and express the reasons why they are offering and administering palliative sedation. The health care professional's intention is ethically relevant and important in the ethical analysis of the proposed use of sedatives.

Against critics who argue that it is always impossible to disengage the health care professional's intention of relieving or managing distressing symptoms from that of hastening the patient's death in those instances when this is foreseen as a likely effect, Lynn A. Jansen has urged a distinction between a narrow and a broad sense of intention: "…on one sense of intention, call it the *broad* sense, an action is intentional if it is done with self-awareness and knowledge of its consequences. But, on another sense of intention, call it the *narrow* sense, an action is intentional only if it is part of the agent's plan in acting." (Jansen 2010)

A moral agent is only responsible for what he or she intends in this narrow sense. This way of ethical reasoning is consistent with the aforementioned Principle of Double Effect, but it could be defended ethically, according to Jansen, even without appeal to this Principle if one accepts that the reason(s) *for which* an agent acts conditions the meaning of his or her action.

In the ethical analysis of palliative sedation, I believe that the health care professional can distinguish between the 'narrow' goal of relieving or managing intractable and intolerable distress in the patient, if this is his plan of care in consultation with the patient and his or her family and other caregivers, from the 'broad' foreseen effect of hastening death in some cases, and express this narrow goal in the health care professional's plan of care.

Focus on discussions regarding goals of care would also exclude the possibility of reasoning by appeal to 'ultimate' intentions. Daniel P. Sulmasy has distinguished between 'the end of the agent' (which could include an 'ultimate intention') and the 'end of the act' (which corresponds to Jansen's 'narrow intention') (Sulmasy 2011). Thus if a health care professional were to reason that he or she 'ultimately' intends the relief of a patient's suffering *by means of* hastening the patient's death, he or she would have to specify this as one of the goals in the plan of care. This would not be an indication for appropriate palliative sedation.

Furthermore, where there are explicit goals discussed regarding the plan of care for the patient, disingenuity is easier to detect in a health care professional than if there has been no such discussion. If sedatives are deliberately given in higher dosages than are necessary for the expressed goal of relieving or managing the patient's distressing symptoms or distress, this would indicate either a medically injudicious practice or a (narrow) intention to hasten the patient's death.

On a policy level, a focus on clarifying the intentions of health care professionals through discussing goals of care would circumvent some policy decisions regarding palliative sedation that I consider to be either inefficacious, if their aim is to protect vulnerable patients, or centred more on serving the interests of health care professionals than those of patients, their family and other caregivers.

Because of an alleged uncertainty related to determining the intention of health care professionals, some policy frameworks and clinical guidelines have urged that continuous palliative sedation should only be given to patients who are imminently dying, often estimated to be within 2 weeks of death (Verkerk et al. 2007). This gives health care professionals the assurance that they did not intend to hasten the patient's death, because there is emerging evidence that there is no statistically significant difference between the survival rates of patients who received palliative sedation and those who did not, within this timeframe (Maltoni et al. 2009; Sykes and Thorns 2003). Estimates of when death is imminent are imprecise and uncertain. Such a policy provision could entail that persons who could benefit from palliative sedation to relieve or manage their distressing symptoms would not receive it on the grounds that they are assessed not to be imminently near death. Discussing and formulating goals of palliative sedation for patients who are at *any* stage of a serious and life-threatening illness is a more practical and ethically just manner of promoting clarity in the intention of the health care professional in administering palliative sedation.

A mirror problem regards policies on the withdrawal of medically-assisted nutrition and hydration with the initiation of continuous palliative sedation in some protocols and clinical pathways (e.g., the Liverpool Care Pathway in the United Kingdom). This practice is justified when death is assessed to be imminent because research shows that such withdrawals do not have a statistically significant impact on the patient's survival. This ethical justification, however, still does not address the fundamental issue of the health care professional's *intention* in withdrawing medically-assisted nutrition and hydration. A moral agent is not less responsible for omissions than actions. If the health care professional's reason for not feeding or hydrating the patient is to have the patient die, then that is what he or she intends. The withdrawal is ethically inappropriate regardless of whether the patient happens to die because of complications due to his or her disease, let's say, rather than from dehydration. (For an explication of this point, see Tollefsen 2006). A policy that stipulates generally that it is appropriate to withdraw medically-assisted nutrition and hydration with the initiation of continuous palliative sedation obscures the distinction between palliative care and euthanasia, which is based, as I have shown above, on the ethical relevance and importance of intention. Discussing and formulating goals for withdrawing medically-assisted nutrition and hydration from patients receiving continuous palliative sedation, on a case-by-case basis, is a more practical and ethically appropriate manner of promoting clarity in the intention of the health care professional. It also serves better the interests of the particular patient.

2.4.2 Promoting Communication and a Shared Understanding of the Overall Good of the Patient

Discussing and formulating goals of care enhances communication among health care professionals, patients, family and other caregivers, and contributes to a shared understanding of the patient's overall good. Research has shown the efficacy of such collaborations in end-of-life decision making in alleviating the burden experienced by many patients and their family and other caregivers, helping them to make sense of various interventions in light of identified and agreed upon goals, prioritizing multiple goals, and resolving goal conflicts (Kadjian et al. 2008). A shared understanding of the overall good of the patient provides guidance regarding whether and when to initiate palliative sedation, and its duration and depth. As noted above, sometimes the medical good that health care professionals aim for might not be the patient's perception of his or her own good. Policy frameworks and guidelines provide general guidance as to the clinical and ethical criteria for appropriate palliative sedation, but health care professionals cannot apply them to justify the appropriateness of palliative sedation for a particular patient without understanding what the patient's goals of care are. Conversely, many families and other caregivers experience significant distress over decisions regarding palliative sedation (Claessens et al. 2008). This could be mitigated by the health care professional's facilitation of discussions regarding ethically appropriate goals of palliative sedation and available alternatives, if any, to meet those goals.

2.4.3 Applying the Canons of Good Health Care Concretely

A focus on discussing and formulating goals of palliative sedation provides a practical basis for applying the canons of good health care. For example, discussing appropriate goals of care for palliative sedation helps to formulate a concrete plan of care in light of those goals. This plan can guide the proportionate administration of palliative sedation according to the patient's condition and response, and the review of those goals when circumstances change.

2.5 The Need for Education, Tools and Other Resources

While affirming the advantages of discussing and formulating appropriate goals of care for palliative sedation, I acknowledge the need for developing education, tools and other resources, to enhance the capacity of health care professionals, patients, family and other caregivers to participate knowledgeably and meaningfully in such discussions. Stone has published, for example, a tool that I have found useful for teaching family physicians to formulate and discuss goals of care at the end of life

(Stone 2001). Peereboom and Coyle have written on communication strategies to facilitate goals of care discussions (Peereboom and Coyle 2012). Other examples of education and tools that would be useful for health care professionals engaged in palliative care are those that will help them to assess distress in patients, to familiarize themselves with a range of interventions and resources possible for addressing such distress, and on the use of sedatives.

2.6 Conclusion

In this chapter, I have argued that, by maintaining the focus in decision making regarding palliative sedation on appropriate goals of care that are informed by well-established principles of good palliative care and ethics, the distinction between palliative sedation and euthanasia can be clarified in practice and the overall good of the patient promoted. I have affirmed that hastening a patient's death is not an ethically appropriate goal of care for palliative sedation. I have argued that clarity regarding the intention of health care professionals in offering and administering palliative sedation can be promoted through goals of care discussions and the formulation of a concrete plan of care in light of those goals. Focusing on appropriate goals of care for palliative sedation also complements the efforts of policy frameworks and clinical guidelines to provide ethical and legal parameters for appropriate palliative sedation on uncertain or contentious issues such as sedation for existential suffering, limiting continuous sedation to those who are imminently dying, or concomitant withdrawal of medically-assisted nutrition and hydration. Focusing on appropriate goals of care for palliative sedation also enhances person- and family-centred holistic care of persons who are seriously ill and dying. It enhances communication among health care professionals, patients, family and other caregivers and provides guidance for decision making regarding palliative sedation based on a shared understanding of the overall good of each patient. It holds health care professionals accountable to a plan of care in palliative sedation that is assessed in light of the patient's condition, response and other circumstances. It allows for flexibility in providing palliative sedation, to take into account changing goals of care over the course of the patient's illness. In summary, two extremes in palliative sedation may be averted by considering and discussing goals of care: sedating inappropriately when the intention is to hasten the patient's death; not sedating appropriately or proportionately to address the patient's goals, such as to relieve or manage distressing symptoms or to prepare for death. I urge developing education, tools and other resources, to enhance the capacity of health care professionals, patients, family and other caregivers to participate knowledgeably and meaningfully in discussions and formulations of goals of care to guide decision making regarding palliative sedation.

Acknowledgments I am grateful for the assistance of Prof. John Heng of King's University College, London, Canada in researching and writing this chapter. I also acknowledge the helpful comments of an anonymous reviewer of the first draft of this chapter, some of whose ideas I have incorporated.

References

Boston, P., A. Bruce, and R. Schriber. 2011. Existential suffering in the palliative care setting: An integrated literature review. *Journal of Pain and Symptom Management* 41(3): 604–618.

Carroll, L., and R.L. Green (eds.). 1998. *Alice's adventures in wonderland*. Oxford: Oxford University.

Chochinov, H.M., T. Hack, T. Hassard, L.J. Kristjanson, S. McClement, and M. Harlos. 2005. Dignity therapy: A novel psychotherapeutic intervention for patients near the end of life. *Journal of Clinical Oncology* 23(24): 5520–5525.

Claessens, P., J. Menten, P. Schotsmans, and B. Broeckaert. 2008. Palliative sedation: A review of the research literature. *Journal of Pain and Symptom Management* 36(3): 310–331.

Greene, W.R., and W.H. Davis. 1991. Titrated intravenous barbiturates in the control of symptoms in patients with terminal cancer. *Southern Medical Journal* 84(3): 332–337.

Haberle, T.H., L.A. Shinkunas, Z.D. Erekson, and L.C. Kaldjian. 2011. Goals of care among hospitalized patients: A validation study. *The American Journal of Hospice & Palliative Care* 28(3): 335–341.

Hauser, K., and D. Walsh. 2009. Palliative sedation: Welcome guidance on a controversial issue. *Palliative Medicine* 23(7): 577–579.

International Association of Catholic Bioethicists. (2011). *The use of sedatives in the care of persons who are seriously ill or dying: Ethical distinctions and practical recommendations.* Consensus Statement of the 5th International Association of Catholic Bioethicists Colloquium, Philadelphia, PA, USA, July 10–14, 2011. *National Catholic Bioethics Quarterly* 2012; 12(3): 489–501.

Jansen, L.A. 2010. Disambiguating clinical intentions: The ethics of palliative sedation. *The Journal of Medicine and Philosophy* 35: 19–31.

Kadjian, L.C., A.E. Curtis, L.A. Shinkunas, and K.T. Cannon. 2008. Goals of care toward the end of life a structured literature review. *The American Journal of Hospice & Palliative Care* 25(6): 501–511.

Maltoni, M., C. Pitureri, E. Scarpi, L. Piccinini, F. Martini, P. Turci, et al. 2009. Palliative sedation therapy does not hasten death: Results from a prospective multicenter study. *Annals of Oncology* 207: 1163–1169.

Peereboom, K., and N. Coyle. 2012. Facilitating goals-of-care discussions for patients with life-limiting disease: Communication strategies for nurses. *Journal of Hospice and Palliative Nursing* 14(4): 251–258.

Pellegrino, E.D. 2006. Toward a reconstruction of medical morality. *The American Journal of Bioethics* 6(2): 65–71.

Quill, T.E., B. Lo, D. Brock, and A. Meisel. 2009. Last-resort options for palliative sedation. *Annals of Internal Medicine* 151: 421–424.

Scott, J. 1991. Submission to the Canadian Legislative Committee on Bill C203, Nov 19, 1991, p. 1.

Stone, M.J. 2001. Goals of care at the end of life. *Proceedings (Baylor University Medical Center)* 14: 134–137.

Sulmasy, D.P. 2011. *Sedative palliation or sedation to death?* Paper for the 5th International Association of Catholic Bioethicists Colloquium, Philadelphia, PA, USA, July 10–14, 2011.

Sykes, N., and A. Thorns. 2003. Sedative use in the last week of life and the implications for end-of-life decision making. *Archives of Internal Medicine* 163(3): 341–344.

Taboada, P. 2011. *Palliative sedation: Analysis of clinical realities, trends and existing guidelines.* Paper for the 5th International Association of Catholic Bioethicists Colloquium, Philadelphia, PA, USA, July 10–14, 2011.

Ten Have, H., and J.V. Welie. 2014. Palliative sedation versus euthanasia: An ethical assessment. *Journal of Pain and Symptom Management* 47(1): 123–136.

Tollefsen, C. 2006. Is a purely first-person account of human action defensible? *Ethical Theory and Moral Practice* 9: 441–460.

Verkerk, M., E. van Wijlick, J. Legemaate, and A. de Graeff. 2007. A national guideline for palliative sedation in the Netherlands. *Journal of Pain and Symptom Management* 34(6): 666–670.

World Health Organization. [cited Sept 28, 2011]. Available at: http://www.who.int/cancer/palliative/en

Chapter 3
Clinical Aspects of Palliative Sedation for Refractory Symptoms

Paul W. Walker

3.1 Introduction

[The patient stated], 'Let me up, get out of my way, I'm leaving. Get your hands off of me.'
  Delirium had settled in with a vengeance now, and I wondered if it was the underlying disease, an infection, or an assemblage of causes that tangled his synapses and made us the enemy.
  Haloperidol, lorazepam (watching for a well described paradoxical reaction), and hydromorphone were administered subcutaneously; he calmed down some, but within 15 to 20 minutes, he was up again, screaming, fighting, and cursing the demons that were taking his last breath. We gave more of the same medications, but nothing seemed to help. I called his surrogate and discussed the limited options that were available. She was quizzical as to what had happened, why his abdomen was infected, and why he was delirious; I told her I didn't know, at least not right now. After a brief conversation, we elected to try a light sedation with midazolam, as he was obviously in the throes of a terminal delirium and needed sedation. The infusion was started and soon he was calm, the evil spirits tossed aside, a therapeutic lethargy calming his soul compliments of the soporific charms of pharmaceuticals. (Rousseau 2009)

This vignette, reported by Rousseau, illustrates the dire situations that palliative care and hospice practitioners can encounter and how important palliative sedation can be to resolve a crisis situation.

Palliative sedation is an important and necessary therapy used by practitioners of palliative care. This treatment of last resort for refractory symptoms is accepted as ethical practice (Burt 1997). Although controversy exists regarding the use of palliative sedation for existential distress, this chapter will not address this controversy in depth, nor will it discuss the ethical and legal issues that are well addressed in other chapters. Instead, this chapter is designed to give the reader a bedside

P.W. Walker (✉)
Palliative Care and Rehabilitation Medicine, MD Anderson Cancer Center,
Houston, TX, USA
e-mail: pwwalker@mdanderson.org

P. Taboada (ed.), *Sedation at the End-of-life: An Interdisciplinary Approach*,
Philosophy and Medicine 116, DOI 10.1007/978-94-017-9106-9_3,
© Springer Science+Business Media Dordrecht 2015

perspective on palliative sedation for the treatment of refractory symptoms, most notably agitated delirium and dyspnea, which are the primary symptoms requiring palliative sedation. Some of the practices used by The University of Texas MD Anderson Cancer Center's acute palliative care unit will be discussed.

3.2 Assessment

A refractory symptom is one that "cannot be adequately controlled despite aggressive efforts to identify a tolerable therapy that does not compromise consciousness" (Cherny and Portenoy 1994). Clearly, practitioners who are experts in symptom management should be involved in the assessment of the patient (Cherny 2006). Once a refractory symptom is determined to be present, it is important to ensure that palliative sedation is appropriate for the situation before it is discussed with the patient and/or family. Braun and colleagues (2003) have outlined four requirements for palliative sedation:

1. A terminal illness must be present.
2. The patient must be suffering from a refractory symptom.
3. Death must be imminent (within days).
4. A do-not-resuscitate order must be in effect.

In many situations it is difficult to estimate accurately prognosis. For this reason, and because of the risks of aspiration, respiratory depression, and cardiovascular compromise associated with palliative sedation, it must be viewed as a treatment with guidelines such as those listed above used to determine the most appropriate situations for its administration.

Any time a physician sedates a patient at the end of life, the potential exists for confusion and misunderstanding of the situation and the goals of care. Thus, the European Association for Palliative Care has published a framework to guide proper practice. It recognizes that "inattention to potential risks and problematic practices can lead to harmful and unethical practice which may undermine the credibility and reputation of responsible clinicians and institutions as well as the discipline of palliative medicine more generally (Cherny and Radbruch 2009)." This framework outlines four "problem practices" to be avoided:

1. Abuse of palliative sedation: sedation is used with the primary goal of hastening the patient's death.
2. Injudicious use of palliative sedation: sedation is used in inappropriate clinical circumstances. This may occur when a physician or caregiver overlooks reversible causes of distress, does not adequately assess or discuss symptom control with other experts, resorts to sedation out of frustration and burnout, or uses sedation to alleviate the family's distress rather than the patient's.
3. Injudicious withholding of palliative sedation: palliative sedation is indicated but not used. Sedation may be deferred while therapeutic options are continued that

do not provide adequate relief. Avoidance of difficult discussions or concerns about hastening death may adversely influence the clinician in this situation.

4. Substandard clinical practice of palliative sedation: sedation is indicated but attention to care is insufficient. Many potential areas of concern exist, including inadequate consultation with the patient, family members, or staff members regarding indications for sedation, goals of care, potential outcomes, and risks; inadequate monitoring of symptom distress or relief; inadequate assessment of psychological, spiritual, or social factors; inadequate monitoring of physiologic parameters and potential for drug toxicity; escalating the drug dosage too quickly without titration to effect; use of inappropriate medications (e.g., opioids) for sedation; inadequate continuing care of the patient's family; and inadequate attention to the emotional and spiritual well-being of distressed staff members.

3.3 Discussion with Patients and Families

Before discussing palliative sedation with the patient or family it is important to consider religious or other specific family concerns. Assistance from a chaplain, social worker, or counselor is helpful in this regard. These professionals are also invaluable in recognizing the psychosocial/spiritual suffering that usually accompanies physical symptoms: as noted by the biopsychosocial model, rarely is one present without the other (Turk et al. 2002; Turk and Fernandez 1990). It is also important to address the option of palliative sedation with the patient in the presence of significant family members, if the patient has the mental capacity to understand the situation. If the patient is experiencing delirium and is unable to participate in the discussion, which can often occur in end-of-life situations, then the patient's surrogate decision maker needs to be consulted.

The timing of this discussion can present a problem for the clinician. On the one hand, it can be helpful to patients and families to have time to consider the option of palliative sedation when the clinician thinks the course of the illness may eventually necessitate it. This can give those involved time to understand what palliative sedation entails and allow important life issues or tasks to be addressed. The knowledge that this option is available can be reassuring in its own right, such as if a patient fears suffocation at the end of life. On the other hand, distressed individuals, especially family members suffering vicariously, may demand the sedation immediately, even if the physician believes that other options are still available to assist the patient.

Educational hand-outs can be used to help the patient and family understand what is being proposed. The acute palliative care team at MD Anderson uses the *Journal of the American Medical Association* Patient Page, which describes palliative sedation (Brender et al. 2005). This 1-page tool, in basic English or Spanish, describes the goals of palliative and hospice care and explains how sedation is used to 'relieve extreme suffering' when "all other means to provide comfort and relief to a dying patient have been tried and are unsuccessful," that "palliative sedation is not intended to cause death or shorten life," that "the timing of death is difficult to predict and could be anywhere from hours to days after palliative sedation is initiated," and that "it is imperative to maintain open communication." It is hoped that families will be reassured by this educational page that palliative sedation is an accepted practice that differs from euthanasia and is appropriate for their situation.

3.4 Documentation

It is important to document the discussion with the patient and family about palliative sedation in the patient's record. The acute palliative care team at MD Anderson has instituted verbal rather than written consent, believing that the presentation of a document requiring a signature at this time of high distress for all involved presents a needlessly over-legalized approach to patient care and may be driven more by physician concern for litigation than by concern for the patient's best interests. After describing to the patient and/or family the symptom and how the treatment is failing, the physician describes palliative sedation and its risks, including the possibility of shortening life. The physician then completes a standardized sticker used to document the discussion in the patient's record (Fig. 3.1)

Palliative Sedation Discussion for the Use of Midazolam for the Relief of Intractable Symptoms
Date:_____
Family/Surrogate present:_____
Intractable symptom(s)_____
_____
Treatments tried prior to use of Palliative Sedation :
_____
Goal of Palliative Sedation: Relief of patient's distressing physical symptoms at the end of life that are refractory to standard palliative treatment. Use of sedation can be cancelled at any time.
Risk/Side Effects
1. Loss of ability to relate to others
2. Loss of consciousness
3. Possible shortness of life
Alternative to Palliative Sedation : Continue to work with other medications, some of which are also sedating.
_____
Physician Signature   Faculty Number

Fig. 3.1 Example of a form used to document discussion of Palliative Sedation

3.5   Symptoms Requiring Sedation

3.5.1   Agitated Delirium

As discussed in Chap. 1, the percentage of patients sedated for refractory symptoms, and the type of symptoms treated, varies widely among different settings. Agitated delirium is one of the most frequently reported symptoms requiring the use of palliative sedation. More than 80 % of advanced cancer patients develop delirium in their last hours to days of life (Elsayem 2011). Elsayem and colleagues published a retrospective report from the MD Anderson acute palliative care unit showing that of a total of 186 patients, 82 % received palliative sedation for delirium, 6 % for dyspnea, and 6 % for other symptoms, including bleeding and seizures (Elsayem et al. 2009).

The progressive nature of delirium is not often discussed in the literature on palliative sedation. When delirium is first diagnosed and is found to be irreversible, the clinician's goal is to control the agitation while allowing the patient to have meaningful interaction with family members. A minimally sedating neuroleptic drug such as haloperidol, prescribed on an around-the-clock basis, is usually the treatment of choice in this situation. Often it reduces hallucinations and agitated thoughts and the family reports improvement in the patient's condition. However, it may become necessary to increase the dose to manage the agitation. Often switching to a stronger neuroleptic drug such as chlorpromazine is required. Doses may need to be increased until the patient is sedated peacefully but is no longer interactive. Attempts to reduce the dose often result in the return of extremely agitated behavior. This is, effectively, palliative sedation. Sometimes this process occurs rapidly, leaving the family with many questions. However, family members are often relieved at this point if they understand that all attempts were made to control the agitation but that the deeply sedating dose of haloperidol or chlorpromazine was necessary.

In other situations, escalating the dose and/or switching to a stronger neuroleptic drug does not effectively control the agitated behavior. At this point, because the patient's agitation can cause extreme stress for family, nurses, and physicians and can result in harm to the patient and those around him or her, an alternative approach to palliative sedation is required to alleviate the patient's distress. In most settings, this is accomplished by starting a midazolam continuous infusion with initial bolus doses (Cherny 2006).

3.5.2   Dyspnea

The sensation of breathlessness can worsen and become terrifying for those with disease involving the lungs and structures supporting respiration. The respiratory function of a patient with lung cancer can progressively deteriorate until the patient is severely disabled. Some patients may develop hypoactive delirium at this late stage, losing awareness and becoming unconscious. Others, unfortunately, remain lucid and have progressively worsening dyspnea. These patients may experience profoundly distressing sensations of gasping for breath or of suffocating. Oxygen administration, inhaled bronchodilators, increased doses of opioids, and a bedside fan can all prove insufficient. Sedation, by altering conscious perception, can provide these individuals with much-needed comfort, sometimes at low enough doses that the patient can still interact with family and friends.

3.5.3 Pain

Although pain is mentioned in the literature as a refractory symptom that may require palliative sedation, the acute palliative care team at MD Anderson has not found the need to sedate patients for poorly controlled pain (Elsayem et al. 2009). This may be related to the availability of other resources within the group to address pain, such as a multidisciplinary psychosocial team and nurses that are skilled in symptom control.

Great attention is given to the multidimensional construct of pain (Lawlor et al. 1997), which recognizes psychosocial and spiritual factors that distress patients and can be expressed as physical pain. This is often termed "total pain" by palliative care/hospice teams and "somatization" in the psychiatric literature. Often this type of pain has a very complicated and difficult presentation; staff with psychosocial expertise are needed to help the patient manage the pain effectively.

In addition, it is helpful to have many strong opioid drug options available to allow sequential opioid rotations, which provide more options for pain management and can greatly assist with management of opioid toxicity. In the acute palliative care unit at MD Anderson, interventional approaches to pain management are rarely needed. Careful maintenance hydration is usually provided to most patients, which may lessen the incidence of opioid-induced neurotoxicity (e.g. confusion, hallucinations, hyperalgesia, allodynia) caused by prerenal failure and accumulation of opioid metabolites. Fortunately, this team has been able to manage pain without the need for palliative sedation as a rule, and some may even find palliative sedation for problems related to pain to be somewhat controversial because it is difficult to exhaust all the options available.

3.5.4 Existential Distress

> To die, to sleep-
> No more- and by a sleep to say we end
> The heartache and the thousand natural shocks
> That flesh is heir to-'tis a consummation
> Devoutly to be wished. (Hamlet (III.i.68–72))

As mentioned in other chapters, palliative sedation for existential distress is a different consideration than for refractory symptoms. The European Association for Palliative Care has published criteria for special consideration of sedation in these situations

(Cherny 2006; Cherny and Radbruch 2009). It recommends that use of sedation for refractory existential or psychological distress abide by the following considerations:

1. Consider only for patients in the advanced stages of a terminal illness with a documented do-not-resuscitate order.
2. Consider only after repeated assessments by experts in psychological care who have established a relationship with the patient and have instituted trials of therapy for anxiety, depression, and existential distress.
3. Evaluate on the basis of opinions from professionals of various disciplines who work with the patient (e.g., social workers chaplains, nurses). An interdisciplinary case conference may facilitate this.
4. In rare situations, sedation may be appropriate and proportional to the situation. Initiate on a respite basis with planned reversal after an agreed interval.
5. Consider continuous sedation only after repeated trials of respite sedation with intermittent therapy.

Presently use of palliative sedation for existential distress remains controversial. A summary of the pros and cons of utilizing this approach include (Cherny 2006; Rousseau 2001):

Pros:

1. The goal of care is to relieve suffering.
2. Existential distress leads to profound distress and debilitation.
3. It is not desirable to offer protracted trials of therapies that do not provide relief.
4. There is no standard therapy for existential distress.
5. Respite sedation (24–48 h) has been reported to break the cycle of anxiety, distress and catastrophizing.

Cons:

1. It can be difficult to establish that existential distress is truly refractory.
2. Existential distress may be very dynamic and idiosyncratic.
3. Treatments have low intrinsic morbidity.
4. Viable alternatives may remain including therapy for depression, anxiety and family discord.
5. Existential distress does not necessarily indicate a state of advanced physiological deterioration.
6. Clinical observation shows that psychological distress and the desire for death may be very variable.
7. Psychological adaptation and coping is common in the clinical setting.

3.6 Medications

Many excellent chapters in palliative medicine texts discuss medication use in palliative sedation (Cherny 2006; Cowan et al. 2009; Krakauer and Quinn 2010). Here is provided an overview with some additional observations.

3.6.1 Medication Route

Although many agents that are used for palliative sedation come in an oral formulation, it is best to use an intravenous or subcutaneous formulation so that the agent is consistently administered regardless of the patient's level of agitation or ability to swallow. The intravenous route is largely used in the hospital setting, and the subcutaneous route is often used in the home setting and when an intravenous site is difficult to access, which is not uncommon with the profound cachexia that occurs with some terminal illnesses. The intramuscular route is not recommended because it requires frequent painful injections, undermining the intent of palliation.

3.6.2 Neuroleptics

These agents represent the first-line drugs used for delirium, the condition that most often results in the need for palliative sedation. An important advantage of the neuroleptic class of drugs is the absence of respiratory depression as a side effect. This may reassure the clinician when rapid escalation is required.

Haloperidol is the drug of choice for the initial treatment of delirium because it is one of the least sedating neuroleptics, although it is possible, if rare, for deep sedation to result from the use of haloperidol alone. Caraceni and colleagues report using haloperidol for palliative sedation in 35 % of cases (Caraceni et al. 2012). This drug is known for its strong dopamine antagonism, which results in possible extrapyramidal side effects (pseudoparkinsonism, acute dystonic reaction, akathisia, tardive dyskinesia). Anticholinergic effects, prolonged QT interval, neuroleptic malignant syndrome, and lowering of the seizure threshold are additional potential adverse effects. The drug may be administered via the intravenous or subcutaneous routes.

Chlorpromazine is a more heavily sedating neuroleptic, often used when the delirium cannot be controlled with escalating doses of haloperidol. Extrapyramidal side effects are less common with chlorpromazine than with haloperidol, but anticholinergic effects (constipation, xerostomia, blurred vision, urinary retention), prolonged QT interval, neuroleptic malignant syndrome, and lowering of the seizure threshold can occur with chlorpromazine as well. Orthostatic hypotension can also occur.

Levopromazine (methotrimeprazine) is another neuroleptic used to induce sedation. Its sedative effect occurs rapidly. This drug also has analgesic properties. However, levopromazine it is not available in the United States.

3.6.3 Benzodiazepines

Midazolam, the agent most commonly used for palliative sedation (Cherny 2006; Burke et al. 1991; Chater et al. 1998; Collins 1997; Johanson 1993; Fainsinger et al. 1998; Morita et al. 1996; Nordt and Clark 1997), is a short-acting benzodiazepine that is reliably absorbed subcutaneously, allowing for administration via continuous subcutaneous or intravenous infusion and intermittent intravenous or subcutaneous boluses. Its ability to be administered subcutaneously is helpful in hospice care, especially in the home setting. Its rapid action and ability to be titrated carefully are additional advantages. One other benefit of midazolam (and benzodiazepines in general) is its anticonvulsant effect, which may provide extra assurance when risk of seizure is also present.

Paradoxical agitation and the development of tolerance are recognized disadvantages of the benzodiazepine drug class. However, respiratory depression is the most dreaded side effect, although this can be avoided by judicious dose increases and careful monitoring.

Determining whether changes in respiratory pattern are due to a recent increase in the drug or to the natural progression of the patient's condition usually falls to the bedside nurse monitoring the sedation. This skilled caregiver must consider temporal events such as recent dose adjustments as well as rely on clinical bedside acumen and experience with patients at the end of life to make this determination. If respiratory depression due to excess benzodiazepine administration is suspected, a decrease in the infusion rate usually remedies this. For seriously concerning episodes, the administration of flumazenil, a benzodiazepine antagonist, can rapidly reverse this effect. However, it will also reverse the sedation; therefore, it is important to be reasonably certain that the midazolam is causing the respiratory depression before administering flumazenil.

In the setting of agitated delirium or dyspnea, when escalating doses of medications have not provided adequate symptom control, the addition of a midazolam infusion to the medications already present is often helpful. The urgency of establishing adequate comfort for the patient usually mandates the addition of the midazolam without subtracting the previously used medications. The medication regimen may be simplified once the symptoms are controlled.

Lorazepam is a common intermediate-duration benzodiazepine agent that may be helpful for controlling severe distress while waiting to have a discussion with the family about palliative sedation. It is often used in the hospital setting for anxiety episodes. Although its short-term use does not imply a plan for palliative sedation as such, it can be a helpful temporizing measure.

3.6.4 Anesthetic Agents

Propofol is the most promising agent in this class of drugs (Collins 1997; Krakauer et al. 2000; Mercadante et al. 1995; Moyle 1995; Tobias 1997). It acts more rapidly and has a shorter duration of action than midazolam, allowing almost instant onset of sedation effects and quick titration (Krakauer and Quinn 2010). Beneficial effects other than sedation include anxiolytic, antiemetic, and anticonvulsant effects (Cowan et al. 2009; Berger et al. 2000). Pharmacokinetics of this agent do not appear to be significantly affected by liver or kidney disease (Krakauer and Quinn 2010; Mirenda and Broyles 1995). Thus, it may be the drug of choice for the rare situations in which other sedating agents have not been effective (Cherny 2006). However, propofol is expensive and can cause pain at the injection site, necessitating reliable intravenous access. In addition, vials are at risk for contamination, which could introduce an infection (Krakauer and Quinn 2010).

3.6.5 Barbiturates

Phenobarbital, pentobarbital, thiopental, and amobarbital are included in this group. These drugs may be used in anesthesia but are often not as readily available outside of the operating room in modern hospitals. However, they may be helpful in settings where other agents are ineffective, unavailable, or too costly. The effective use of thiopental and amobarbital for palliative sedation is reported by Greene and Davis (Greene and Davis 1991). The advantages of these agents are their low cost and anticonvulsant properties. Phenobarbital also has the advantage that it can be administered subcutaneously. Disadvantages of barbiturates include drug interactions and tolerance (Cowan et al. 2009). Truog and colleagues suggest that this class of drugs could be used in the care of the terminally ill but note that the use of barbiturates for palliative sedation may be confused with their use for euthanasia and physician-assisted suicide; these agents are well known as the principal drugs used to induce death by physicians performing euthanasia in the Netherlands as well as in physician-assisted suicide and the execution of prisoners by lethal injection in the United States (Truog et al. 1992).

3.7   Implementation and Monitoring

Although many guidelines have been published about palliative sedation in general terms, very little information is available to guide a clinician through dose escalation and monitoring of this therapy (Cherny and Portenoy 1994; Braun et al. 2003; Rousseau 2001). Palliative care trainees and young physicians in the field may find themselves at a disadvantage because the type and level of training offered for palliative sedation varies by institution. In addition, nursing staff responsible for patient care can encounter significant difficulties if the severe agitation or distress of a patient is not managed rapidly and safely.

Although Krakauer and Quinn (2010) as well as Cherny (2006) have outlined some basic starting points for drug administration, the acute palliative care team at MD Anderson has developed a standardized approach based on its own experience and the pharmacokinetics of midazolam. This approach uses bolus doses and a continuous infusion of midazolam, dose changes may be guided by an algorithm at the discretion of the practitioner (Table 3.1). The aim is for rapid but safe dose escalation until the patient's symptoms are controlled. Accompanying nursing guidelines for monitoring palliative sedation with midazolam are presented in Table 3.2.

Table 3.1 Palliative sedation with midazolam dose escalation guidelines

Step	Dosage (mg/h)	Step	Dosage (mg/h)
Step 1:	1	**Step 6:**	8
Step 2:	2	**Step 7:**	10
Step 3:	3	**Step 8:**	13
Step 4:	4	**Step 9:**	16
Step 5:	6	**Step 10:**	19

A loading dose and bolus doses of Midazolam 1–2 mg may be administered every 15 min IV or
  every 60 min S.Q. Notify physician if symptoms are not controlled after 2 consecutive boluses.

NOTE: Continuous IV infusion may be titrated every 2 h per physician

NOTE: Continuous SQ infusion may be titrated every 4 h per physician

*Disclaimer: These guidelines are not intended to replace independent medical or professional
  judgement of physicians or other healthcare providers.*

Table 3.2 Nursing monitoring guidelines for palliative sedation with Midazolam

**Monitor and record respiratory rate and RASS every 30 min until desired symptom
  control/sedation is achieved**

Then q1 h for first 24 h

Then q2 hourly

If respiratory rate becomes <8/min unexpectedly

(i.e. Assessed as due to midazolam and not the patient expiring)

The infusion is to be stopped and the physician notified.

Flumazenil 0.2 mg will be available at the bedside for the reversal of respiratory depression as needed.

Physician to assess status of palliative sedation daily.

**Continue appropriate nursing care (e.g. turning, mouth care, bed baths, skin care and
  bowel management)**

Table 3.3 The Richmond agitation sedation assessment scale (RASS)

+4	Combative	Overtly combative, violent, immediate danger to staff
+3	Very agitated	Pulls or removes tube(s) or catheter(s); aggressive
+2	Agitated	Frequent non-purposeful movement, fights ventilator
+1	Restless	Anxious but movements not aggressive or vigorous
0	Alert and calm	
−1	Drowsy	Not fully alert, but has sustained awakening (eye-opening /eye contact) to voice (≥10 s)
−2	Light sedation	Briefly awakens with eye contact to voice (<10 s)
−3	Moderate sedation	Movement or eye opening to voice (but no eye contact)
−4	Deep sedation	No response to voice, but movement or eye opening occurs to physical stimulation
−5	Unarousable	No response to voice or physical stimulation

The Richmond agitation sedation scale is used to monitor the level of sedation
and ensure that agitation is adequately controlled (Sessler et al. 2002; Ely et al.
2003). This bedside tool rates the level of agitation and arousal on the basis of the
patient's response to verbal (stating the patient's name and asking him/her to open
his/her eyes and look at the speaker) and physical stimulation (shaking the patient's
shoulder and/or rubbing the patient's sternum) (Table 3.3).

Table 3.4 Suggested goals of care for palliative sedation

Delirium	Richmond Agitation Sedation Scale (RASS)	RASS of 0 to –4 (i.e. no evidence of restlessness or agitation allowing for light or deep sedation as required but avoiding sedation to the point of the patient being unarousable)
Dyspnea		Options vary depending on the level of communication possible
		1. Patient gives a numerical score for dyspnea that he/she has previously said would be acceptable
		2. Patient states "No" to the question: "Are you short of breath?"
		3. Patient indicates (nods head or use of other body language) that he/she is comfortable/not short of breath.
		4. If patient is unresponsive he/she appears calm and restful.
Control of distress from: Pain, Bleeding, Seizures, Existential Distress		Each goal to be determined individually (e.g. absence of seizure activity, patient not distressed by bleeding, no voiced existential distress, reduction of pain to an acceptable score)

A score of 0 to –4 on the Richmond agitation sedation scale indicates adequate control of agitation while avoiding sedation to the point of complete unresponsiveness.

As a general rule, the lowest level of sedation necessary to achieve the desired goal should be administered. Relief from dyspnea, for example, may occur with light or deep sedation. The level of communication possible with the patient may vary with the level of sedation. The acute palliative care team at MD Anderson has proposed a strategy to determine whether adequate relief from dyspnea has been achieved; the strategy varies depending on the level of patient interaction possible (Table 3.4).

While palliative sedation is being administered, assurance of pain control, requiring the continuation of opioid medications, is also needed. Attention should also be given to nutrition and hydration. The general consensus is that although nutrition and hydration needs vary for each particular situation, they should not simply be stopped because palliative sedation has been initiated. Reports on palliative sedation in terminally ill patients show that median survival times from initiation of the sedation range from 1.9 to 6.1 days (Cowan et al. 2006; Cowan and Walsh 2001; Fainsinger et al. 2000). Survival duration has not been shown to be reduced when sedation is titrated to the point of comfort (Ventafridda et al. 1990; Stone et al. 1997; Rousseau 2000; Sykes and Thorns 2003). Two studies showed no difference in survival duration between patients who received palliative sedation and those who did not (Chiu et al. 2001; Maltoni et al. 2009).

3.8 Conclusions

Palliative sedation is an accepted and important therapy of last resort for management of distressing refractory symptoms at the end of life. Adherence to medical and ethical guidelines is important to prevent misuse of this therapy. Until we reach a time when a solution to all difficult symptoms is available in all cases, palliative sedation will continue to be a necessary and ethical strategy to ensure the comfort of the terminally ill.

References

Berger, J.M., A. Ryan, N. Vadivelu, P. Merriam, L. Rever, and P. Harrison. 2000. Ketamine-fentanyl-midazolam infusion for the control of symptoms in terminal life care. *The American Journal of Hospice & Palliative Care* 17(2): 127–134.

Braun, T.C., N.A. Hagen, and T. Clark. 2003. Development of a clinical practice guideline for palliative sedation. *Journal of Palliative Medicine* 6(3): 345–350.

Brender, E., A. Burke, and R.M. Glass. 2005. JAMA patient page. Palliative sedation. *JAMA* 294(14): 1850.

Burke, A.L., P.L. Diamond, J. Hulbert, J. Yeatman, and E.A. Farr. 1991. Terminal restlessness–its management and the role of midazolam. *Medical Journal of Australia* 155(7): 485–487.

Burt, R.A. 1997. The Supreme Court speaks–not assisted suicide but a constitutional right to palliative care. *New England Journal of Medicine* 337(17): 1234–1236.

Caraceni, A., E. Zecca, C. Martini, G. Gorni, T. Campa, C. Brunelli, et al. 2012. Palliative sedation at the end of life at a tertiary cancer center. *Support Care Cancer* 20: 1299–1307.

Chater, S., R. Viola, J. Paterson, and V. Jarvis. 1998. Sedation for intractable distress in the dying–a survey of experts. *Palliative Medicine* 12(4): 255–269.

Cherny, N.I. 2006. Palliative Sedation. In *Textbook of palliative medicine*, ed. E. Bruera, I. Higginson, C. Ripamonti, and C. von Gunten, 976–987. New York: Edward Arnold.

Cherny, N.I., and R.K. Portenoy. 1994. Sedation in the management of refractory symptoms: guidelines for evaluation and treatment. *Journal of Palliative Care* 10(2): 31–38.

Cherny, N.I., and L. Radbruch. 2009. European Association for Palliative Care (EAPC) recommended framework for the use of sedation in palliative care. *Palliative Medicine* 23(7): 581–593.

Chiu, T.Y., W.Y. Hu, B.H. Lue, S.Y. Cheng, and C.Y. Chen. 2001. Sedation for refractory symptoms of terminal cancer patients in Taiwan. *Journal of Pain and Symptom Management* 21(6): 467–472.

Collins, P. 1997. Prolonged sedation with midazolam or propofol. *Critical Care Medicine* 25(3): 556–557.

Cowan, J.D., and D. Walsh. 2001. Terminal sedation in palliative medicine–definition and review of the literature. *Support Care Cancer* 9(6): 403–407.

Cowan, J.D., L. Clemens, and T. Palmer. 2006. Palliative sedation in a southern Appalachian community. *The American Journal of Hospice & Palliative Care* 23(5): 360–368.

Cowan, J., T. Palmer, and L. Clemens. 2009. Palliative Sedation. In *Palliative medicine*, ed. D. Walsh, A.T. Caraceni, R. Fainsinger, K. Foley, P. Glare, C. Goh, et al., 983–988. Philadelphia: Saunders Elsevier.

Elsayem, A. 2011. Delirium. In *The MD Anderson supportive and palliative care handbook*, 4th ed, ed. E. Bruera and A. Elsayem, 97–105. Houston: The University of Texas – Houston Health Science Center.

Elsayem, A., E. Curry, J. Boohene, M.F. Munsell, B. Calderon, F. Hung, et al. 2009. Use of palliative sedation for intractable symptoms in the palliative care unit of a comprehensive cancer center. *Supportive Care in Cancer* 17(1): 53–59.

Ely, E.W., B. Truman, A. Shintani, J.W. Thomason, A.P. Wheeler, S. Gordon, et al. 2003. Monitoring sedation status over time in ICU patients: reliability and validity of the Richmond Agitation-Sedation Scale (RASS). *JAMA* 289(22): 2983–2991.

Fainsinger, R.L., W. Landman, M. Hoskings, and E. Bruera. 1998. Sedation for uncontrolled symptoms in a South African hospice. *Journal of Pain and Symptom Management* 16(3): 145–152.

Fainsinger, R.L., A. Waller, M. Bercovici, K. Bengtson, W. Landman, M. Hosking, et al. 2000. A multicentre international study of sedation for uncontrolled symptoms in terminally ill patients. *Palliative Medicine* 14(4): 257–265.

Greene, W.R., and W.H. Davis. 1991. Titrated intravenous barbiturates in the control of symptoms in patients with terminal cancer. *Southern Medical Journal* 84(3): 332–337.

Johanson, G.A. 1993. Midazolam in terminal care. *The American Journal of Hospice & Palliative Care* 10(1): 13–14.

Krakauer, E., and T. Quinn. 2010. Sedation in palliative medicine. In *Oxford textbook of palliative medicine*, 4th ed, ed. G. Hanks, N.I. Cherny, N.A. Christakis, M. Fallon, S. Kaasa, and R.K. Portenoy, 1560–1568. Oxford: Oxford University Press.

Krakauer, E.L., R.T. Penson, R.D. Truog, L.A. King, B.A. Chabner, and T.J. Lynch Jr. 2000. Sedation for intractable distress of a dying patient: acute palliative care and the principle of double effect. *The Oncologist* 5(1): 53–62.

Lawlor, P., P. Walker, E. Bruera, and S. Mitchell. 1997. Severe opioid toxicity and somatization of psychosocial distress in a cancer patient with a background of chemical dependence. *Journal of Pain and Symptom Management* 13(6): 356–361.

Maltoni, M., C. Pittureri, E. Scarpi, L. Piccinini, F. Martini, P. Turci, et al. 2009. Palliative sedation therapy does not hasten death: results from a prospective multicenter study. *Annals of Oncology* 20(7): 1163–1169.

Mercadante, S., F. De Conno, and C. Ripamonti. 1995. Propofol in terminal care. *Journal of Pain and Symptom Management* 10(8): 639–642.

Mirenda, J., and G. Broyles. 1995. Propofol as used for sedation in the ICU. *Chest* 108(2): 539–548.

Morita, T., S. Inoue, and S. Chihara. 1996. Sedation for symptom control in Japan: the importance of intermittent use and communication with family members. *Journal of Pain and Symptom Management* 12(1): 32–38.

Moyle, J. 1995. The use of propofol in palliative medicine. *Journal of Pain and Symptom Management* 10(8): 643–646.

Nordt, S.P., and R.F. Clark. 1997. Midazolam: a review of therapeutic uses and toxicity. *Journal of Emergency Medicine* 15(3): 357–365.

Rousseau, P. 2000. The ethical validity and clinical experience of palliative sedation. *Mayo Clinic Proceedings* 75(10): 1064–1069.

Rousseau, Paul. 2001. Existential suffering and palliative sedation: A brief commentary with a proposal for clinical guidelines. *The American Journal of Hospice & Palliative Care* 18(3): 151–153.

Rousseau, P. 2009. Complications. *Palliative & Supportive Care* 7(3): 379–380.

Sessler, C.N., M.S. Gosnell, M.J. Grap, G.M. Brophy, P.V. O'Neal, K.A. Keane, et al. 2002. The Richmond Agitation-Sedation Scale: validity and reliability in adult intensive care unit patients. *American Journal of Respiratory and Critical Care Medicine* 166(10): 1338–1344.

Stone, P., C. Phillips, O. Spruyt, and C. Waight. 1997. A comparison of the use of sedatives in a hospital support team and in a hospice. *Palliative Medicine* 11(2): 140–144.

Sykes, N., and A. Thorns. 2003. Sedative use in the last week of life and the implications for end-of-life decision making. *Archives of Internal Medicine* 163(3): 341–344.

Tobias, J.D. 1997. Propofol sedation for terminal care in a pediatric patient. *Clinical Pediatrics (Philadelphia)* 36(5): 291–293.

Truog, R.D., C.B. Berde, C. Mitchell, and H.E. Grier. 1992. Barbiturates in the care of the terminally ill. *New England Journal of Medicine* 327(23): 1678–1682.

Turk, D.C., and E. Fernandez. 1990. On the putative uniqueness of cancer pain: do psychological principles apply? *Behaviour Research and Therapy* 28(1): 1–13.

Turk, D., E. Monarch, and A. Williams. 2002. Cancer patients in pain: considerations for assessing the whole person. *Hematology/Oncology Clinics of North America* 16: 511–525.

Ventafridda, V., C. Ripamonti, F. De Conno, M. Tamburini, and B.R. Cassileth. 1990. Symptom prevalence and control during cancer patients' last days of life. *Journal of Palliative Care* 6(3): 7–11.

Chapter 4
The Use of Palliative Sedation to Treat Existential Suffering: A Reconsideration

Aron Portnoy, Punam Rana, Camilla Zimmermann, and Gary Rodin

4.1 Introduction

Palliative sedation refers to the monitored use of medications intended to induce a state of decreased awareness or unconsciousness in order to relieve otherwise intractable suffering in a manner that is ethically acceptable to the patient, family and health-care providers (Cherny et al. 2009). This sedation may be categorized as mild (the patient is awake but the level of consciousness is lowered), intermediate (the patient is asleep but can be wakened for communication), or deep (coma) (Materstvedt and Bosshard 2009). Proportionality is considered to be an essential ingredient of palliative sedation such that the amount and duration of medication used should be only that which is necessary to adequately relieve one or more symptoms (Broeckaert 2011).

Although palliative sedation is most often used to relieve physical suffering at the end of life, many guidelines for palliative sedation specify that existential suffering is also a legitimate indication for this intervention. This chapter is focused on existential suffering as an indication for palliative sedation, with a consideration of its assessment and application in the practice of palliative sedation in different settings and the clinical and ethical questions and controversies that this practice may raise. The use of deep, continuous palliative sedation prior to the end of life is not addressed here, because such an intervention would inevitably shorten life and therefore would raise different ethical, legal and clinical questions.

A. Portnoy • P. Rana • C. Zimmermann • G. Rodin (✉)
Department of Psychosocial Oncology and Palliative Care, Princess Margaret Cancer Centre, University Health Network, Toronto, Canada

Faculty of Medicine, University of Toronto, Toronto, Canada
e-mail: Gary.Rodin@uhn.ca

P. Taboada (ed.), *Sedation at the End-of-life: An Interdisciplinary Approach*, Philosophy and Medicine 116, DOI 10.1007/978-94-017-9106-9_4, © Springer Science+Business Media Dordrecht 2015

4.2   What Is Existential Suffering?

Existentialism is a philosophical attitude associated with nineteenth and twentieth century European philosophers, especially Martin Heidegger, Karl Jaspers and Jean-Paul Sartre, who stressed the unique position of the individual as a self-determining agent with personal responsibility for authenticity and meaning in their life (Guignon 2005). The term existential suffering has most often been used in the palliative care literature to connote the loss of hope and meaning in the context of impending mortality. For example, The National Hospice and Palliative Care Organization (NHPCO) has defined existential suffering as that which arises from a loss or interruption of meaning, purpose, or hope in life (Kirk et al. 2010). Yalom (1980) refers to existential pain as an individual's confrontation with his or her ultimate fears and concerns, and Schuman-Olivier et al. (2008) consider that an individual's confrontation with the dying process is essential in the diagnosis of existential suffering.

Schuman-Olivier et al. (2008) suggest that existential distress may be categorized as acute, which occurs when the threat of imminent death triggers fear and panic; subacute, which occurs when death would be imminent only if treatment were withdrawn or withheld; and chronic, when prognosis is greater than two weeks. However, psychological distress of all kinds is not necessarily maximal near the end of life. In fact, some research suggests that while depression may increase near the end of life (Lo et al. 2010), anxiety is most common at the onset or recurrence of a life-threatening illness (Li et al. 2011; Rodin et al. 2013).

Some, such as Rousseau (2001), have included a wide range of psychological symptoms in the definition of existential distress, including hopelessness, disappointment, loss of self-worth, remorse, meaninglessness, and disruption of personal identity. In that regard, Morita (2004a) found that existential suffering for which palliative sedation was administered in palliative care units in Japan included not only intractable feelings of meaninglessness or worthlessness, but also a sense of burden, dependency, death anxiety, fear, panic, the wish to control the time of death, and social isolation. Such broader definitions may come to include almost all psychological disturbances that may occur near the end of life. Indeed, some have questioned whether existential suffering at the end of life is simply part of the human condition (Hauser and Walsh 2009). This variability of definitions across settings is understandable, since there are no widely accepted measures or clinical criteria to define existential suffering, nor any agreed upon thresholds for its refractoriness.

4.3   Clinical Conceptualizations of Existential Suffering

A review of the literature suggests that not only is there no universally accepted definition or measure of existential suffering, but also that this term overlaps substantively with other clinical constructs, particularly demoralization and impaired spiritual well-being. Demoralization was initially defined by Jerome Frank (1974) as a psychological state characterized by feelings of impotence, isolation, despair and meaninglessness of life.

Kissane et al. (2004a) developed and validated a measure of demoralization in palliative care settings, although its use has not been reported in relation to palliative sedation. Spiritual well-being, according to Canada et al. (2008), is a related multidimensional construct applied to health care that refers to the comfort that is derived from one's values and beliefs, the sense of inner peace and the sense of meaning about one's life and the world. We have shown (Lo et al. 2011) that spiritual well-being is linked not only to religiosity, but also to self-esteem, social relatedness, and to freedom from physical suffering. However, the boundaries between impaired spiritual well-being and demoralization are not clear and both are indistinguishable from existential suffering.

4.4   Disturbances That May Contribute to or Overlap with Existential Suffering

The etiology of existential suffering is not well-understood, perhaps because this state has not been well-defined nor systematically investigated. Existential issues are likely to become salient in the context of impending mortality (Rodin and Zimmermann 2008), as we have shown with regard to spiritual well-being in patients with cancer (Lo et al. 2011), and reflect the capacity to find meaning, comfort from personal beliefs and a sense of connection to others.

The loss of the will to live is explicitly or implicitly included in most definitions of existential distress, although the latter may also arise from depression and other psychological disturbances, a relative lack of social relatedness, and/or inadequately treated physical suffering (Khan et al. 2010). In that regard, we demonstrated (Lo et al. 2010; Rodin et al. 2009) that depression, hopelessness, and the desire for a hastened death all may arise from a final common pathway of disease-related, individual and social factors. The desire for a hastened death arises in the context of multiple risk factors, including physical suffering, lowered self-esteem, loss of meaning, depression and demoralization. Further, although existential suffering has been distinguished from other psychological disturbances by its relationship to the end of life by Schuman-Olivier et al. (2008), we (Lo et al. 2010) found that both the cognitive–affective and somatic symptoms of depression grow toward the end of life in patients with advanced cancer. Thus, proximity to death may not be a valid distinction between depression and existential distress and impending mortality may instead be an irreducible contextual factor for all psychological disturbances at this stage of disease.

Major depression is the psychiatric disorder that may overlap most with existential suffering. Indeed, some of the symptoms of existential distress are included in the Diagnostic and Statistical Manual of Mental Disorders (DSM-IV-TR) criteria for major depression (American Psychiatric Association 2000). These include the presence, for at least two weeks, of either depressed mood or anhedonia, and at least four additional symptoms that include: changes in appetite or weight, sleep and psychomotor activity; decreased energy; feelings of worthlessness or guilt; difficulty thinking, concentrating, or making decisions; or recurrent thoughts of death or suicide. There is considerable overlap between the clinical features of depression and the broader definitions of existential suffering and they may be considered to be mutually reinforcing states. It has also been suggested that the diagnostic threshold for major depression is so low that it has caused normal sadness to be regarded as a psychiatric disorder (Horwitz and Wakefield 2007). In a similar vein, it has been suggested that the designation of existential distress as a clinical disorder represents the medicalization of normative distress (Betts and Smith-Betts 2009).

4.5 Existential Suffering as an Indication for Palliative Sedation

Despite ambiguity about its definition, features, thresholds of severity, appropriate treatment and criteria for proportionality or refractoriness, existential suffering has been accepted as an indication for palliative sedation by many governing bodies, such as the Royal Dutch Medical Association (2009), the European Association of Palliative Care (Cherny et al. 2009), the NHPCO (Kirk et al. 2010), and by an international consensus panel (de Graeff and Dean 2007). It has not been endorsed by the American Medical Association (Levine and the American Medical Association 2011: AMA CEJA Report 5-A-08) which has indicated that existential or emotional distress is best treated by other means. Other bodies, such as the Calgary Health Region (Braun et al. 2003) have reserved judgment, stating only that the role of palliative sedation for the treatment of existential suffering deserves further study. Similarly, the Palliative Sedation Task Force of the NHPCO Ethics Committee was unable to reach agreement on the use of palliative sedation for existential suffering that is "primarily nonphysical in nature" (Kirk et al. 2010). In fact, that organization urged great caution and multiple careful discussions among interdisciplinary team members, families, and patients when considering the use of sedation for existential suffering. In view of the dynamic nature of existential suffering, it was also recommended that trials of intermittent sedation for respite be instituted first when a decision to proceed with sedation is reached.

4.6 Survey of Palliative Sedation to Treat Existential Suffering

The earliest studies that examined palliative sedation indicated that it was used for the alleviation of physical symptoms in dying patients, but did not mention psychological or existential indications. These surveys found that palliative sedation for terminally ill patients was employed in 16–50 % of patients at the end of life (Ventafridda et al. 1990; Fainsinger et al. 1991). Questions have been raised subsequently about the higher end of this range, since palliative sedation is intended to be only a last-resort treatment option in rare cases that are refractory to all other treatments (Kirk et al. 2010). A German seven-year retrospective review of 548 patients in the last 48 h of life (Muller-Busch et al. 2003) demonstrated an increase in the general use of palliative sedation from 7 % in 1995 to 19 % in 2002, and also an increase in patients' and relatives' requests for sedation in the final phase of life. They noted that whereas palliative sedation was primarily used in the 1990s to treat physical symptoms, particularly dyspnoea, gastrointestinal pain, bleeding, and agitated delirium, there has been growing trend for it to be used to treat psychological symptoms after the turn of this century.

More recent studies have demonstrated considerable variability in the use of palliative sedation within and among different countries. In a 2004 study of all palliative care units in Japan (Morita 2004a), continuous deep sedation was found to be used in 1 % of all patients who died in these settings. However, whereas palliative sedation was used to treat "psycho-existential distress" in more than 10 % of these deaths in 3 of the institutions and in 0.5–5 % in 26 others, it was not used at all for this purpose in 52 institutions. The psychological disturbances for which it was used included feelings of meaninglessness and worthlessness (61 %), burden on others and discomfort with dependency (48 %), death anxiety (33 %), the wish to control the timing of death (24 %), and social isolation (22 %). A Dutch study (Van Deijck et al. 2010) indicated that existential suffering was the indication for palliative sedation in 16 % of 316 cases. A multinational study (Fainsinger et al. 2000) that examined sedation for uncontrolled symptoms in 387 palliative patients in inpatient palliative care programs in Israel, South Africa, and Spain found that palliative sedation was used for existential distress in 5 % of these cases in Madrid, 1 % in each of Cape Town and Durban, and not at all in Israel. This wide variation in the use of palliative sedation to treat existential distress may reflect cultural differences in attitudes toward this practice, assessment and documentation, or overall treatment approaches.

4.7 Understanding Differences in the Use of Palliative Sedation to Treat Existential Suffering

Methodological limitations and variability across studies of palliative sedation often limit the comparisons that can be made among them (Muller-Busch et al. 2004). In particular, there has been variability and ambiguity about the types of palliative sedation that were used and in the definition of existential suffering. Further, some studies do not specify the use of palliative sedation for existential suffering but mention that it was used for similar or related problems. For example, in a review of 13 series and 14 case reports, Cowan and Walsh (2001) found that existential distress was not listed as one of the indications for palliative sedation but that in 9 % of cases the indication was "anguish." However, anguish was not defined in this study or in an earlier study by Stone et al. (1997), which found it to be the indication for palliative sedation in 27 % of cases.

There has been consensus in guidelines and in the literature that palliative sedation should only be used to treat symptoms that are unbearable and refractory to treatment. Cherny and Portenoy (1994) describe a refractory symptom as one that cannot be adequately controlled despite aggressive efforts to identify a tolerable therapy that does not compromise consciousness. However, the criteria to establish refractoriness are rarely specified in reported studies. In the Morita (2004a) study of palliative sedation for "psycho-existential distress" in Japan, virtually no information was provided regarding the severity or duration of the symptoms for which palliative sedation was used, and only 59 % of the patients who were treated with palliative sedation had received prior specialized psychiatric, psychological or religious care. Although 89 % of those who were depressed had received antidepressant medication, the dose and duration of treatment and nature of these medications was not described. In their retrospective review of palliative sedation in Germany, Muller-Busch et al. (2004) found that palliative sedation was used for refractory physical symptoms, but psychological symptoms were not specified as refractory nor was the duration or severity of symptoms and previous treatments documented. Similarly, the criteria for refractoriness were not reported in other studies of palliative sedation (Fainsinger et al. 1991; Stone et al. 1997; Rosengarten et al. 2009).

4.8 Ethical Issues

Much of the ethical debate surrounding palliative sedation for existential distress and for other indications is related to whether or not it shortens survival. A large number of studies have found that palliative sedation does not affect the survival of patients at the end of life (Stone et al. 1997; Maltoni et al. 2009; Sykes and Thorns 2003), although Rady and Verheijde (2010) note there are a variety of mechanisms by which continuous deep sedation may do so. These include the effect of deep continuous sedation, in hypoxic and dehydrated patients, on circulation and respiration, on airway and pharyngeal tone and on the ability to swallow or cough, all of which may increase the likelihood of aspiration and hypoxia. It has been reported that approximately one third of palliative care physicians believe that continuous deep sedation can shorten life (Morita 2004b). Stone et al. (1997) note that a lack of observed difference in survival times between sedated and nonsedated patients does not necessarily mean that sedation does not alter survival, since the demonstration of such an effect would require the design of a randomized controlled trial. It may be more feasible to determine the impact of palliative sedation on survival in patients with an otherwise longer expected survival, but the gravity of the intervention and the difficulty obtaining informed consent in this circumstance may preclude the possibility of applying such methodology.

It has been suggested that palliative sedation is a complex intervention that is closer to physician-assisted suicide and involuntary active euthanasia than is ordinarily acknowledged (Baumann et al. 2011) and deep continuous palliative sedation has been referred to as "slow euthanasia" (Billings and Block 1996; Douglas et al. 2008). In that regard, a recent study indicated that the growing use of palliative sedation in the Netherlands after the legalization of euthanasia may reflect its use as an alternative to euthanasia (Rietjens et al. 2008). However, although the potential effect of palliative sedation on survival continues to be debated, it has been noted that deep continuous sedation results in the "social death" of the patient (de Graeff and Dean 2007) and that, from the patient's point of view, it makes little difference whether they are dead or continuously sedated (Materstvedt and Bosshard 2009).

Whereas assisted suicide or euthanasia refers to the ending of the life of a competent patient who has requested such an intervention, the paradigm of palliative sedation is that of a medical treatment of last resort for a state of suffering for which there is medical responsibility. However, the validity of the distinction between palliative sedation and euthanasia is undermined when it has not been determined that the symptoms that it is being used to treat are unbearable and refractory. Palliative sedation is also distinguished from euthanasia and assisted suicide by the absence of an explicit intention of the medical caregiver to end or shorten the life of the patient. However, this distinction may be only theoretical, since the presence of such an intention is difficult, if not impossible, to ascertain both because such an intent is illegal in most jurisdictions and because the intention of clinicians in this context may be multiple, ambiguous, and uncertain, even to themselves (Jansen 2010). Some have suggested (Cherny 1998) that inference about intentions can be made based on clinical actions, although such determinations are inevitably speculative. However, since continuous deep sedation at the end of life produces the psychological or social death of the patient, it may be argued that the same safeguards that are applied to assisted suicide or euthanasia should be applied to palliative sedation, particularly when used to treat existential distress. This may be particularly important in the current context in which criteria for duration, severity or refractoriness of existential suffering are rarely documented or reported.

All of the guidelines for palliative sedation require that the suffering which it is used to treat be intolerable to the patient and refractory to all other means of intervention. Therefore, the judgment to apply palliative sedation requires a comprehensive diagnostic assessment of the symptom and its potential causes and an adequate consideration and trial of all other treatment possibilities. Asking the patient which symptoms have been refractory, as reported in some studies (Claessens et al. 2011) does not meet medical criteria for the determination of refractoriness. According to accepted guidelines, palliative sedation is not intended to be merely an accession to the wishes of a competent patient to temporarily obliterate consciousness or to permanently end their life. Although it has been suggested that existential suffering can be as distressing and refractory as physical suffering near the end of life (Rousseau 2001), its nature has not been clearly or consistently defined in the consideration of palliative sedation and there are no well-established strategies for evaluating and managing refractoriness (Crenshaw 2009). Indeed, the absence of clear criteria for the assessment and treatment of existential distress have left some to suggest that its treatment with deep continuous sedation until death may blur the boundary with assisted suicide or euthanasia and to express concern that palliative sedation not become a substitute for intensive treatment of existential suffering (Bruce and Boston 2011).

4.9 Interventions for Existential Suffering

The relief of existential suffering is considered to fall within the general framework of palliative care, defined by the World Health Organization (2002) as an approach that improves the quality of life of individuals and their families facing problems associated with a life limiting illness, through prevention and relief of suffering by means of identification and impeccable assessment and treatment of pain and other problems, physical, psychosocial and spiritual. It should be emphasized that physical and existential suffering may be inextricably linked and that relief of pain and other physical symptoms may be the most effective intervention to relieve existential suffering and improve quality of life. However, some (Materstvedt and Bosshard 2009) have argued that consciousness is a necessary component of quality of life and therefore that the state of unconsciousness produced by palliative sedation may not qualify as one in which the quality of life has been improved.

Schuman-Olivier et al. (2008) suggest that initial management of existential distress should include psychopharmacologic interventions, hypnosis, meditation, relaxation, imagery, brief psychotherapy, pastoral or spiritual interventions, and nursing interventions. Spiritual care may include empathic listening, support in the search for personal meaning, reframing one's perspective of suffering in the context of life's incongruities (Puchalski et al. 2006), and aspects of spirituality related to peace and coping. There is empirical evidence that psychological and pharmacological interventions can diminish symptoms of depression and anxiety in patients with advanced and terminal disease (Li et al. 2011). This is relevant in view of the association and overlap of existential distress with these symptoms. Supportive-expressive therapy with the terminally ill (Rodin 2009) may also help patients to process the meaning of the illness, the sense of loss, the disruption in personal relationships, and the damage to the sense of competence or mastery. It may also enhance reflective awareness and help patients find meaning in both their prior and current life experiences.

A recent systematic review by LeMay and Wilson (2008) suggests that there is promise in a number of manualized interventions to treat existential distress in patients with advanced disease. These include Supportive-Expressive Group Therapy (SEGT) (Spiegel and Spira 1991), the Healing Journey (Cunningham 2002), the Life Threatening Illness Supportive-Affective Group Experience (LTI-SAGE) (Miller et al. 2005), Cognitive Existential Group Therapy (CEGT) (Kissane et al. 2003, 2004b), Meaning Centered Group Psychotherapy (Greenstein 2000;

Greenstein and Breitbart 2000), Meaning Making Intervention (MMI) (Lee et al. 2006), and Dignity Therapy (Chochinov et al. 2005). However, it has not been reported that any of these treatments have been systematically applied to patients who are being considered for palliative sedation for existential distress. Most importantly, it may be optimal to intervene earlier to prevent existential distress at the end of life, since the clinical deterioration closer to the end of life may not allow participation in such interventions at that time.

Semi-structured psychotherapeutic interventions delivered prior to the end of life have also been developed to prevent subsequent existential suffering. Dignity Therapy is an example of such an intervention, which makes use of a narrative approach to bolster the patients' sense of worth, meaning, and purpose, with the hope of decreasing their level of despair (Chochinov et al. 2005, 2011). Another promising intervention that may help to prevent existential distress in patients with advanced cancer is termed CALM (Managing Cancer And Living Meaningfully) (Nissim et al. 2012). CALM is a brief, individual psychotherapy that is designed to address the specific problems and risk factors and to decrease symptoms of depression and death anxiety and to improve spiritual well-being (Lo et al. 2014).

4.10   Guidelines for the Use of Palliative Sedation to Treat Existential Suffering

To assist in decision-making regarding palliative sedation for existential suffering, the following clinical guidelines were proposed by Rousseau (2001): (i) The patient must have a terminal illness; (ii) a do-not-resuscitate (DNR) order must be in effect; (iii) all palliative treatments must be exhausted including treatments for depression, anxiety, and any other contributing maladies; (iv) a psychological assessment by a skilled clinician should be completed; (v) an assessment for spiritual issues by a skilled clinician should be completed; (vi) if nutritional support or intravenous or subcutaneous hydration is present, discussion should be initiated regarding the benefits and burdens of such therapy in view of impending palliative sedation; (vii) informed consent should be obtained from the patient for a predetermined interval, such as 24–48 h, then downwardly titrating the sedative until consciousness reappears.

The temporary use of palliative sedation prior to the initiation of continuous increasing sedation is not well documented in the reported surveys of palliative sedation. Rousseau (2001) recommends that once palliative sedation has been initiated, the dosage of the sedative agent should not be increased unless the patient awakens and has findings that could reasonably be interpreted as evidence of suffering. It has been suggested that the use of temporary sedation may break a cycle of anxiety and distress that precipitated the request for palliative sedation and nullify the need for further sedation (Cherny 1998). When the dosage of medication is increased without an overt clinical indication, Cherny suggests that this might imply that the clinician is intending to hasten death. In that regard, because of the risk that palliative sedation may be instituted as a response to physician burn-out, he also recommends the importance of routine case conferences and/or consultation with other palliative care consultants before palliative sedation is initiated.

4.11 Conclusions

The principle that psychological distress be given the same importance as physical distress seems justifiable in view of its impact on quality of life and well-being and its potential contribution to suffering at the end of life. From that perspective, the use of palliative sedation to relieve intractable suffering of this kind seems as valid as that to relieve physical suffering. However, the consideration of deep continuous sedation for the treatment of existential suffering at the end of life raises many unanswered questions.

Most importantly, the validity of existential suffering as a criterion for palliative sedation is undermined by ambiguity in its definition. This term has been used by some to include virtually all psychological symptoms. The suggestion (Schuman-Olivier et al. 2008) to limit this term to mortality-related concerns may not improve specificity in its usage, since mortality is inevitably a context that shapes all psychological concerns near the end of life. The variability in the definitions and applications of the term existential suffering or distress may also limit comparisons that can be made across studies. We have developed a self-report measure of existential distress, now being evaluated, that may be of value both in judgments about palliative sedation and in the evaluation of the impact of interventions to relieve distress.

The use of deep continuous sedation to treat existential suffering also raises questions about its being used as a covert form of slow euthanasia, particularly when the criteria of refractoriness and unresponsiveness to other interventions, including temporary sedation, have not been met. Although the withholding of artificial nutrition and hydration has been regarded as a separate decision (Geppert et al. 2010), this intervention most commonly accompanies deep continuous sedation. Deep continuous sedation until death may, in any case, be regarded as a form of euthanasia in that it causes a "social death" and the permanent loss of awareness and personhood. It has been suggested that a trial of intermittent sedation be used, in addition to other forms of treatment, before implementing continuous sedation until death. However, the effectiveness and risk of intermittent palliative sedation in such patients have not been systematically evaluated. The justification of palliative sedation for existential distress will require greater uniformity and clarification regarding the definitions of existential distress, the criteria for intolerability and refractoriness to treatment, and the routine earlier referral to mental health experts for the evaluation and treatment of existential distress.

Existential suffering is most often considered to be a symptom within the patient, but should also be considered to arise from the social context. Mobilizing support of the family, significant others and the multi-disciplinary palliative care team at the end of life may all help to diminish or alleviate existential suffering at the end of life. The occurrence of intolerable suffering at the end of life may be secondary to the failure to institute appropriate interventions earlier in the course of the disease. Continued advocacy for the routine early referral and evaluation of existential distress by mental health experts specialized in end of life care may prevent or diminish such suffering at the end of life.

References

American Psychiatric Association. 2000. *Diagnostic and statistical manual of mental disorders, Fourth Edition Text Revision (DSM-IV-TR)*. Washington, DC: American Psychiatric Association Press.

Baumann, A., F. Claudot, G. Audibert, P.M. Mertes, and L. Puybasset. 2011. The ethical and legal aspects of palliative sedation in severely brain-injured patients: A French perspective. *Philosophy, Ethics, and Humanities in Medicine* 6: 4. Published online 2011 February 8. (Electronic version: http://www.peh-med.com/content/6/1/4).

Betts, C.E., and A.F.J. Smith-Betts. 2009. Scientism and the medicalization of existential distress: A reply to John Paley. *Nursing Philosophy* 10(2): 137–141.

Billings, J.A., and S.D. Block. 1996. Slow euthanasia. *Journal of Palliative Care* 12(4): 21–30.

Braun, T.C., N.A. Hagen, and T. Clark. 2003. Development of a clinical practice guideline for palliative sedation. *Journal of Palliative Medicine* 6(3): 345–350.

Broeckaert, B. 2011. Palliative sedation, physician-assisted suicide, and euthanasia: "Same, same but different"? *American Journal of Bioethics* 11(6): 62–64.

Bruce, A., and P. Boston. 2011. Relieving existential suffering through palliative sedation: Discussion of an uneasy practice. *Journal of Advanced Nursing* 67(12): 2732–2740. Epub 2011 Jun 1.

Canada, A.L., P.E. Murphy, G. Fitchett, A.H. Peterman, and L.R. Schover. 2008. A 3-factor model for the FACIT-Sp. *Psychooncology* 17(9): 908–916.

Cherny, N.I. 1998. Commentary: Sedation in response to refractory existential distress: Walking the fine line. *Journal of Pain and Symptom Management* 16(6): 404–406.

Cherny, N.I., and R.K. Portenoy. 1994. Sedation in the management of refractory symptoms: Guidelines for evaluation and treatment. *Journal of Palliative Care* 10(2): 31–38.

Cherny, N.I., L. Radbruch, and Board of the European Association for Palliative Care. 2009. European Association for Palliative Care (EAPC) recommended framework for the use of sedation in palliative care. *Palliative Medicine* 23(7): 581–593.

Chochinov, H.M., T. Hack, T. Hassard, L.J. Kristjanson, S. McClement, and M. Harlos. 2005. Dignity therapy: A novel psychotherapeutic intervention for patients near the end of life. *Journal of Clinical Oncology* 23(24): 5520–5525.

Chochinov, H.M., L.J. Kristjanson, W. Breitbart, S. McClement, T.F. Hack, T. Hassard, and M. Harlos. 2011. Effect of dignity therapy on distress and end-of-life experience in terminally ill patients: A randomised controlled trial. *Lancet Oncology* 12(8): 753–762. Epub 2011 Jul 6.

Claessens, P., J. Menten, P. Schotsmans, B. Broeckaert, on behalf of the Palsed Consortium. 2011. Palliative sedation, not slow euthanasia: A prospective, longitudinal study of sedation in Flemish palliative care units. *Journal of Pain and Symptom Management* 41(1): 14–24. Epub 2010 Sept 9.

Cowan, J.D., and D. Walsh. 2001. Terminal sedation in palliative medicine – Definition and review of the literature. *Support Care Cancer* 9(6): 403–407.

Crenshaw, J. 2009. Palliative sedation for existential pain: An ethical analysis. *Journal of Hospice and Palliative Nursing* 11(2):101–106.

Cunningham, A.J. 2002. *Bringing spirituality into your healing journey*. Toronto: Key Porter Books Limited.

de Graeff, A., and M. Dean. 2007. Palliative sedation therapy in the last weeks of life: A literature review and recommendations for standards. *Journal of Palliative Medicine* 10(1): 67–85.

Douglas, C., I. Kerridge, and R. Ankeny. 2008. Managing intentions: The end-of-life administration of analgesics and sedatives, and the possibility of slow euthanasia. *Bioethics* 22(7): 388–396. Epub 2008 Jun 28.

Fainsinger, R., M.J. Miller, E. Bruera, J. Hanson, and T. Maceachern. 1991. Symptom control during the last week of life on a palliative care unit. *Journal of Palliative Care* 7(1): 5–11.

Fainsinger, R.L., A. Waller, M. Bercovici, K. Bengtson, W. Landman, M. Hosking, J.M. Nunez-Olarte, and D. deMoissac. 2000. A multicentre international study of sedation for uncontrolled symptoms in terminally ill patients. *Palliative Medicine* 14(4): 257–265.

Frank, J.D. 1974. Psychotherapy: The restoration of morale. *The American Journal of Psychiatry* 131(3): 271–274.

Geppert, C.M., M.R. Andews, and M.E. Druyan. 2010. Ethical issues in artificial nutrition and hydration: A review. *Journal of Parenteral and Enteral Nutrition* 34(1): 79–88. Epub 2009 Nov 6.

Greenstein, M. 2000. The house that's on fire: Meaning-centered psychotherapy pilot group for cancer patients. *American Journal of Psychotherapy* 54(4): 501–511.

Greenstein, M., and W. Breitbart. 2000. Cancer and the experience of meaning: A group psychotherapy program for people with cancer. *American Journal of Psychotherapy* 54(4): 486–500.

Guignon, C.B. 2005. Existentialism. In *The shorter Routledge encyclopedia of philosophy*, ed. E. Craig, 252–260. London: Routledge.

Hauser, K., and D. Walsh. 2009. Palliative sedation: Welcome guidance on a controversial issue. *Palliative Medicine* 23(7): 577–579.

Horwitz, A.V., and J.C. Wakefield. 2007. *The loss of sadness: How psychiatry transformed normal sorrow into depressive disorder*. New York: Oxford University Press.

Jansen, L.A. 2010. Disambiguating clinical intentions: The ethics of palliative sedation. *Journal of Medicine and Philosophy* 35(1): 19–31. Epub 2010 Jan 6.

Khan, L., R. Wong, M. Li, C. Zimmermann, C. Lo, L. Gagliese, and G. Rodin. 2010. Maintaining the will to live of patients with advanced cancer. *The Cancer Journal* 16(5): 524–531.

Kirk, T.W., M.M. Mahon, and Palliative Sedation Task Force of the National Hospice and Palliative Care Organization Ethics Committee. 2010. National Hospice and Palliative Care Organization (NHPCO) position statement and commentary on the use of palliative sedation in imminently dying terminally ill patients. *Journal of Pain and Symptom Management* 39(5): 914–923.

Kissane, D.W., S. Bloch, G.C. Smith, P. Miach, D.M. Clarke, J. Ikin, A. Love, N. Ranieri, and D. McKenzie. 2003. Cognitive-existential group psychotherapy for women with primary breast cancer: A randomised controlled trial. *Psychooncology* 12(6): 532–546.

Kissane, D.W., S. Wein, A. Love, X.Q. Lee, P.L. Kee, and D.M. Clarke. 2004a. The Demoralization Scale: A report of its development and preliminary validation. *Journal of Palliative Care* 20(4): 269–276.

Kissane, D.W., A. Love, A. Hatton, S. Bloch, G. Smith, D.M. Clarke, P. Miach, J. Ikin, N. Ranieri, and R.D. Snyder. 2004b. Effect of cognitive-existential group therapy on survival in early-stage breast cancer. *Journal of Clinical Oncology* 22(21): 4255–4260. Epub 2004 Sep 27.

Lee, V., S.R. Cohen, L. Edgar, A. Laizner, and A.J. Gagnon. 2006. Meaning-making and psychological adjustment to cancer: Development of an intervention and pilot results. *Oncology Nursing Forum* 33(2): 291–302.

LeMay, K., and K.G. Wilson. 2008. Treatment of existential distress in life threatening illness: a review of manualized interventions. *Clinical Psychology Review* 28(3): 472–493. Epub 2007 Aug 7.

Levine, M.A., and the American Medical Association. 2011. Report of the Council on Ethical and Judicial Affairs (CEJA) Report 5-A-08: Sedation to Unconsciousness in End-of-Life Care; June 2008. http://www.ama-assn.org/ama/pub/about-ama/our-people/ama-councils/council-ethical-judicial-affairs/ceja-reports.page. Accessed 18 Aug 2011.

Li, M., V. Boquiren, C. Lo, and G. Rodin. 2011. Depression and anxiety in supportive oncology. In *Supportive oncology*, ed. M.P. Davis, P. Feyer, P. Ortner, and C. Zimmermann, 528–540. Philadelphia: Elsevier.

Lo, C., C. Zimmermann, A. Rydall, A. Walsh, J.M. Jones, M.J. Moore, F.A. Shepherd, L. Gagliese, and G. Rodin. 2010. Longitudinal study of depressive symptoms in patients with metastatic gastro-intestinal and lung cancer. *Journal of Clinical Oncology* 28(18): 3084–3089. Epub 2010 May 17.

Lo, C., C. Zimmermann, L. Gagliese, M. Li, and G. Rodin. 2011. Sources of spiritual well-being in advanced cancer. *BMJ Supportive & Palliative Care* 1: 149–153. doi:10.1136/bmjspcare-2011-000005.

Lo, C., S. Hales, J. Jung, A. Chiu, T. Panday, A. Rydall, R. Nissim, C. Malfitano, D. Petricone-Westwood, C. Zimmermann, and G. Rodin. 2014. Managing Cancer and Living Meaningfully (CALM): Phase 2 trial of a brief individual psychotherapy for patients with advanced cancer. *Palliative Medicine* 28(3): 234–242. Epub 2013 Oct 29.

Maltoni, M., C. Pittureri, E. Scarpi, L. Piccinini, F. Martini, P. Turci, L. Montanari, O. Nanni, and D. Amadori. 2009. Palliative sedation therapy does not hasten death: Results from a prospective multicenter study. *Annals of Oncology* 20(7): 1163–1169.

Materstvedt, L.J., and G. Bosshard. 2009. Deep and continuous palliative sedation (terminal sedation): Clinical-ethical and philosophical aspects. *Lancet Oncology* 10(6): 622–627.

Miller, D.K., J.T. Chibnall, S.D. Videen, and P.N. Duckro. 2005. Supportive-affective group experience for persons with life-threatening illness: Reducing spiritual, psychological, and death-related distress in dying patients. *Journal of Palliative Medicine* 8(2): 333–343.

Morita, T. 2004a. Palliative sedation to relieve psycho-existential suffering of terminally ill cancer patients. *Journal of Pain and Symptom Management* 28(5): 445–450.

Morita, T. 2004b. Differences in physician-reported practice in palliative sedation therapy. *Support Care Cancer* 12(8): 584–592. Epub 2004 Feb 28.

Muller-Busch, H.C., I. Andres, and T. Jehser. 2003. Sedation in palliative care – A critical analysis of 7 years experience. *BMC Palliative Care* 2(1): 2.

Muller-Busch, H.C., F.S. Oduncu, S. Woskanjan, and E. Klaschik. 2004. Attitudes on euthanasia, physician-assisted suicide and terminal sedation – A survey of the members of the German Association for Palliative Medicine. *Medicine, Health Care and Philosophy* 7(3): 333–339.

Nissim, R., E. Freeman, C. Lo, C. Zimmermann, L. Gagliese, A. Rydall, S. Hales, and G. Rodin. 2012. Managing Cancer and Living Meaningfully (CALM): A qualitative study of a brief individual psychotherapy for individuals with advanced cancer. *Palliative Medicine* 26(5): 713–721.

Puchalski, C.M., B. Lunsford, M.H. Harris, and R.T. Miller. 2006. Interdisciplinary spiritual care for seriously ill and dying patients: A collaborative model. *Cancer Journal* 12(5): 398–416.

Rady, M.Y., and J.L. Verheijde. 2010. Continuous deep sedation until death: Palliation or physician-assisted death? *The American Journal of Hospice & Palliative Care* 27(3): 205–214. Epub 2009 Dec 14.

Rietjens, J., J. van Delden, B. Onwuteaka-Philipsen, H. Buiting, P. van der Maas, and A. van der Heide. 2008. Continuous deep sedation for patients nearing death in the Netherlands: Descriptive study. *BMJ* 336(7648): 810–813. Epub 2008 Mar 14.

Rodin, G. 2009. Individual psychotherapy for the patient with advanced disease. In *Handbook of psychiatry in palliative medicine*, 3rd ed., ed. HM Chochinov, W Breitbart, 443–453. New York: Oxford University Press; Chap 26.

Rodin, G., and C. Zimmermann. 2008. Psychoanalytic reflections on mortality: A reconsideration. *The Journal of the American Academy of Psychoanalysis and Dynamic Psychiatry* 36(1): 181–196.

Rodin, G., C. Lo, M. Mikulincer, A. Donner, L. Gagliese, and C. Zimmermann. 2009. Pathways to distress: The multiple determinants of depression, hopelessness, and the desire for death in metastatic cancer patients. *Social Science and Medicine* 68(3): 562–569. Epub 2008 Dec 7.

Rodin, G., D. Yuen, A. Mischitelle, M.D. Minden, J. Brandwein, A. Schimmer, C. Marmar, L. Gagliese, C. Lo, A. Rydall, and C. Zimmermann. 2013. Traumatic stress in acute leukemia. *Psychooncology* 22(2): 299–307. Epub 2011 Nov 13.

Rosengarten, O.S., Y. Lamed, T. Zisling, A. Feigin, and J.M. Jacobs. 2009. Palliative sedation at home. *Journal of Palliative Care* 25(1): 5–11.

Rousseau, P. 2001. Existential suffering and palliative sedation: A brief commentary with a proposal for clinical guidelines. *American Journal of Hospice and Palliative Care* 18(3): 151–153.

Royal Dutch Medical Association (KNMG) Committee on National Guideline for Palliative Sedation. 2009. Guideline for Palliative Sedation. January 2009. http://knmg.artsennet.nl/Diensten/knmgpublicaties/KNMGpublicatie/Guideline-for-palliative-sedation-2009.htm. Accessed 18 Aug 2011.

Schuman-Olivier, Z., D.H. Brendel, M. Forstein, and B.H. Price. 2008. The use of palliative sedation for existential distress: A psychiatric perspective. *Harvard Review of Psychiatry* 16(6): 339–351.

Spiegel, D., and J. Spira. 1991. *Supportive-Expressive Group Therapy: A treatment manual of psychosocial intervention for women with recurrent breast cancer*. Stanford: Stanford University School of Medicine.

Stone, P., C. Phillips, O. Spruyt, and C. Waight. 1997. A comparison of the use of sedatives in a hospital support team and in a hospice. *Palliative Medicine* 11(2): 140–144.

Sykes, N., and A. Thorns. 2003. Sedative use in the last week of life and the implications for end-of-life decision making. *Archives of Internal Medicine* 163(3): 341–344.

Van Deijck, R.H., P.J. Krijnsen, J.G. Hasselaar, S.C. Verhagen, K.C. Vissers, and R.T. Koopmans. 2010. The practice of continuous palliative sedation in elderly patients: A nationwide explorative study among Dutch nursing home physicians. *American Geriatrics Society* 58(9): 1671–1678. Epub 2010 Aug 24.

Ventafridda, V., C. Ripamonti, F. De Conno, M. Tamburini, and B.R. Cassileth. 1990. Symptom prevalence and control during cancer patients' last days of life. *Journal of Palliative Care* 6(3): 7–11.

World Health Organization (WHO). 2002. *National cancer control programmes: Policies and managerial guidelines*, 2nd ed. Geneva: World Health Organization.

Yalom, I.D. 1980. *Existential psychotherapy*. New York: Basic.

Chapter 5
The Relevance of Double Effect to Decisions About Sedation at the End of Life

Joseph Boyle

5.1 Introduction: Definitions and Clarifications

Let me begin with (a) some clarifications about how I will understand and use the key terms in clinical and moral discussions of sedation at the end of life, and (b) a brief account of what the ethical doctrine of the double effect is.

5.1.1 Terminal Sedation

I understand 'sedation' to refer to medical steps taken to reduce a patient's level of awareness or consciousness, including those steps taken for the sake of reduction of consciousness to complete lack of awareness or unconsciousness. This term does not make reference to the reasons why sedation is chosen, but I will focus on one common goal of sedation, namely to provide palliative care, that is, care designed to promote the comfort of patients by limiting or eliminating pain and other suffering. Palliative care is an ingredient within many health care treatments. Palliative care is not limited to cases in which curing the patient is not possible, but plays a central role in the treatments of such patients. It has an especially prominent role within hospice care for those facing death. Thus, patients who (1) cannot be cured of illness, (2) are in pain and other distress, and (3) face imminent death are among those for whom palliative care is a central element of treatment. Sedation as an element in palliative care for these patients will be the focus of my discussion.

Sedation can be provided in various degrees. One can decrease a person's level of conscious awareness without causing that person to be unconscious; such sedation

J. Boyle (✉)
St. Michael's College, University of Toronto,
81 Saint Mary Street, Toronto, ON M5S 1J4, Canada
e-mail: josephmboylejr@gmail.com

P. Taboada (ed.), *Sedation at the End-of-life: An Interdisciplinary Approach*,
Philosophy and Medicine 116, DOI 10.1007/978-94-017-9106-9_5,
© Springer Science+Business Media Dordrecht 2015

might be sufficient for the palliative treatment goals for some patients. Sedation to some level of unconsciousness is also possible and achieving that end point may be necessary for palliative treatment for some patients. Sedation to unconsciousness can be temporary or continuous and potentially permanent; again the former may be sufficient palliation for some patients and the second may be necessary for other patients.

I will focus on decisions to undertake and sustain continuous sedation aimed at maintaining the patient in an unconscious condition until he or she dies. I will call continuous sedation at the level of unconsciousness until death simply, 'terminal sedation'. This measure raises especially puzzling moral issues.

My definition differs from some commonly in use. Perhaps the most important competing definition is that in which the withholding of nutrition and hydration is taken as part of the definition of terminal sedation, even though it does not itself contribute to sedating the patient (Rietjens et al. 2004; Tannnsjo 2010). My objection to this definition is that since the withholding of nutrition and hydration does not contribute to sedating the patient, it raises moral questions distinct from those raised by the terminal sedation itself. Another competing definition settles a question which my definition leaves open by defining 'terminal sedation' as a form of palliative care and by assuming that palliative care is distinct from euthanasia (Hawryluck et al. 2002). Although I agree that the stipulated purpose is palliation, that purpose can also be realized by ending the patient's life. Stipulations are not sufficient to separate terminal sedation from euthanasia, as is clear from the fact that it sometimes is a case of intentional killing.

I will address just two kinds of moral issues raised by decisions to use terminal sedation. These issues are hardly exhaustive of the moral questions that arise in these decisions. However, they seem to me very important for the general ethical assessment of terminal sedation.

Issues of the first kind arise from the characterization of terminal sedation, as I have defined it. They arise because continuous sedation at the level of unconsciousness up to the point of death seems to involve permanently depriving the patient of a central human good. So central a human good, in fact, that definitively removing the possibility of conscious life seems not very different from ending life. That causes people to wonder how in principle terminal sedation can be morally justified.

Issues of the second kind do not arise in all cases of terminal sedation but when the sedation, or other conjoined measures, such as withholding nutrition and hydration or perhaps some uses of opioids for pain management, are expected to shorten the patient's life. In these cases terminal sedation may seem to be a euphemism for euthanasia, 'slow euthanasia' as it has been called (Sumner 2011).

I will address these two moral questions through the lens of the ethical doctrine of the double effect, as developed within the Catholic tradition of moral reflection. Many people both within the Catholic tradition and outside it make use of some of the concepts of this doctrine to approach these and related moral issues. More generally, ideas connected to double effect have gained a place within common sense morality. In this chapter I will try to show how double effect helps clarify the moral issues surrounding terminal sedation.

5.1.2 Double Effect

Before developing the application it is necessary to say something about the doctrine of the double effect itself. In the case before us double effect provides that it can be morally good to shorten a patient's life as a foreseen and accepted but unintended side effect of an action undertaken for a good reason, even if it is agreed that intentionally killing the patient or shortening the patient's life is wrong.

This doctrine began in Catholic moral theology. The expression 'double effect' was used by St. Thomas Aquinas (Aquinas) in his discussion of killing in self defense; in this early, perhaps original, philosophical use of the term St. Thomas referred to the fact that actions have a plurality of results, not all of which need be intended. This idea has played a role in Catholic moral thinking ever since, and in the mid-nineteenth century was formulated as a set of conditions for the permissibility of actions having bad side effects: the classic formulation is that of the Jesuit moralist J. P. Gury (1869):

> It is licit to posit a cause which is either good or indifferent from which there follows a twofold effect, one good the other evil, if a proportionately grave reason is present, and if the end of the agent is honorable – that is, if he does not intend the evil.[1]

Gury elaborated these three conditions into four, by construing the condition of honorable intention as two. The first addressed the distinction between a means and a side effect: if the bad effect – that is, the result which would render that action simply wrong were it intended – is the means to the good effect, then it cannot be a side effect and is intended. Thus, the key requirement that the good effect be brought about 'immediately', that is, not by means of the bad effect. The second of these extrapolated conditions – that one intend only the good effect – excludes cases in which the bad effect is not brought about as a means to the good effect, but is nevertheless intended because it functions an independent goal. An example would be 'bonus' effects – results that emerge as side effects of bringing about a goal but then recognized as independently useful or beneficial and so (ordinarily) intended.

Gury's first two conditions – that the 'cause' be morally good or indifferent and that there be a proportionately grave reason for doing what brings about evil side effects–refer to the further moral considerations that are needed for a complete assessment of an action meeting the conditions for upright intention. An action done with an honorable intention might still be wrong if either of these conditions is not satisfied. The first condition rules out actions that are morally wrong independent of any consideration of the action's further results that might be intended or accepted as side effects but not intended. Perhaps his thought here is that since the behavior a person chooses to activate – for example, for the sake of self-defense – has both defensive and destructive results, one can distinguish the chosen performance from the results and ask of it whether that performance is morally permissible. In some cases, telling a lie or committing adultery, for example, the action is impermissible

---

[1] This is my translation of Gury (1869, p. 7) in Boyle (1980) at 528; this textbook went through many revisions well into the twentieth century. It was first published in 1850.

in virtue of considerations logically prior to those concerning intended or accepted results. To take a relevant case, a physician's prescribing analgesics, described in just that way, is morally indifferent; therefore, it meets this first condition and so the results, intentions and other circumstances of this chosen behavior will determine its permissibility or impermissibility. In this respect the action is unlike acts of adultery or lying, which as so described are wrong.[2] The second condition requires that the action which has the bad effect be important enough to justify the bad effect. So, for example, it excludes actions that would impose very harsh burdens on some people as side effects of actions that promise only small benefits to others.

At least in this original conception, the doctrine holds that absolute moral prohibitions refer to intentional acts of certain kinds, but not to actions having results of the same kind as the results of actions of the prohibited kind, if those results are not intended. For example, an action that involves intentional killing of an innocent person is held to be absolutely prohibited. But that prohibition does not necessarily apply to an action that brings about the death of an innocent as a side effect of doing something else. Killing some bystanders as side effects of a military action can be morally permissible; it will be if the action is necessary and focused, and if the deaths of the bystanders are not intended as a bonus or a larger plan to demoralize the enemy. 'No intentional killing' does not imply 'No killing as a side effect'. In bioethics, much of traditional morality, including traditional medical ethics, holds that euthanasia, understood as intentionally ending or shortening a person's life for the sake of removing suffering, is simply impermissible; however, using pain killing drugs, such as opioids, is not euthanasia but possibly palliation that might be morally justified, even if one thinks that earlier death is a likely risk of the intervention. Again: 'No intentional killing' does not imply 'No causing of death as a (non-intended) side effect of doing something otherwise good.' This central element of the doctrine of the double effect was named 'the principle of the side effect' by Elizabeth Anscombe (2001).[3]

Relatively little has been said about why this specific and very important normative significance is attributed to the distinction between what an agent intends in acting and what the agent accepts as a side effect of doing something else. Nevertheless, I believe that in the context provided by a commitment to the existence of absolute prohibitions plausibly does have this moral significance. These are prohibitive norms that exclude acts of certain kinds, and do so on the basis of elements contained within the description in virtue of which acts are of that kind. Consequently, moral absolutes apply prior to the all-things-considered assessment of an action; such considerations cannot remove or overturn the impermissibility of the action.

---

[2] This account of the Catholic formulations of double effect is lightly adapted from Boyle (2004); for a fuller story with references see Boyle (1980).

[3] Anscombe's (2001) definition of the principle of the side effect is the following: "the prohibition on murder does not cover *all* bringing about of deaths that are not intended. Not that such deaths are not often murder. But the quite clear and certain prohibition on intentional killing (with the relevant 'public' exceptions) does not catch you when your action brings about an unintended death." So much seems clear. But notice that the principle is modest: it says "where you must not aim at someone's death causing it does not necessarily cause guilt." (p. 61)

The reference of moral absolutes, however, must be limited so as to avoid contradiction, if they are to guide our choices. For example, an absolute prohibition of killing, if understood broadly as prohibiting causing death, will lead to contradiction in cases where refusing to kill one will cause the death of another. The need to limit moral absolutes does not imply that the limitation must be to intentional acts of the kind prohibited. However, the distinction between what one intends in acting and what one brings about as a side effect that is not intended marks a relevant difference in human power, since one can always choose not to perform an intentional action, but often cannot avoid doing what has bad side effects. That distinction, therefore, provides a reasonable limit to the reference of absolute prohibitions, and so avoids the potential for contradiction in a moral system that includes absolute prohibitions.[4]

As noted above, double effect doctrine includes more than this 'principle of the side effect' which limits the reference of absolute moral norms. Serious moral justification is obviously in order when one does what will bring about a bad side effect. For a bad side effect is a result of one's action which, if intended, would render the action simply wrong. If it is a side effect of a morally bad action or a trivial action, it cannot be justified morally; if there is anything else about bringing about a side effect that might make doing so wrong, for example, that it would be unfair to those on whom the bad side effect falls, then it is not justified.

Variations on this traditional conception of the doctrine of double effect have become quite common in modern normative and applied ethics. But virtually all these variations reject the absolutist context of Catholic and other forms of traditional morality. That, I have just suggested, is an essential part of the context in which double effect was justified in the Catholic tradition (however implicit that justification has remained). Outside that context the objections to various versions of double effect seem to me to be overwhelming, and so, for this discussion of the relationship between terminal sedation and double effect, I will work with the understanding of double effect as limiting the application of absolute prohibitions to intentional actions. I will briefly suggest at the end of this chapter why this is not a retreat into sectarian ethics.

5.2 Norms for Inducing Unconsciousness and the Value of Consciousness

I now turn to the first of the moral issues I plan to address: the moral justification of sedation, and, in particular, of terminal sedation, as I defined it above.

Everybody, not only medical personnel in clinical settings, often takes steps to reduce or remove, at least temporarily, their own or others' level of conscious awareness; most find no moral issue in doing so. Taking sleeping pills or using relaxation

---

[4]For a development of the issues raised by this way of justifying double effect see Boyle (2008) and Boyle (2011).

techniques to facilitate sleep is intentionally acting for the sake of the health and other benefits being asleep provides and causes; abuses surely are possible, but just as such acting to reduce or remove consciousness seems permissible. Similarly, anesthesia is sometimes used for the sake of achieving a therapeutically beneficial level of unconsciousness for the sake of enhancing the prospects of the success of a surgery.

Therefore, however valuable consciousness may be, common sense morality seems to indicate that seeking unconsciousness, that is, intentionally acting for the sake of inducing unconsciousness, is not generally morally problematic. Terminal sedation to the point of unconsciousness, does, however, raise a more serious moral question, because the sedation intended is to be continuous until death.

The reasons for this special concern about intentional terminal sedation are not mysterious. The person facing death ordinarily has issues to deal with, good-bys to say, religious actions to carry out – such as prayers to offer, sacraments to receive, and suffering to be offered up. These actions are sometimes morally required, and these responsibilities cannot be fulfilled by one who is unconscious. Such considerations do not, however, ground an absolute prohibition against terminal sedation. They would at most ground a prohibition against terminal sedation for those capable of rational human action such as prayer and conversation. However, even for those who can think and choose as they face death, these considerations do not reasonably ground a duty heroically to maintain the condition of consciousness once final prayers and goodbyes are completed and the prospects of agonizing death or complete incapacity are imminent.[5]

These considerations suggest that suppressing the consciousness of a dying person is not absolutely prohibited, but can be morally done (1) if there is a serious palliative reason for this step, (2) if there is no palliative option to inducing unconsciousness, and (3) if fulfillment of grave responsibilities is not prevented. The common sense moral evaluations I mentioned above support the stringency of the

---

[5]The relevant teaching of the Catholic Church, especially the papal magisterium since Pope Pius XII (1957), supports the skepticism expressed here about the existence of an absolute prohibition of terminal sedation (although I should add that the specific procedures I have called terminal sedation has not been expressly addressed by the Church's papal magisterium or that of the Catholic bishops of the whole world). Pope John Paul II, in the encyclical, *Evangelium Vitae* (John Paul II 1995) – which contains the most recent full-scale papal teaching on end of life matters – reaffirmed the constant modern teaching of the Church: "Pius XII affirmed that it is licit to relieve pain by narcotics even when the result is decreased consciousness and a shortening of life, "if no other means exist and if in the given circumstances, this does not prevent the carrying out of other religious and moral duties." In such a case, death is not willed or sought, even though for reasonable motives one runs the risk of it; there is simply the desire to ease pain effectively by using the analgesics which medicine provides. All the same "it is not right to deprive the dying person of consciousness without a serious reason": as they approach death people ought to be able to satisfy their moral and family duties, and above all they ought to be able to prepare in a fully conscious way for their definitive meeting with God."(John Paul II 1995) Paragraph 65. The internal quotes are from Pope Pius XII (1957); also cited is the Congregation for the Doctrine of the Faith's 1980 "Declaration on Euthanasia" (Sacred Congregation of the Doctrine of faith). The later does not add to Pius's teaching.

conditions that must surround this moral permission, since it permits much more than actions with temporary sedative goals such as using sleeping pills and anesthesia. These do not compromise, but ordinarily are a part of, a plan of living in which responsibilities to God and others are carried out. By contrast, terminal sedation compromises and often renders impossible those essential activities at an especially important time in life, so the continuous or permanent character of terminal sedation implies that undertaking it must be justified by very stringent conditions, such as those I have suggested above.

It is worth noting that the moral assessment I have been developing does not make use of the doctrine of the double effect; there is no suggestion that causing unconsciousness may be permissible only if it is a side effect of doing something else. Inducing reduced or complete unconsciousness seems to be the point of sedation, in the case of terminal sedation as in the morally unproblematic cases.[6]

5.2.1   The Goodness of Consciousness

Consciousness is obviously a great good; and if basic human goods are somehow the basis of moral obligation, it might seem that acting to suppress consciousness is simply wrong. Some explanation of the precise goodness of being conscious is, therefore, required.

Consciousness is evidently a human good. A person's being conscious plainly is a precondition for human action, and for distinctively human activities. Consciousness is clearly a pre-condition for the realization of the distinctively human activities that are important as a person faces death – especially religious actions, facing up to one's situation and making peace with and reaching out to others suffering because of one's predicament. This fact about consciousness does not, however, establish that consciousness as such is more than an all purpose empowerment, a means to what is more basically and finally good and fulfilling for human beings.

If consciousness were itself a component of the human good, not simply a pre-condition for the realization of some of the human goods, then I agree that it would be simply wrong to choose permanently to suppress it. But I believe consciousness is not a basic human good but instead two things that are closely related; first, as already noted, it is an empowerment that allows the pursuit of several basic human goods, notably goods such as friendship, moral integrity, and religion. Second, it is an element in a temporally significant pattern which is part of the good of biological health.

---

[6] This point seems to be supposed by Pope John Paul's differential treatment of suppressing consciousness on the one hand and shortening life on the other (John Paul II 1995), quoted above note 5. He uses double effect language to explain what is going on in the latter – death is not willed or sought – but not in the former. Pope John Paul is careful not to suggest the morally important intentional strictures of these actions are not the same.

The relationship between consciousness and human goods such as moral integrity and religion is no more than that of a necessary condition for their realization for the following reason. The consciousness that can be suppressed by human action is an aspect of the biological reality of humans as animals. Only such human powers can be directly accessed by manipulating the human body, as happens in sedation. The specifically spiritual powers of human persons – free will, knowledge and under-standing of truth – are not biological realities, and so are not identical with the conscious awareness humans share with higher animals. This is shown by the fact that conversation, study and reflection are the ways a person activates, and others access, these more spiritual powers. The exercise of rationality and choice certainly presuppose biologically based consciousness, but these remain ontologically and causally irreducible to biological events and structures. It is the exercise of these spiritual powers in which the morally and spiritually central human goods that are so emphasized by the popes as important at the time of death can be realized.

The partially constitutive role of consciousness within the human good of biological life and health, but only within a pattern of alertness and rest, is indicated by observations such as the following: The biological flourishing of animals such as humans obviously includes conscious awareness. Being especially alert on some occasions is necessary for life and health; on other occasions some diminution of alertness is needed for healthy living; and at others sleep or states of unresponsive-ness are needed. It is the pattern, not simply consciousness by itself, that is part of the good of health.

It follows that when one acts for the sake of greater or complete unresponsive-ness, that can be a healthy and a morally justified or even required choice. Therefore, the choice of sedation is not as such against the only human good that embraces (but only within the pattern I have described) the awareness human beings have as animals.

Consequently, a family or physician might choose terminal sedation for the sake of the only health one might pursue for a person so wracked with pain or upset that anything like normal biological functioning is out of the question. Here the appear-ances of good, the removal of this pain and distress, is the best that can be done – is all that can be done. When that is all of the good available, acting for it is not irrational.

Of course, this account of the value of consciousness will not sit well with those who hold that positive experiences are the foundation of what makes anything good, and negative experiences the foundation of what makes things bad. However, such broadly 'hedonistic' conceptions of value seem incapable of explaining the central goodness of substantive achievement by making good choices and developing virtue (which often does not register as pleasurable), and a person's deep interest not only in experiences, but in the survival and welfare of his or her fullest self in its full reality.

Moreover, on this experiential view of human good the difference between terminal sedation and euthanasia is bound to vanish, since being alive is valuable only as a condition for having those positive experiences. On that conception of the value of human living, the absolute prohibition against intentional killing will be irrational. The existence of a general, morally significant difference between terminal sedation and euthanasia presupposes that the latter is simply wrong while because of the difference in intention the former might be morally permissible. If euthanasia is not wrong, then separating terminal sedation from it is morally pointless.

To sum up the line of reasoning of this section so far: consciousness refers ambiguously to: (a) the awareness humans have of themselves and their environment insofar as they are sophisticated animals having a developed central nervous system, and (b) the human capacities to conceptualize, judge and choose. The former awareness is part of the basic human good of health, but only as an element in a pattern of wakefulness and sleep. One does not necessarily choose contrary to this human good when one chooses sedation, even terminal sedation. The latter awareness is what is essentially exercised in the realization of several important goods, but whatever its complicated relationship to the central nervous system, this level of consciousness involves an order of reality not in the reach of actions on the human body, such as medical interventions, but is accessible only in discussion and reflection. The consciousness explainable in biological terms is surely necessary for choice and understanding but it is not an ingredient in the goods realizable by exercising these powers.

5.2.2   Some Implications of This Account: Applying Double Effect

When one believes that a patient's condition is unlikely to allow for a level of consciousness that would sustain acts of understanding and choice, then it is not possible that suppressing consciousness will be flawed morally because it prevents the realization of these goods. These goods are simply not available in the patient's condition; indeed in this condition it would be irrational to hold that terminal sedation is undertaken to suppress the realization of the goods that can be realized in choosing and understanding. This is the clear case in which the condition that terminal sedation should not prevent the carrying out of moral and religious duties is met.

So far, double effect has not proved necessary for assessing the permissibility of the suppressing of consciousness that is central to the moral understanding of terminal sedation. But it does seem to be relevant in some cases similar to but importantly different from the clear case in which the terminal sedation is called for medically and does not prevent the execution of moral and religious duties.

What should we say about cases where some real possibility – but hardly a certainty – remains that a dying person might have the chance to make important choices and do important things if not terminally sedated? Suppose that the situation otherwise calls for terminal sedation.

In cases of this kind, I think double effect considerations do apply. For the prevention of the opportunity for executing moral duties occurs only as a side effect and is not intentional prevention. That prevention is a side effect of choosing to provide palliative care for the dying person. The other conditions of double effect will be satisfied if the other conditions are observed. However, when the likelihood is significant that choosing terminal sedation would have the effect of preventing carrying out such responsibilities – that is, when the patient's condition is such that without terminal sedation, the patient very likely will be able to understand duties and make free choices in respect to them – the terminal sedation is much more difficult to justify. Even in such cases, the prevention will not be intended but a side effect because probability or improbability of an outcome does not settle whether or not it is intended or accepted as a side effect. However, if the patient can think and choose or be expected to do so before death, the seriousness of the palliative reasons for sedation are likely to be doubtful, and other palliative options are likely to be available. In such cases, the reasonable conditions for justifiably suppressing consciousness until death are not met, even supposing that the prevention of thought and choice is a side effect only.

This analysis is relevant for assessing a perplexing form of terminal sedation, namely its use as a solution to one particular kind of case within the loosely defined category of is called 'existential suffering'.

The kind of existential suffering I have in mind is the form of suffering often distinguished from pain. Suffering in this sense includes a more rational assessment of one's predicament as bad, or in the extreme, as hopeless. It also involves a person's practical response to that assessment, sadness in the face of an evil one cannot get around. This particular form of 'existential suffering' is obviously a part of what many dying people experience. The reasoning of the previous paragraphs suggests that this form of terminal sedation cannot be justified as a general remedy for existential suffering, even on the supposition that the interventions involved in the sedation did not include the intention of death. The application of the double effect that could justify accepting as a side effect the removal of the capacity to choose and understand in cases where the terminal sedation is chosen for the sake of dealing with debilitating pain and biologically based distress *cannot* be easily extended to its use to remove the consciousness one has of one's unhappy situation. In such cases of terminal sedation (to unconsciousness) the aim would remain palliation, but the palliative effect would be sought and intentionally realized by making it impossible precisely to think and will.

For the kind of existential suffering on which I am focusing is not simply pain or other distress, as when one cannot catch one's breath, but suffering, which essentially includes judgment and volition, and is an element in a person's self in such a way that the goods of self integration, relating to others and to God are implicated in dealing with it. If this form of existential suffering is in fact an element that emerges within the human self as a free and responsible agent, and challenges the person to deal with God, others and him or herself in appropriate ways, it follows that the removal of consciousness to avoid precisely meeting these challenges is not undertaken for the sake of the biological health available, but precisely to make impossible those activities for which it is a pre-condition. In that case consciousness is suppressed so that further thought and willing – the substance of this form of existential suffering – cannot exist.

Suppressing a function of the human person has seemed morally questionable to many traditionally minded moralists. But that is not the normative foundation of the preceding argument. I agree that thought and choice, intelligence and will, are important human functions to say the least. But the normatively central fact is that suppressing the capacity to think and choose *so as not to deal with* the thoughts, choices and reactions that would be called for appears to be choosing against the goods of personal integrity, sociality, and religion.

I believe that resisting terminal sedation for the sake of dealing with this form of existential suffering is a perspicuous example of the concern that there be a very serious reason for suppressing consciousness at the end of life. Choosing terminal sedation for this reason appears to be a case of refusing to live life to its end. That said, I have given a sharp definition of a form of 'existential suffering', and have supposed that it is easily distinguishable from more biologically based misery. Sorting this out in practice is likely to be very difficult. But dealing with severe pain and other biological distress is a different matter than dealing with suffering in the larger sense; medicine is proportioned to the former; talk, prayer and conversion are what address the latter on its own terms.

5.3 Terminal Sedation and Euthanasia

The second moral issue to be addressed concerns the relationship between euthanasia and terminal sedation. Euthanasia is intentional killing for the sake of relieving pain and suffering. Terminal sedation is inducing unconsciousness for palliative reasons. These are obviously distinct kinds of human action. They can be difficult practically to distinguish only when terminal sedation is expected to hasten, or involves the risk of hastening, death. In such cases double effect will be useful by directing decision makers to the question whether the terminal sedation in fact involves the intention to shorten life. If it does then the action is morally indistinguishable from euthanasia; if not, it remains palliative care only.

I emphasize that double effect is needed for this clarification *only when* terminal sedation is expected to have life shortening effects. In fact the clinical literature I have seen suggests that such cases are not the rule but exceptional (Fohr 1998; McIntyre 2009, 2011).[7] Apparently, opioids in large doses can suppress breathing; but opioids are not normally used for sedation. Other analgesics and sedatives do not generally have life shortening effects (Regnard et al. 2011).

---

[7] See Fohr "It is important to emphasize that there is no debate among specialists in palliative care and pain management on this issue. There is a broad consensus that when used appropriately, respiratory depression from opioid analgesics is a rarely occurring side effect. The belief that palliative care hastens death is counter to the experience of physicians with the most experience in this area. No studies have shown that patient's lives have been shortened through the administration of appropriate pain medication." (p. 319) My attention was drawn to this statement by Sumner (2011), pp. 50–55.

In the cases of terminal sedation in which sedating the patient is expected to have life shortening effects (however rare they may be), it might seem that it is arbitrary whether one calls the action palliative terminal sedation or euthanasia. In both cases death is hastened; in both cases the suffering is ended. Supposing that the morally significant differences are to be found in the agents' intentions, there are likely to be at least some cases in which it is very difficult, especially for third parties, to determine what action is being done.

However, the kinds and doses of analgesics and sedatives used for the sake of ending a person's life are ordinarily distinguishable from the kinds and doses used for continuous sedation (Hawryluck et al. 2002). Given that these matters are not interior to agents but public, and given that the intentional meaning of such public matters as the size of a dose, and the increases in dosage as recorded in a patient's chart can be clarified in conversation, the intentions involved are generally accessible.

The conversational and forensic articulation of intentions considers the agent's account of what he or she did and why. If the agent's means, that is, the chosen behavior (including refraining from doing something or stopping doing it) is revealed as obviously and straightforwardly contributing to the acknowledged goal, then the intention is clear, but when it remains unsettled after conversation about how what the agent did was thought to contribute to what the agent proposed as the goal, one has ground for suspecting that the full intention is not acknowledged. In the case at hand, if the expected shortening of life caused by the sedation is a side effect only, no further sedatives beyond those required to realize the state of unresponsiveness in which the patient is comfortable should be used. If further painkillers or sedatives were used, one might then ask why, and pursue the possibility that they might have life shortening effects and that those effects were sought as a bonus to the sedation. If it emerges that shortening life is being treated as a bonus, the terminal sedation involves intentional killing.

This clarification of intentions is especially important in cases of terminal sedation in which nutrition and hydration are withheld. As I noted in my initial definition of terms, some who discuss terminal sedation define it as including the withholding of nutrition and hydration. These steps are no doubt closely conjoined in clinical practice; nevertheless, they seem to me practically and morally distinct – a point that seems to be acknowledged by the fact that those who regard the conjoined items as one clinical reality nevertheless separate them for moral purposes (Rietjens et al. 2004).[8]

Moreover, it is, I believe, a mistake to suppose that, because withholding nutrition and hydration is not an action but a choice not to act, it belongs in the morally separate category of an omission, of allowing rather than doing. One can choose not to do something or to stop doing it. Often that will mean doing something else. Clearly that is a choice; instead of doing something one can do for some purpose one embraces, one chooses not to realize that goal.

---

[8] See quotation in note 9 below.

Such choices are quite different from cases in which a person just does not do what he or she could and should do. These latter are omissions in the strict sense. They do require special moral consideration (Aquinas; Boyle 2008). But choices not to act have the same structure as choices to act. Our responsibility for them is of the same kind as in other choices, as is clear from cases in which one chooses not to do something beneficial for another and refrains for the sake of seeing the other harmed.

So, the intentions precisely of the decision to withhold nutrition and hydration also need to be articulated as required by double effect. The key to this articulation is identifying the precise reason for withholding the nutrition and hydration. Is the reason that the dying patient cannot absorb the nourishment or hydration? Is it that the provision of hydration and nutrition makes the patient uncomfortable, or risks other undesirable events such as vomiting? Is it that the dying patient cannot benefit and will not be harmed by withholding these things? Or is the reason that the absence of nutrition and hydration will end the patient's life sooner and so end sooner the ordeal for all concerned?

Luke Gormally (2010) objects to the withholding of nutrition and hydration conjoined to terminal sedation on the supposition that the general reason for withholding nutrition and hydration in this context is shortening life. I agree that this is a reason for some, particularly among those who see terminal sedation with withholding nutrition and hydration as an option preferable to euthanasia. Moreover, there is evidence that some physicians who practice terminal sedation conjoined to withholding nutrition and hydration intend the shortening of life, in the withholding, the sedating or both (Rietjens et al. 2004).[9]

However, the possibility that there are other reasons for withholding nutrition and hydration in this context cannot be excluded a priori. I believe that the possible reasons I suggested in the two paragraphs above cannot be excluded without paying attention to the actual intentions of the actors in the situation. I suggest, therefore, that clear headed conversation about the reasons for withholding nutrition and/or hydration in various clinical circumstances cannot be cut short. The fact that the expected shortening of life due to withholding nutrition and hydration is sometimes very brief, together with my own experience in speaking to clinicians who have proposed as reasons considerations very like those I have suggested, warns against a general exclusion of conjoining terminal sedation and withholding nutrition and hydration as necessarily a case of euthanasia.

---

[9] "Of all physicians, 36 % reported having made their most recent decision to perform terminal sedation without the intention of hastening death. The physicians partly had the intention to hasten death in 47 % of cases and had the explicit intention in 17 % of cases. This explicit intention involved sedation only in 2 % of the physicians' most recent cases, only the foregoing of artificial nutrition or hydration in 14 % of cases, and both sedation and the foregoing of artificial nutrition or hydration in 1 % of cases." (Rietjens et al. 2004, pp. 180–181).

5.4   The Public Relevance of Double Effect
   Based Moral Analysis

The approach to the moral issues surrounding terminal sedation which I have taken in this chapter has been unabashedly Catholic. I approach double effect as formulated and understood within the Catholic tradition of moral inquiry. This might lead some to believe that my assessments are essentially religious and theological, and so incapable of being ingredients within the so called 'public reason' that is the basis for law and the policies of pluralistic institutions and professions.

As noted above, double effect emerged within Catholic moral thinking. However, there is nothing about that doctrine as such that is specifically religious. As I explained double effect, it is a procedural rule that guides the formulation and application of moral norms. The heart of double effect is the principle of the side effect which limits the reference of moral absolutes to intentional acts, and thereby blocks their application to actions having side effects of a kind that would render impermissible an act of intentionally being them about. This rule, therefore supposes that there are norms that are absolute.

Moral absolutes are out of favor among secular moralists nowadays, and Catholicism seems to be one of a relatively few current communities in which moral absolutes are accepted as an essential part of the foundation of moral life.[10] But even this conviction is not strictly religious. The existence of moral absolutes is not a matter of religious dogma, but of morality that Catholics believe to be rationally defensible and accessible generally to human beings.

Double effect is a further step removed from religion or sectarian ethics. For it does not pretend to establish the truth of those absolutes, being instead a rule for limiting and applying them. Double effect does not say that intentional killing is always wrong, it says rather that this moral truth does not and cannot imply that any action that leads to death is always wrong; sometimes whatever we do, some lives will be lost or some other very great goods damaged. So, double effect blocks the move from intentional killing is wrong to all causing death is wrong.

It follows that double effect can have application wherever a norm is put forward as absolute. That norm need not be anything as strategic or general as the norm prohibiting intentional killing of the innocent, nor need such a norm be as central to an ethical system as the absolutes of Catholic morality are within that system.

The point is that any prohibition which a society, institution or profession has reason to hold to be absolute, that is, as infeasible by considerations not included in the characterization of the kind of act prohibited, would be reasonably limited by the principle of the side effect. The objection that double effect is religious dogma is, therefore, off target, and the supposition that its application presupposes

---

[10] Elizabeth Anscombe (1958) noted that the existence of moral absolutes is central to Christian morality; that the unanimous rejection of moral absolutes by philosophers of all stripes in contemporary moral philosophy is the most salient feature of this movement; and that silence on the importance of this salient fact is a sign of a certain provinciality of mind.

traditional Catholic justifications and very general absolute prohibitions against such things as idolatry, adultery, murder and lying is false.

Double effect regulates the application of prohibitions that are reasonably judged to be absolute, that is, not defeasible by other moral considerations. The relevance of double effect is not affected by the particular moral reasoning in support of holding any prohibition to be absolute. Consequently, the question about the public use of double effect, in the larger euthanasia debate and elsewhere, reduces to the question whether there are reasons for maintaining some public rules as absolute. It does appear that there are cases where it is reasonable for a society, institution or profession to treat as absolute some of the norms by which it operates. For example, in the area of private killing, a polity may have good reason to adopt a public norm forbidding all private killing of one person by others. The ground for this might be quite far removed from a general ethical doctrine such as the sanctity of life doctrine, and it might include a number of pragmatic and institutional considerations, such as the importance of communicating to everybody that individuals do not have any discretion about the matter.

In the more limited context of a profession's ethics, the medical profession might judge that for the sake of its integrity and the trust of the public its ethical codes must include some absolute prohibitions such as that against intentional killing.[11] I believe that the medical profession and society in fact have very strong reasons to prohibit certain actions by doctors. Killing patients, even at their request and for benevolent motives, is one of those plausibly prohibited actions. Now, how far can such a ban extend? To all intentional killing of patients? Surely. Should the prohibition extend to those decisions to treat and not to treat that predictably shorten life? Surely not, since the principle of the side effect will remind us that absolute prohibition will require limitation. Medical professionals can avoid intentionally killing patients, but there are many situations in which however they decide their decisions will have life shortening side effects or other unacceptable effects.

The arguments only suggested and surely not developed in the preceding few paragraphs seem to me to be at the heart of the public debate about end of life issues.[12] Neither the complaint that double effect, a rule for limiting the conclusions of such arguments, is unsound nor the objection that a religious sanctity of life doctrine is being imposed is reasonably taken to be center stage. If double effect points to a reasonable limitation of moral absolutes, it is not out of line to appeal to it to block inferences from the moral permissibility of withholding extraordinary treatments or taking risks to patient's lives to help them (where the bad effects are not intended) to the public legitimacy of euthanasia or assisted suicide (where death is the intended goal).

---

[11] See Edmund Pellegrino's (2005) list, based not on a general sanctity of life doctrine but the requirements of good medical practice.

[12] See Grisez and Boyle (1979) for a development of such considerations, especially those based on justice and respect for individual liberty, but not, as a public policy matter, on the sanctity of life.

Consequently, double effect is an important tool both clinically and in public debate for situating end of life treatments, and for getting clear about whether or not actions that look like intentional killing really are that. In the light of that clarification, the acceptance of terminal sedation as a part of palliative care for the dying is not precedent for euthanasia, although some questionable uses of terminal sedation may in fact be intentional killing.

References

Anscombe, E. 1958. Modern moral philosophy. *Philosophy* 33(124): 1–19.
Anscombe, E. 2001. Medalist's address: Action, intention and double effect. In *The doctrine of double effect*, ed. P.A. Woodward. Notre Dame: University of Notre Dame Press.
Aquinas, T. Summa Theologiae. 2–2, q. 64, a. 7.
Aquinas, T. Summa Theologiae, 1–2, q. 6, a. 3.
Boyle, J. 1980. Toward understanding double effect. *Ethics* 90: 527–538.
Boyle, J. 2004. Medical ethics and double effect. The case of terminal sedation. *Theoretical Medicine and Bioethics* 25: 53–54.
Boyle, J. 2008. The moral meaning and justification of the doctrine of the double effect: A response to Robert Anderson. *The American Journal of Jurisprudence* 53: 69–84.
Boyle, J. 2011. On defining 'side effects: A response to Adam Bailey. *The American Journal of Jurisprudence* 56: 169–182.
Fohr, S. 1998. The double effect of pain medication: Separating myth from reality. *Journal of Palliative Medicine* 1: 315–328.
Gormally, L. 2010. Terminal sedation and the doctrine of the sanctity of life. In *Terminal sedation: Euthanasia in disguise?* 81–86, ed. T. Tannsjo. Dordrecht: Kluwer.
Grisez, G., and J. Boyle. 1979. *Life and death with liberty and justice: A contribution to the Euthanasia debate*. Notre Dame: University of Notre Dame Press.
Gury, J.P.S.J. 1869. *Compendium theologiae moralis*, 2nd ed., 6–8. (revised by A/. Ballerieni, SJ) (Rome and Turin, 1869).
Hawryluck, L.A., W.R. Harvey, L. Lemieux-Charles, and P.A. Singer. 2002. Consensus guidelines on analgesia and sedation in dying intensive care unit patients. *BMC Medical Ethics* 3: 3. Available at: http://www.biomedcentral.com/1472-6939/3/3.
John Paul II. 1995. Encyclical Letter Evangelium Vitae. Vatican. Available at: http://www.vatican.va/holy_father/john_paul_ii/encyclicals/documents/hf_jp-ii_enc_25031995_evangelium-vitae_en.html.
McIntyre, A. 2009. The doctrine of double effect. In *The Stanford encyclopedia of philosophy* (Spring 2009 Edition), ed. E. Zalta. Available at: http://plato.stanford.edu/archives/spr2009/entries/doubleeffect.
McIntyre, A. 2011. Doing away with double effect. *Ethics* 111: 255.
Pellegrino, E. 2005. Some things ought never to be done: Moral absolutes in clinical ethics. *Theoretical Medicine and Bioethics* 26: 469–486.
Pope Pius XII, AAS 49, 24 November 1957.
Regnard, C., R. George, E. Grogan, T. Harlow, S. Hutchison, J. Keen, S. McGettrick, C. Manson, S.A. Murray, V. Robinson, P. Stone, and C. Tallon. 2011. So, farewell then, doctrine of double effect. *BMJ* 343: d4512. doi:10.1136/bmj.d4512.
Rietjens, J.A.C., A. van der Heide, A.M. Vrakking, B.D. Onwuteaka-Philipsen, P.J. van der Maas, and G. van der Wal. 2004. Physician reports of terminal sedation without hydration or nutrition for patients nearing death in the Netherlands. *Annals of Internal Medicine* 141(4): 178–185.

Sacred Congregation of the Doctrine of faith. Declaration on Euthanasia. Available at: http://www.vatican.va/roman_curia/congregations/cfaith/documents/rc_con_cfaith_doc_19800505_euthanasia_en.html.

Sumner, L.W. 2011. *Assisted death. A study in ethics and law*. Oxford: Oxford University Press.

Tannnsjo, T. 2010. Terminal sedation. A substitute for Euthanasia. In *Terminal sedation: Euthanasia in disguise?* ed. T. Torbjorn, 15–31. Dordrecht: Kluwer.

.

Chapter 6
The Field of Application of the Principle of the Double Effect and the Problem of Palliative Sedation

Alejandro Miranda

6.1 Introduction

A question arises in relation to the problem of palliative sedation as to whether the administration of drugs that have the effect of deprivation of consciousness in the patient, is or is not an action that could (or should) be justified by the application of the so called "principle of the double effect" (PDE). To answer this question it is necessary to establish exactly the field of application of this principle, that is to say, what are the bad effects whose production must be justified under the PDE. Is it necessary to justify, by virtue of the PDE, every human action which has an effect that in any sense could be called "bad"? If the answer is No, then what bad effects are to be included in the field of its application? In this chapter, I seek to demonstrate that the field of application of the PDE is more limited than what is sometimes thought, to conclude finally that the deprivation of consciousness, in itself, does not have to be justified by virtue of the PDE. With this objective, I will proceed as follows: firstly, I will briefly expose the meaning of the PDE and the elements that constitute it; secondly, I will analyse the link between the PDE and the doctrine of intrinsically evil acts; thirdly, I will show some improper uses of the PDE and I will explain why they are improper; fourthly, I will answer certain possible objections to the thesis that I am defending; fifthly, I will refer to the relationship between PDE and the principle of totality; and finally, I will present the arguments which, in my view, prove that the deprivation of consciousness is not an effect which, in itself, should be justified by virtue of the PDE.

A. Miranda (✉)
Faculty of Law, Universidad de los Andes, Santiago, Chile
e-mail: amiranda@uandes.cl

P. Taboada (ed.), *Sedation at the End-of-life: An Interdisciplinary Approach*,   73
Philosophy and Medicine 116, DOI 10.1007/978-94-017-9106-9_6,
© Springer Science+Business Media Dordrecht 2015

6.2 The Principle of the Double Effect: Meaning and Elements

The PDE establishes that a bad effect which will always be immoral to intend—that is, to procure as the end of the action or as a means to achieve a further end—could, however, be justifiably tolerated or accepted if it arose only as the side effect of an in itself permissible action which is necessary to achieve a good of proportionate importance.[1] The paradigmatic example of this type of effect is the death of an innocent human being. He who *intentionally* kills an innocent human being necessarily commits a "homicide", an action always evil or unjust and which, therefore, is absolutely forbidden. On the other hand, a person who carries out an in itself permissible action that has the foreseen side effect of the death of an innocent person, not always commits homicide: the person acts justifiably if the action is necessary to achieve a good of proportionate importance.

The PDE emerges and makes sense, therefore, in the context of a tradition of moral thinking according to which there are some bad outcomes that can never permissibly be intended, neither as a means to an end nor, *a fortiori*, as ends in themselves. This tradition (from now on: double effect tradition) maintains that: (i) there are some human actions which are absolutely forbidden, and (ii) that those human actions are always described in terms of the effects or state of affairs that the agent intends when carrying them out.

The main element on which PDE is based is the thesis that sustains that the distinction between intended effects and side effects is morally relevant. This moral relevance is explained as follows: if a voluntary action is considered absolutely forbidden by virtue of the effect or state of affairs which it brings about, this absolute prohibition can only refer to an action in which that effect is procured as an end or as a means, but not to an action from which this effect follows collaterally or indirectly, even when the effect has already been foreseen with certainty. To briefly state it, the moral relevance of the distinction between intended effects and side effects (hereafter: IE/SE distinction) is that in relation to certain effects or states of affairs, the end never justifies the means, but it can justify the side effects. If, instead, we talk about effects that could be permissibly procured as a means to an end, the IE/SE distinction has no moral relevance.

The moral relevance of the IE/SE distinction is the *central* element of the PDE, but it is not the only one. In fact, the PDE does *not* say that it is permissible to bring

---

[1] An extended formulation of the PDE could be the following: "If by a human action there are two effects, a good one and a bad one, and the latter is one of those that is never permissible to intend, that action could only be justified when all the following requirements are fulfilled simultaneously: first, that the action, if considered independently from the bad effect, will be permissible; second, that only the good effect would be the aim of the action; third, that the bad effect is not chosen as a means of achieving the good effect; fourth, that there is no other way less harmful to achieve the good effect; and fifth, that the agent is not compelled more to avoid the bad effect than to attain the good effect". PDE also gets called the principle of indirect voluntary, and, on other occasions, doctrine, rule, law or reasoning of the double effect.

about any kind of bad effect provided only that the effect is purely collateral: it also demands that there should be a proportionally important reason or serious moral reason to justify the action. This supposes, firstly, that there should not exist a less harmful way to achieve the good effect, and, secondly, that the good effect should be sufficiently important in relation to the bad effect, so that the agent is not under more obligation to avoid the bad effect than to achieve the good effect (Aquinas, *ST*, II-II, q. 64, a. 7c; Cavanaugh 2006, p. 12, 33–34).[2] However, this requirement for a proportionate reason is not an element confined to the double effect doctrine. In general, moral theories agree that it is not permissible, gratuitously or for trivial motives, to bring about damages or bad effects, that is to say, they agree that if an agent is going to carry out an action where damage or bad effect follows, this agent must have a proportionate reason to act. Of course, the different moral theories could differ over the ways to establish the proportionate reason. For example, for some kinds of consequentialism the proportion is established according to a calculation of the good and bad in a pre-moral sense. On the contrary, for the double effect tradition the proportion is determined by also addressing moral considerations, like the obligations deriving from the state or activity of the acting person, and other commitments previously agreed by that person.

6.3   Principle of the Double Effect and Intrinsically Evil Acts

Not all actions that have a bad effect require justification through the PDE. This is due to the fact that there are many bad effects—or bad states of affairs—which is permissible to set up as objects of the will (*i.e.* of intention and choice). Accordingly, when an action brings about a bad effect of this sort, the only thing necessary for its justification is that the agent has a valid reason to act. Among the bad effects that could be permissibly intended are, for example, the destruction of a material good (even someone else's property), the destruction or death of a vegetative living, and the destruction or death of a non-rational animal. Thus, a fire-fighter can licitly intend to destroy a wall to rescue people in a house on fire; an individual may licitly intend to destroy a tree in his garden (*v. gr.*, by burning it) if he is allergic to that tree; and a subject can licitly intend to slaughter and butcher a cow to feed himself. In none of these cases the agent needs to invoke the PDE to justify his actions: it is sufficient to act with a proportionate motive, which is a general requirement to justify any action which produces a bad effect. Therefore, in these cases the IE/SE distinction lacks relevance. In the end, what happens is that if the named effects or states of affairs could, somehow, be considered "bad", they are not so in the sense that they render immoral the choice that falls on them.

That said, what are the effects or states of affairs which make immoral the choice that falls on them? Those which the double effect tradition has presented as such can

---

[2] The first class proportion could be characterized as a proportion between the action and its end, and the second as a proportion between the good effect and the bad effect.

be known by looking at those actions considered to be intrinsically evil. In fact, an action is intrinsically evil when the will is directed, as to its object, to one of these states of affairs. If such a hypothesis occurs, the choice of the will is judged intrinsically disordered, always evil, and therefore, absolutely forbidden. For each intrinsically evil action there is, thus, an effect or state of affairs which it is not permissible to choose (or intend).[3] If we take two examples of intrinsically evil actions proposed by Aristotle, namely, homicide and adultery,[4] it can be observed that, in the case of homicide, which is the intentional or direct killing of an innocent human being, the effect or state of affairs chosen, and which it is not permissible to choose, is the death of an innocent human being; and in the case of adultery, which means choosing to have sexual intercourse with a person not your own spouse or with a person married to a third party, the effect or state of affairs chosen, and which is not permissible to choose, is precisely the extramarital intercourse.

The classical double effect tradition did not have a precise rule of general application to determine which states of affairs are never permissible to choose, or, equally, when an object is bad or when an act is intrinsically evil. For each case there is always a special argument (and, sometimes, these arguments are clearly physicalistic[5]) (Sánchez 1605; Gury 1862). Some contemporary theoreticians of natural law have proposed a precise rule of general application for such purpose. This is the case of Germain Grisez, Joseph Boyle, and John Finnis for whom is intrinsically evil any action which "involves a choice to destroy, damage or impede some instance of a basic human good" (Finnis et al. 1987, p. 293), Each time that the description of an action reveals such a choice, the intrinsic malice of that action is established. In this way, if the basic human goods are adequately identified, it could be known that any action in which the intention is to destroy one of them is intrinsically evil. This is the reason why the following examples of actions fall under this condition: homicide, which destroys directly the basic human good of life; lie, which impedes directly the basic human good of practical reasonableness or authenticity; and contraception, which infringes directly the basic human goods of life and marriage (Finnis et al. 1987; Finnis 1998; Grisez 1993).[6] Robert Spaemann also appears to present a criterion to recognize intrinsically evil actions. The German

---

[3] This is nothing but a corollary of the thesis that human actions are specified morally by their object, that is to say, by the state of affairs chosen by the acting person's will, and that a human action is intrinsically evil when it is evil because of its species.

[4] Cf.Aristotle 1984, *Nicomachean Ethics*. II, 6, 1107a8 et seq.

[5] This is what happens, for example, in the case of direct pollution. The moralist of the double effect tradition used to declare that the direct pollution, that is, the intentional effusion of semen outside the marital act, is intrinsically evil because it is opposed to the end for which semen was destined by nature, which is procreation (Sánchez 1605; Gury 1862, p. 166).

[6] About homicide, cf. Finnis et al. 1987, pp. 298–300. At this point, the authors diverge from the traditional concept, because they consider intrinsically evil any direct killing of a human being, and not only that of the innocent (cf. Finnis et al. 1987, p. 317 and Finnis 1998, pp. 279–282). The lie inhibits practical reasonableness (*bonum rationis*), as this good involves "the person's integrity or authenticity —harmony of inner with outer aspects of the person—" (Finnis 1998, p. 161). About contraception, cf. Grisez 1993, pp. 509, 633 and Finnis 1998, p. 181.

author maintains that if the traditional canon of this type of actions is reviewed, it appears that they are actions which instrumentalize spheres of life where personality is expressed directly and naturally. These spheres are the organic life, language and sexuality. This is why, according to Spaemann, "in the classical philosophical and theological tradition the action of intentionally and directly killing innocent and unarmed men, intentional betrayal of trust saying untruthful things, and the separation of sexuality from its integral human context have been kept out of any weighing of goods and declared always unjustifiable" (Spaemann 2003, pp. 223–224).

6.4 Use and Abuse of the Double Effect Principle

In any case, independently of whether it is or is not a precise rule of general application to determine which bad effects are never permissible to be intended, the field of application of the PDE is more limited than what is sometimes thought. It is not unusual, however, to overlook this fact and to invoke the PDE in issues that are out of its field of operation. For example, some defenders of the principle illustrate it through examples in which the bad effect is environmental pollution. The PDE—it is claimed—would allow the justification of environmental pollution caused by industrial activity or vehicle traffic, because environmental pollution is only a side effect of such activities, and there is, also, a proportionate reason to carry them out (Oderberg 2000, p. 102; 2010, pp. 324–325). But this is a mistake. To make the pollution action permissible it is only necessary to have a proportionate reason to act, but it is not necessary that the pollution is a side effect. Here we have the same situation as in the case of an action which damages property: for the permissibility of the action damaging property it is only necessary to have a proportionate reason to act, but it is not necessary that the damage is a side effect. A fireman, as stated above, can licitly intend to destroy the property as a means of saving a person. It is rare, of course, that pollution could be a means to a sufficiently important end, but it is not impossible.[7]

The PDE, therefore, as a justification principle, only operates where a double effect action is justified, precisely and uniquely, because the bad effect produced is merely collateral. If the justification of an action that produces a bad effect does not demand that such effect be collateral, the PDE is not truly operating, because the action is not justified *by virtue of it*. In other words, the fact that an action (i) brings about a good and a bad effect, (ii) brings about the bad effect merely collaterally, and (iii) is justified, does not necessarily mean that such an action is justified by virtue of the PDE, because for this it is required that such action *is only justified by*

---

[7] Following the classical examples of blackmailing tyrants, consider here the case of a terrorist who says that if we do not start to operate the polluting chimney of our enterprise so as to reach a certain level of particles in the air, he will detonate a powerful bomb that he has hidden at the children's playgroup in town. There is no doubt that in this case it would be permissible, in principle, to intend to contaminate as a means of avoiding that the terrorist carries out his threat.

the fact that the bad effect is merely collateral. So, to know if it is the PDE which is justifying an action it is possible to ask the following counterfactual question: Could a good end justify an action in which this same bad effect was intended as a means? Only in case of a negative answer is it the PDE what provides the justification.

Otherwise, the action is justified because the agent has a proportionate reason to act, and not *because* the bad effect is collateral, even though the effect is collateral. If the proportionate reason were enough to justify the action, we would be in a case in which someone could deny the PDE (or the moral relevance of the IE/SE distinction) and even so could offer a *truthful* justification for that action.[8]

The abuse of the PDE—that is to say, its invocation in cases in which it is not applicable—seems to be due to a great extent to the irruption of proportionalism. In fact, the discussion with proportionalism has meant that some authors in tune with the classical tradition of the natural law fall victim to an urge to correct the PDE, thinking that the morality of an action can never be determined solely by the proportion between good and evil. Nevertheless, the classical tradition of natural law—and the double effect tradition that emerges within it—does not deny the relevance of the proportionate reason; neither has it denied that certain bad effects could be procured as means to a good end. The *fundamental* difference between the proportionalist or consequentialist moral doctrine and the moral doctrine of the double effect tradition lies in that, for the first, the calculation of the consequences or balance of proportionality is always the only relevant factor to establish the morality of human actions, while for the second, this calculation is important, but it has a radical limit: the person's dignity. That is to say, according to the double effect tradition, each time that the choice of a certain state of affairs implies reducing a person to a condition of thing, or of mere instrument, the calculation of proportion or consequences ceases: that action must always be omitted. But it is evident that not every human action in which is intended an effect that, in some way, could be called "bad", implies a violation of the human dignity. For example, to intentionally contaminate the environment as a means of saving a person is not an action that violates in itself human dignity. The action of intentional pollution, therefore, is not intrinsically evil or always morally disordered: it will only be immoral if there is no proportionate reason, that is, if the pollution of the environment is done as a means for a bad end or as a means for an end which is not sufficiently important. Neither is the intentional destruction of another person's property an action which, in itself, violates human dignity. Hence, the destruction

---

[8] From what was explained recently, it follows that the moral relevance of the IE/SE distinction, as it is used by the double effect tradition, cannot be proved by any argument based on the fact that the rejection of that distinction will take us to the almost complete inactivity or paralysis. This argument, which does not prove, is called upon, for example, in: (Zalba 1987, p. 687; Oderberg 2000, p. 90; 2010, p. 342); and, in some way, in (Anderson 2009, p. 263). The argument fails because it overlooks the existence of many bad effects which is permissible to intend as means to an end, in such a way that even without assigning any moral relevance to the IE/SE distinction they could continue to be brought about. Again: to bring about bad effects like the death of a non-rational animal, the destruction of property, the air pollution or, in general, any damage to a non-rational being, it is only necessary to have a proportionate or serious moral reason.

of property and the other "bad" effects referred to above could be permissibly procured as means to a good end.

To sum up, only human dignity, which is absolutely inviolable, can be the foundation of absolute prohibitions, that is to say, prohibitions that are kept out of all calculation of consequences. The value of sub-human realities is not absolute. These realities are essentially instrumental, and therefore can be treated as mere means to achieve sufficiently important ends. The first proponents of the PDE, nonetheless, did not invoke human dignity to explain the foundation of the intrinsically evil acts and the resulting principle's scope. However, the idea that the human being is a certain end in him/herself and should never be treated as a mere means clearly underlies the thesis of the intrinsic malice of the direct or intentional killing of an innocent person (homicide), because what is stated in this way is precisely that it is in itself unjust to kill an innocent as a means to any end.

So, the actions that are intrinsically evil or always morally disordered are specified by the effects or the state of affairs which the agent intends or chooses, not by the effects produced in a collateral, indirect or incidental form when licit, necessary and proportionate actions are carried out. However, this point refers to the justification of the moral relevance of the IE/SE distinction, which will not at this time be dealt with.[9]

6.5 Objections

The idea that the PDE deals only with effects or states of affairs which would be always immoral to intend has been defended, in the contemporary discussion, mainly by Joseph Boyle. Boyle declares that the principle establishes the conditions that make it licit to bring about certain types of damage to people. To the tradition, continues Boyle, these damages are of different kinds—including corporal damage, like death or injury to the agent or a third party, and moral damage, like helping another person to commit sin or get oneself in a situation of sinning—, "but they have in common that they are all harms which would be absolutely impermissible to bring about intentionally" (Boyle 1991, p. 476). By virtue of these considerations, Boyle concludes that "[o]utside the absolutist context of the Catholic tradition, DDE [doctrine of the double effect] is not needed; and those who reject this context are not entitled to use it" (Boyle 1991, p. 477).

As has been presented by Boyle, the thesis that the PDE applies only to effects that would never be permissible to intentionally bring about has received objections from two different sides. Firstly, it has been claimed that apart from an absolutist context (that is to say, the context of a moral theory that defends the existence of absolute prohibitions) the double effect doctrine is also meaningful. Secondly, and from an absolutist context, it has been said that the doctrine also applies to types of evils which in some cases would be permissible to intend, as long as it is not

---

[9]The argument does seem conclusive to me is explained, in a summary form in (Miranda 2012, pp. 263–265).

permissible to intend them when the choice is made. The first of these objections is presented by Mark Aulisio. The second, by Robert Anderson.

According to Aulisio, Boyle unjustifiably limits the PDE's home. For Aulisio, "[t]he intention/side effect distinction may operate within a non-absolutist framework provided that it functions as a deontic constraint over a certain range of action" (Aulisio 1997, p. 154). Some types of rule utilitarianism would constitute an example of this non-absolutist framework. So, adds Aulisio, "[i]t is not hard to envision a rule utilitarianism in which agents might be forbidden from ever intentionally harming another" (Aulisio 1997, p. 154). Without dealing here with the question of whether, and when, the rule utilitarianism is truly a utilitarianism (Spaemann 1991, pp. 185–187), supposing that such doctrine were to formulate an absolute prohibition, even though in a limited field, then Aulisio's criticism could be valid, but only against the limitation of the PDE to the absolutist context of the Catholic tradition which Boyle makes, and not against the more general statement which I sustain here, namely, that the principle refers to bad effects that it would never be permissible to intend.

An example of a non-absolutist framework in which the PDE could, in principle, operate, is Richard McCormick's moral doctrine. McCormick—who recognizes himself as a teleologian or proportionalist moralist—does not entirely deny the relevance of the IE/SE distinction, and, at the same time, states that there are virtually absolute moral norms, such as that which forbids terror bombing (McCormick 1978).[10] That is why, in McCormick's theory, the PDE would indeed be relevant to judge the morality of the killing of non-combatants in war, because such killing would only be permissible if it were indirect and there is a proportionate reason to bring it about. However, this redirects the problem to whether a moral doctrine such as McCormick's or the rule utilitarianism can soundly be sustained. Boyle (with reason in my view) thinks not, and therefore could still maintain that both theories are not entitled to the PDE.

Robert Anderson's objection is that the PDE applies to anything which, when the choice is made, would be impermissible to intend, to bring about, or to intend not to pursue (Anderson 2007, pp. 265, 270).[11] So, for example, even if it is not

---

[10] For McCormick (1978), the IE/SE distinction is generally applicable, in relation to all kinds of evils, and not only to those whose intentional search is considered forbidden in a virtually absolute way. McCormick thinks that "since evil-as-means and evil-as-effect are different realities, they may demand different proportionate reasons. What is sufficient for allowing an evil [as a side effect] may not in all cases be sufficient for choosing it as a means" (McCormick 1978, p. 40). However, this thesis also could be subscribed detached of its utilitarian context, in which case it simply means that the IE/SE distinction is equally relevant to judge the morality of actions that bring about evils which in certain circumstances could be permissible to intend as means. The only difference between intending a certain evil of that kind as means and accepting it as a side effect would be that the proportionate reason must be stronger in the first case than in the second case.

[11] Anderson (2007) exposes his criticism in terms of the moral theory of Grisez, Boyle, and Finnis. As it was presented before, for these authors the absolute moral prohibitions fall on actions which directly attempt against the basic human goods. Therefore, Anderson's criticism is that the PDE also would be relevant to judge the attempt against the non-basic goods.

always immoral—but only frequently immoral, adds Anderson—to intend to bring about the destruction of property or cause physical pain, both effects could be also side effects justified by the PDE. In this way, a woman combing her long hair knows that it will cause her physical pain, but such action is permissible because the pain is only the side effect of an action in itself good. Equally—continues Anderson—policemen regularly destroy property as a side effect of carrying out their work.

The difference between Anderson's idea and the one presented in this chapter is that he adds the qualification "when the choice is made". This qualification would imply that the PDE could be applied to a much wider spectrum of bad effects, because, in certain circumstances, almost anything could become impermissible to be chosen or intended. Consequently, the PDE would not be applied only to bad effects that having been sought intentionally make the action intrinsically evil or evil in its species, but also to those effects which, if intended in the action, make it evil in the concrete case in which it is carried out.

In his answer to Anderson, Boyle affirms that the PDE applies to these cases "only because the considerations that might justify intentionally damaging the non-basic good have already been made and found incapable of justifying the intentional damage" (Boyle 2008, p. 76). This inability could be due, according to Boyle, to the fact that the agent has a further intention to harm a basic human good, or that the reasons for overturning the general respect for the non-basic good are not sufficiently strong. Therefore, what happens here is that "the norm in question has been specified so as to be, at this point of the deliberation, practically speaking a moral absolute" (Boyle 2008, p. 77) and because of that it is possible to assess, according to the double effect doctrine, the harm referred to by this norm. From this Boyle concludes that "adding damage to non-basic goods to the items about which double effect is usefully applied makes sense, but only when the norms governing choices in which they are damaged are specified so as to become quasi absolute" (Boyle 2008, p. 77).

I disagree, both with Anderson's objection and Boyle's answer. About the latter, it has to be considered that, if the inability to justify the intentional damage to the non-basic good derives from the malice of the agent's further intention, then such damage cannot be justified as side effect, because a bad remote end cannot justify any action, no matter if the bad effect brought about is procured as a means or accepted as a side effect; and if the inability derives from the fact that the reasons by which the agent acts are not sufficiently strong to justify the intentional damage of the non-basic good, then neither will they be sufficiently strong to justify it as a side effect. So, although it is undoubtful that in their work policemen will regularly destroy property as a side effect of actions which are directed to an important end, this does not mean that if they intentionally destroy it—as a means for that same end—they would be acting morally badly. For example, with the end of catching a dangerous criminal, a policeman could permissibly fire at him to subdue him, despite the fact that he could foresee that, as side effect, the shots will break a neighbour's window in whose house the criminal is hiding. But with the same end, the same policeman could fire at the same window *to destroy it*, when that window obstructs the entry to the room where the criminal is hiding. The reason for this is that the property, even the third party's property, being instrumental, can be licitly destroyed as a means for a proportionately important end (Finnis 1995, p. 244). Therefore, contrary to Anderson's views, it seems to me that there is no case in which, in the exercise of his work and searching for an equally important end, it would be immoral for a policeman to destroy a third party's property as a means whereas it would be permissible for him to destroy it as a certain side effect of the action which allows him to reach his end.[12] On the other hand, the case of the woman who combs her hair is not appropriate to demonstrate that the PDE is not applicable solely to damages which are absolutely forbidden to intend. It is not appropriate simply because the physical pain caused by that action could not be a means to the end of having tidy hair. In other words, what we are comparing here is (i) to procure the physical pain as an end, with (ii) to accept it as side effect. But the PDE does not refer specifically to the moral relevance of the distinction between (i) to intend a bad state of affairs as an end—*i.e.*, procure it for its own sake—and (ii) to accept that same bad state of affairs as side effect (because such relevance is also recognized by those who deny the PDE)[13] but to the moral relevance of the distinction between (i) to intend a bad state of affairs as a means to a good end and (ii) to accept that same bad state of affairs as a side effect of an action directed to the same good end.[14]

In short, when Anderson asks " If the distinction between what is intentional and what is a side effect is so important, Why does the distinction never show up except in the well-known, much-debated, tough cases in which moral absolutes seem to be violated?" (Anderson 2007, pp. 271–272), it can be answered that it is because, apart from the cases which refer to a bad effect which is absolutely forbidden to intend, the IE/SE distinction has no relevance as a criterion to determine if an action is or is not justified, because the judgement of proportionate reason is sufficient.

---

[12] In the hypothetical case that the window of the last example were to be so valuable which is better to leave the criminal to escape rather than break the window, then —supposing that this circumstance were known by the policeman— it would not be justified to break it in the first case nor in the second, that is, neither as a means nor as a side effect foreseen with certainty.

[13] See, for example, Mackie 1977, p. 160; Bennett 1995, p. 215; McIntyre 2001, pp. 226, 229.

[14] For this identical reason, it is not correct to argue in favour of the PDE invoking cases that oppose (i) to intend a bad effect for its own sake, to (ii) to accept it as side effect. For example, Aulisio points out that "[t]he doctor may foresee that the child will be caused pain by the shot, but if the doctor makes it her purpose to cause the child pain we should think ill of her" (Aulisio 1996, p. 195). But Aulisio's comparison is inadequate because it seems to oppose accept pain as side effect and intend pain as an end (as something that is sought for its own sake). No-one, on the other hand, would think badly of the doctor if she causes pain to a child when that is a necessary means for a good and important end; for example, pain is necessary so that the child's body liberates a substance whose analysis is indispensable to make the diagnosis of a serious illness which the child probably suffers.

6.6   The Principle of the Double Effect and the Principle of Totality

If it is true that all sub-human realities, because they lack dignity, may be intentionally damaged for serious moral reasons, is it also true that man, by being endowed with dignity, cannot be intentionally damaged as a means for any end? Or are there cases, on the contrary, in which a proportionately important or morally serious reason justifies damage to a human as a means? Here, I will leave aside the cases of private lethal defence, war, tyrannicide and capital punishment, to concentrate only on the cases involving innocent human beings, that is to say, human beings who (i) are not *guilty* of a serious crime punishable with the death penalty (ii) are not aggressors or *nocents* who can only be repelled by lethal force.

John Finnis maintains that it is never permissible to intend human harm. This leads him to sustain that in any licit action which involves human harm this is in fact a side effect (Finnis 1991, pp. 74–81). An exact assessment of this thesis requires a precise definition of the meaning of the word "harm" (or "damage"). Indeed, the word "harm" contains a certain ambiguity that could make the analysis difficult. Thomistic ethics teaches that, according to the "principle of totality" (PT), a physician could, permissibly, intentionally amputate a gangrened leg from his patient (Aquinas, *ST*, II-II, q. 65, a. 1c). But, does that physician intend any harm?

If intending harm means to intend that a person is brought to be, in absolute terms, in a worse situation than that in which he/she was, then it is clear that the doctor who amputates a gangrened leg does not intend to do harm to his patient. But if intend to harm means intend to remove or destruct a part of the body of an organism when this removal or destruction causes, in itself, a decrease in the physical capacities, then it is also clear that the doctor of the example is intending to harm (*i.e.*, intends to cut off the leg). Moreover, it is important to keep in mind that the PT authorizes also the removal or destruction of a healthy limb. For example, according to the PT it is permissible to cut or destroy a leg stuck on a railway line, when that is the only way to stop the person stuck from being crushed by the train. Again it is evident that, according to the second meaning of "harm", here the intention is also to harm, insofar as it is intended to cut or destroy the leg as a means to liberate the person and take him/her away from the railway line.

Surely Finnis uses the word harm in the first sense indicated above, because he writes that "therapeutic amputation is not doing harm but preventing the further harm that a limb already doomed would do to the health or life of the person" (Finnis 1991, p. 79). However, this seems to indicate that, according to the first meaning of harm, in therapeutic amputation there is no harm at all done to the patient. But then it seems to me that it is inaccurate to maintain, as Finnis does, that the PT "is simply an application of the proper analysis of the third-order [*i.e.*, moral order] distinction between intention and side-effect" (Finnis 1998, p. 280). If in therapeutic amputation there really is no harm, then the need does not arise to justify any harm as side effect.

The double effect tradition states that, in cases covered by the PT, it is permissible to intend precisely the destruction or removal of the limb or body part. For example, trying to make clear the difference between the PDE and the PT, Juan de Lugo maintains that "the person who cuts off an infected hand to preserve health intends the very amputation of the hand" (Lugo 1893).[15] Mausbach and Ermecke add explicitly: "The norms governing actions with double effect refer exclusively to the permissibility of a bad consequence, which *is not directly willed* in itself, but only indirectly in its cause. On the other hand, the principle of totality refers to the justification of the *directly willed* loss of a limb, as a means to save the organism" (Mausbach and Ermecke 1971, pp. 204–205). Finnis, certainly, would agree with Lugo and would concede that the amputation is intended, but will add that there is no intention to cause harm. I think, instead, that there is no problem with saying in this case that there is an intentional harm, because the second meaning of "harm" mentioned above is a correct one. It seems to me that it is more exact, therefore, to say that, in the cases that are a matter for the PT, it is permissible to intend damage or physical harm (the removal or destruction of a human body part), and that this permissibility is based on the fact that the action responds to the order according to which the human body limbs are parts which exist for the good of the whole. When Thomas Aquinas refers to these cases, he says without a problem that here one *chooses* a lesser evil to avoid a bigger one:

> … according to the Philosopher in Book V of the *Ethics*, the lesser evil, in as much as it is preferred to the greater evil, acquires the reason of the greater good; and for this reason the corporal doctor of man, if he can, frees him entirely of sickness, but if he cannot, he chooses the lesser evil in order to prevent the greater evil (*eligit minus malum, ut occurrat magis malo*), such as amputating a limb so that it may not infect the whole body. (Aquinas, *In IV Sent.*, d. 19, q. 2, a. 3, qc. 1c)[16]

And also says, in the same sense, that it is licit to inflict harm to avoid a greater evil:

> … medicine never removes a greater good in order to promote a lesser; thus the medicine of the body never blinds the eye in order to repair the heel. However, sometimes it inflicts harm (*infert nocumentum*) in lesser things if it may be helpful in things of greater importance. (Aquinas, *ST*, II-II, q. 108, a. 4c)[17]

---

[15] Cf. Lugo 1893, disp. 10, sec. 6, n. 149.

[16] In the same sense, Aquinas says that "a wise workman induces a lesser evil in order to prevent a greater (*sapiens artifex inducit minus malum ad vitandum maius*); as the surgeon cuts off a limb to save the whole body" (*S. Th.*, I, q. 48, a. 6, s. c.; cf. *De malo*, q. 1, a. 5, c.). And none of this is contradictory with the fact that the first principle of practical reason is "*bonum est faciendum et prosequendum, et malum vitandum*" (*S. Th.*, I-II, q. 94, a. 2, c.), neither with the fact that Saint Thomas affirms repeatedly that "evil must not be done that good may come" (cf. *In IV Sent.*, d. 6, q. 1, a. 1, qc. 1, ad 4; *S. Th.*, II-II, q. 64, a. 5, ad 3; *S. Th.*, III, q. 68, a. 11, ad 3). The reason why there are no contradictions is that Thomas Aquinas was using different senses for the word "evil". In the first set of cases he is referring to something that is an evil *secundum quid*, while in the second he is talking of something that is an evil *simpliciter*. This distinction is what also allows him to say that "evils of fault must not be done that good may come; but evil of punishment must be inflicted for the sake of good (*mala poenae sunt inferenda propter bonum*)" (*S. Th.*, I-II, q. 79, a. 4, ad 4). The evil of punishment is, in fact, a characteristic case of the evil *secundum quid* (cf. *S. Th.*, II-II, q. 19, a. 1, c.).

[17] This is not contradictory with the fact that Saint Thomas says that "any harm caused to another person is repulsive to charity, which wants the good for the other" (*S. Th.*, II-II, q. 59, a. 4, c.),

The traditional authors, therefore, do not have the need to justify these situations in the light of the PDE. Using a common language, it could be said that in these situations the chosen object, even though it includes a *physical* evil, it is not a disordered object that makes the choice immoral, because such physical evil is within a rational order: the order of subordination of the parts to the whole.

A similar argument demonstrates that there are some cases in which it is permissible to intend physical pain as a means to a good end. Alison McIntyre gives the example of dentists, who are allowed, in order to make a diagnosis, to seek physical pain as a means, as happens when they instruct their patient with the phrase "tell me when it hurts" (McIntyre 2004).

6.7 The Privation of Consciousness

Finally, it is time to ask oneself if the deprivation of consciousness is a bad effect that is never permissible to intend, not even as a means to a good end, or if, on the contrary, it is a state of affairs that could be licitly intended as a necessary means to a proportionately important end. The main source on which I will base my reasoning is the speech by Pope Pius XII about the religious and moral implications of analgesia (Pius 1957). This speech constitutes a fundamental contribution to bioethics, as it exposes a set of arguments of natural reason useful for achieving a correct conclusion in the matters in hand.

Pope Pius XII states, as the first point, that it is morally permissible to suppress or diminish painful sensations, using analgesia, and also to suppress general sensitivity, through general anaesthesia, when such effects are sought precisely in order to alleviate the patient's pain. The reason for this is based on the fact that man retains "the right of control over the forces of nature, of employing them for his own use, and consequently of deriving benefit from all the resources which it offers him either to avoid or to suppress physical pain" (Pius 1957). Indeed, pain produces adverse effects and can prevent the procurement of greater goods. From this it also follows that pain never should be considered as an end in itself, but only "as a means more or less suited to the end that is intended" (Pius 1957).

Right away the Roman Pontiff makes clear that the suppression or lessening of consciousness and of the use of higher faculties are *phenomena which accompany* the loss of sense-perception, that is to say, its side effects. This is evident, because what the physician normally wants is to achieve a loss of sense-perception and not the loss of consciousness, even though that would be an effect that sometimes

---

neither with the fact that he says that the prohibition of homicide "forbids at the same time all harm to other persons (*omne nocumentum in personam prohibetur*)" (*In III Sent.*, d. 37, q. 1, a. 2, qc. 2, c.). It is evident that Saint Thomas thinks that, in other sense, it could be permissible to cause harm to another person: "No-one should despise or cause harm to another without a cause that constrain him" (*S. Th.*, II-II, q. 60, a. 4, c.); "It is not permissible to cause harm to anyone, unless it is caused as a punishment for justice" (*S. Th.*, II-II, q. 65, a. 2, c.).

cannot be achieved "without bringing about at the same time total or partial loss of consciousness" (Pius 1957).

However, from the fact that the usual relationship is the one mentioned before—that is, that the loss of sense-perception is intended and the loss of consciousness is accepted only as a side effect—it does not follow that it always occurs like that. That is why the Pope adds that "outside the sphere of surgery, this relationship is often inverse, not only in medicine, but also in psychology and in criminal investigations. Here, a lowering of consciousness, and through it of higher faculties, is intended" (Pius 1957). That is to say, in many permissible activities the privation or lessening of consciousness is intended as a means to achieve an end. The Pope warns of the *dangers* of such situation and suggests some ways to avoid them, but does not state that the intentional privation of consciousness is intrinsically immoral.

On the other hand, Pius XII notes that "in sleep, nature itself interrupts more or less completely intellectual activity" (Pius 1957). Sleep deprives us of *dominium rationis*, and, nevertheless, "it does not follow that, if a man gives way to sleep, he is acting contrary to the moral order in depriving himself of consciousness and mastery over himself in the use of his higher faculties" (Pius 1957). In this same line, Joseph Boyle (in this book, Chapter 5) has provided another suitable counter-example: if it were intrinsically immoral to procure the state of unconsciousness as a means for any end, then it would be possible to consider immoral the use of sleeping pills, which does not seem reasonable. Likewise, through hypnosis there is an intentional suppression of the patient's consciousness, and, nevertheless, there are no moral reasons to oppose a "hypnosis practiced by the doctor to serve a clinical purpose, while he observes the precautions which medical science and ethics demand" (Pius 1957). Therefore, intentional privation of consciousness through hypnosis would only be impermissible if the end pursued with it is not morally serious or proportionately important, as would happen if a hypnosis were sought "for the sake of a mere experience, or even as a simple hobby" (Pius 1957).

In the context of these reasonings, Pius XII draws his conclusion in the following terms:

> Since the natural energies and the blind instincts, left to themselves, are incapable of guaranteeing a regulated activity, it follows that the use of the reason and of the higher faculties is indispensable both for seeing clearly the precise norms of obligation and for applying them to particular cases. Hence derives the moral obligation of not depriving oneself of consciousness *without true necessity*. (Pius 1957)[18]

---

[18] Italics added. The teaching that there are some actions that are bad in general or according to an absolute consideration, but that could become good for some necessity or reasonable cause, is a constant in the classical tradition of the natural law. These actions are not the object of an absolute or unconditional prohibition. Considered in abstract, they can only be the object of a conditional prohibition. That is to say, in contrast to the *ex genere* evil actions, which are not justified by any utility (*pro nulla utilitate*), the actions that are here discussed can be justified by the utility that follows from them. When Thomas Aquinas discusses one kind of these actions, he maintains: "… something can be evil in two ways: either *per se* or by the consequences that it produces. Thus, that which is *ex se* evil, never can be permissible, no matter how great the necessity (*quantumcumque necessitas incumbat*), as is shown in the case of rape and other *ex genere* evil actions. But in relation to those that are evil due to the danger that follows (*propter periculum sequens*), two things are

Thus, to make permissible the administration of narcotics that produce the suppression or lessening of consciousness in the patient it is *not* required that such effects are merely collateral. In other words, it is morally licit to administer the narcotics with the intention of producing unconsciousness, provided that this was a *necessary* means to achieve a *proportionately serious* end. As was said before, these two requirements must always be fulfilled when knowingly bringing about a bad effect (and the privation of consciousness is a bad effect), independently of the fact that the effect can or cannot be intended as a means. In this way, if the end that is sought can be achieved equally effectively by means that do not cause the suppression of the patient's consciousness, then these have to be adopted. Likewise, if the good that wants to be achieved as a remote end of the action is not important, critical or serious, the action will become corrupted by disproportion. Pius XII states that, for example, "one may not weaken consciousness, or suppress it, with the sole end of gaining pleasurable sensations", (Pius 1957) and then he adds: "… the dying person should not, *without serious reasons*, be deprived of consciousness. When this state is produced by natural causes, men must accept it; but it is not for them to bring it about, *unless they have serious motives for so doing*" (Pius 1957).

The requirement of proportionality must take into account not only the evil of privation of consciousness and the good of pain relief; for a prudent judgement, the set of obligations that the dying person has to fulfil come also into play; for prudent judgement, the set of obligations that the dying person has to fulfil. That is why it could be said with Pius XII that "the dying person cannot allow, still less ask the doctor, to procure him unconsciousness if he thereby renders himself incapable of fulfilling some serious moral duties" (Pius 1957). But, *a contrario sensu*, the dying person could allow or ask the doctor to *procure* him unconsciousness if he/she has already fulfilled his/her final moral duties, or if he/she could not fulfil them even when conscious due to the extent of his/her sufferings. On the other hand, it must be said that, as it is not permissible to seek physical pain for its own sake, but only as a means to a good end, neither is it permissible to deprive the patient of consciousness with the only objective that he/she avoids a conscious end. At the time before death, as in other important moments, human beings need the full use of their intellectual faculties, so that their moral strength can keep them in the exercise of virtue. But, when there is an intention of avoiding serious pain, it is permissible to induce unconsciousness

---

required so that it is permissible to do it. One is enough caution to avoid that danger. The other is the consequent utility (*utilitas consequens*)" (*In III Sent.*, d. 39, q. 1, a. 2, qc. 2, c.). From this Aquinas concludes that, in relation to actions that are evil in themselves (*per se mala*), all will is forbidden, that is, both the absolute will and the conditional will (*voluntas ex suppositione*); in relation to actions that are good in themselves (*per se bona*) there is no will forbidden; and in relation to actions that are good for some need (*bona propter necessitatem aliquam*) only the absolute will is forbidden, but not the will *ex suppositione* (*In III Sent.*, d. 39, q. 1, a. 2, qc. 2, ad 2). This means that the agent can carry out that last kind of action, but whenever they are chosen he/she must have a justifying cause. (For other examples on actions that are generally forbidden but that can be permissibly done *propter aliquam necessitatem aut rationabilem causam*, cf. *In IV Sent.*, d. 32, q. 1, a. 2, qc. 1, ad 4; *S. Th.*, II-II, q. 40, a. 4, 3 a. y c.; *S. Th.*, II-II, q. 90, a. 1, c.; *S. Th.*, II-II, q. 95, a. 8, c.; *S. Th.*, II-II, q. 169, a. 2, ad 3).

precisely because these pains, far from allowing the peaceful use of reason, many times "increase the state of weakness and physical exhaustion, check the ardour of soul and sap the moral powers instead of sustaining them" (Pius 1957).

Therefore, in itself the deprivation of consciousness is not an effect that is never permissible to intend. Such privation can be licitly intended as a means to a proportionately important end, and, in that way, is an effect that is out of the scope of the PDE. Of course, when the drug also produces the effect of accelerating the death of the patient then the PDE becomes relevant, because this state of affairs can only be justifiably brought about if it is a side effect of a palliative action in itself permissible, necessary and proportionate. But death (or its acceleration) and unconsciousness are two different states of affairs (Watt 2000, p. 30).

It could also be argued that what is intrinsically immoral or absolutely forbidden is not the intentional deprivation of consciousness, but the intentional total and permanent deprivation of consciousness. This has a solid basis, because to deprive someone completely and perpetually of his/her consciousness does not differ much from killing that person. As it is impermissible to intend the death of a patient, it is also impermissible to intend the perpetual suppression of their consciousness. I think that this could be conceded, but from this the impermissibility of the terminal palliative sedation does not follow. To justify the permanent character that palliative sedation can have, the PDE is invoked again. Indeed, in terminal sedation the only thing that the doctor needs to intend is lessering consciousness as much as required for pain relief. The fact that the patient's unconsciousness lasts until their death is only something that happens *per accidens*, due to their critical state. In other words, the doctor foresees, but does not intend, that the patient never recovers consciousness. The doctor only intends the *complete* deprivation of consciousness, because it is necessary for pain relief.

Therefore, I disagree with the idea that in this kind of case there are not two effects, but only two degrees of the same effect (Sullivan in this book, Chap. 2). Rather, one effect is the complete deprivation of consciousness in the patient (necessary, *ex hypothesi*, for pain relief) and another different effect is the fact that the patient, because of their terminal state, is never going to recover consciousness before death. These are two different effects, and, thus, the total suppression of consciousness can be perpetual or transitory, and consciousness can be suppressed totally or partially in perpetuity. A consequence of what I have just stated is that, if there was a drug destined to suppress totally the patient's consciousness *once and forever*, it would not be licit to use it as a means for pain relief. In this case, there would be an intention to suppress consciousness in perpetuity; but this is not what happens in the usual situation.

6.8   Conclusions

The PDE is not applicable in relation to all effects that can, in some sense, be called "bad". Only those effects that are never permissible to intend, not even as a means to a good end, are within its field of application. The deprivation of consciousness is not an effect of this kind, because it can be brought about intentionally if it were necessary to achieve a proportionate good end, as is the pain relief of a terminal patient. However, the PDE is relevant when the drug used to deprive the patient of consciousness produces also the effect of accelerating death, or when the patient, after being sedated, and due to health deterioration, will not recover consciousness before death. Both the death of the patient and the perpetual suppression of his/her consciousness are effects that never are permissible to intend, but can be accepted as side effects of actions in themselves permissible and necessary to achieve a good of proportionate importance.

References

Anderson, R. 2007. Boyle and the principle of double effect. *The American Journal of Jurisprudence* 52: 259–272.

Anderson, R. 2009. The moral permissibility of accepting bad side effects. *American Catholic Philosophical Quarterly* 83: 255–266.

Aquinas, T. *Summa theologica*. II-II, q. 64, a. 7, c.

Aquinas, T. *Summa theologica*. II-II, q. 65, a. 1, c.

Aquinas, T. *In IV Sent.*, d. 19, q. 2, a. 3, q. c. 1, c.

Aquinas, T. *Summa theologica*. II-II, q. 108, a. 4, c.

Aristotle. 1984. Nicomachean ethics. In *The complete works of Aristotle*, ed. J. Barnes. Princeton: Princeton University Press.

Aulisio, M. 1996. On the importance of the intention/foresight distinction. *American Catholic Philosophical Quarterly* 70: 189–205.

Aulisio, M. 1997. One's Persons *Modus Ponens*: Boyle, Absolutist Catholicism, and the Doctrine of Double Effect. *Christian Bioethics* 3: 142–157.

Bennett, J. 1995. *The act itself*. Oxford: Oxford University Press.

Boyle, J. 1991. Who is entitled to double effect? *The Journal of Medicine and Philosophy* 16: 475–494.

Boyle, J. 2008. The moral meaning and justification of the doctrine of double effect: A response to Robert Anderson. *The American Journal of Jurisprudence* 53: 69–84.

Cavanaugh, T. 2006. *Double-effect reasoning: Doing good and avoiding evil*. Oxford: Oxford University Press.

Finnis, J. 1991. *Moral absolutes: Tradition, revision, and truth*. Washington, DC: The Catholic University of America Press.

Finnis, J. 1995. Intention in tort law. In *Philosophical foundations of tort law*, ed. D.G. Owen, 229–247. Oxford: Clarendon.

Finnis, J. 1998. *Aquinas: Moral, political, and legal theory*. Oxford: Oxford University Press.

Finnis, J., J. Boyle, and G. Grisez. 1987. *Nuclear deterrence, morality and realism*. Oxford: Oxford University Press.

Grisez, G. 1993. *The way of the Lord Jesus. Vol. 2. Living a Christian life*. Quincy: Franciscan Press.

Gury, J.P. 1862. *Compendium theologiae moralis*. Ratisbona: Manz.

Lugo, J. 1893. *Disputationes scholasticae et morales. De justitia et jure*. Paris: Ludovicum Vivés.

Mackie, J. 1977. *Ethics: Inventing right and wrong*. London: Pelican Books. Repr., Penguin Books, 1990.

Mausbach, J., and G. Ermecke. 1971. *Teología moral católica* (T. III, Translated into Spanish by M. García). Pamplona: Eunsa.

McCormick, R. 1978. Ambiguity in moral choice. In *Doing evil to achieve good: Moral choice in conflict situations*, ed. R. McCormick and P. Ramsey, 7–53. Chicago: Loyola University Press.

McIntyre, A. 2001. Doing away with double effect. *Ethics* 111: 219–255.

McIntyre, A. 2004. Doctrine of double effect. In *Stanford encyclopaedia of philosophy.* http://plato.stanford.edu/entries/double-effect/. Published on 28 July 2004.

Miranda, A. 2012. Eutanasia, suicidio asistido y principio del doble efecto. Réplica al profesor Rodolfo Figueroa. *Revista Médica de Chile* 140: 261–265.

Oderberg, D. 2000. *Moral theory: A non-consequentialist approach.* Oxford: Blackwell Publishers.

Oderberg, D. 2010. The doctrine of double effect. In *A companion to the philosophy of action*, ed. T. O'Connor and C. Sandis. Oxford: Blackwell Publishing.

Pius, XII. 1957. *Address at the IX National Congress of the Italian Society of the Science of Anesthetics: Responses to three religious and moral questions regarding analgesia*, 24 February.

Sánchez, T. 1605. *Disputationum de sancto matrimonii sacramento.* l. 9, disp. 17, nn. 12–15. Madrid: Ludovicum Sanchez.

Spaemann, R. 1991. *Felicidad y benevolencia.* Spanish Trans. J.L. del Barco. Madrid: Rialp.

Spaemann, R. 2003. ¿Quién es responsable y de qué? Reflexiones críticas acerca de la distinción entre ética de los principios y ética de la responsabilidad. In *Límites: Acerca de la dimensión ética del actuar,* ed. R. Spaemann. Trans. into Spanish J. Fernández y J. Mardomingo. Barcelona: Eunsa.

Watt, H. 2000. *Life and death in healthcare ethics. A short introduction.* London: Routledge.

Zalba, Marcelino. 1971–1987. voluntario, acto. In *Gran Enciclopedia Rialp.* XXIII. Rialp: Madrid.

Chapter 7
'Palliative Sedation', Ethics and the Law: An Overview of the 'Sanctity of Life', 'Best Interests' and 'Autonomy'

John Keown

7.1 Introduction

'Palliative sedation' raises several profound ethical and legal questions. Is it compatible with the 'sanctity of life'? When is it in a patient's 'best interests'? To what extent should a patient's autonomous wishes determine when it is or is not carried out? This chapter does not attempt to resolve these questions directly. This is in no small measure because 'palliative sedation' is protean concept with no universally agreed definition. For example, it may involve sedation which is or is not 'deep'; which is or is not administered with the consent of the patient; which is or is not associated with the withdrawal of tube-feeding; which involves or does not involve the 'terminally ill'; and which is or is not administered with intent to shorten life. In short, 'palliative sedation' can embrace many, many distinct scenarios.

Rather than attempt to address the ethical and legal dimensions of each of these scenarios, this chapter confines itself to offering a broad overview of some basic concepts central to any sound legal and ethical analysis of palliative sedation in any of its many forms. In particular, it offers a simple explanation of the 'sanctity of life', 'best interests' and 'autonomy', concepts which are key to any sound understanding of when palliative sedation is legally and ethically defensible. Only when these basic concepts have been soundly understood is it sensible to address specific questions such as whether the administering sedation with intent to shorten the patient's life, or when the patient is not 'terminally ill', or as a response to 'existential'

This chapter was originally published as "'The Sanctity of Life', 'Best Interests' and 'Autonomy': An Overview" in John Keown, *The Law and Ethics of Medicine: Essays on the Inviolability of Human Life* (Oxford University Press, 2012). I am grateful to Oxford University Press for permission to reproduce it in this volume.

J. Keown (✉)
Kennedy Institute of Ethics, Georgetown University, Washington, DC, USA
e-mail: ijk2@georgetown.edu

suffering, is ethical and lawful. None of these basic concepts is more important than that of the 'sanctity of life', with which we shall begin.

The 'sanctity' or 'inviolability of life' is, as has been repeatedly judicially affirmed, a fundamental principle of the common law. Since the phrase 'sanctity of life,' though judicially hallowed, may have distracting theological connotations, 'inviolability of life' (IOL) will be used hereafter. The doctrine and the principle of the IOL were originally formulated by theologians, but can stand on purely philosophical grounds. In *Re A*, the 'Conjoined Twins' case, Lord Justice Brooke referred to a brief the court had received from the Archbishop of Westminster. The brief referred to a number of 'overarching moral considerations,' the first of which was: "Human life is sacred, that is inviolable, so one should never aim to cause an innocent person's death by act or omission."[1] Brooke LJ observed:

> There can, of course, be no doubt that our common law judges were steeped in the Judaeo-Christian tradition and in the moral principles identified by the Archbishop when they were developing our criminal law over the centuries up to the time when Parliament took over the task. There can also be no doubt that it was these principles, shared as they were by the other founder members of the Council of Europe 50 years ago, which underlay the formulation of article 2 of the European Convention on Human Rights.[2]

The principle appears, accordingly, in declarations on human rights as the 'right to life'. Indeed, a prohibition on intentional killing is central to the pre-Christian fount of Western medical ethics, the Hippocratic Oath[3] (and the modern reaffirmation of that Oath by the Declaration of Geneva[4]), and many non-believers recognize the right of human beings not to be intentionally killed.[5]

Although foundational to the common law, the IOL has rarely if ever been accurately formulated—put in propositional form—either in judicial decisions or in textbooks on medical/health law. Precisely what it involves is, indeed, mired in confusion, in the academy, at the Bar, and on the Bench. This chapter seeks to outline the principle, summarize its relevance to the law governing medical decision-making at the end of life, and sketch its implications for the important concepts of 'best interests' and 'autonomy'.

---

[1] *Re A* (2001) Fam 147, 211. The IOL has historically been formulated in terms of the wrongness of intentionally taking 'innocent' life. 'Innocent' excludes anyone actively contributing to unjust aggression. The principle has, therefore, traditionally allowed the use of lethal force in self-defense, the prosecution of a just war, and the execution of capital offenders. This has little relevance to doctor-patient context, which is the concern of this book.

[2] ibid 212.

[3] "To please no-one will I prescribe a deadly drug, nor give advice which may cause his death. Nor will I give a woman a pessary to procure abortion.": Mason and McCall Smith (1994: 429).

[4] "I will maintain the utmost respect for human life from the time of conception; even under threat, I will not use my medical knowledge contrary to the laws of humanity." ibid 430.

[5] A prohibition on killing is not, of course, exclusive to Western ethics. See Keown (1995).

7.2   Three Competing Approaches to the Valuation of Human Life

There are three main, competing approaches to the valuation of human life.

(a) *Vitalism*

Human life is the *supreme* good and one should do everything possible to preserve it. The core principle, therefore, is: 'try to maintain the life of each patient at all costs'. Whether the life be that of an anencephalic newborn (one lacking the cerebral hemispheres) or a dying centenarian, vitalism prohibits its shortening and requires its preservation. Regardless of the pain, suffering, or expense that life-prolonging treatment entails, it must be administered: human life is to be preserved at all costs. Vitalism is as ethically untenable as its attempt to maintain life indefinitely is physically impossible. Its error lies in isolating the genuine and basic good of human life, and the duty to respect and promote that good, from the network of standards and responsibilities which make up our ethics and law as a whole; and its neglect of concepts and distinctions (such as between intention and foresight) vital to that network.

(b) *'Quality of life' (QOL)*

On this approach, there is nothing supremely or even inherently valuable about the life of a human being. The dignity of human life, such as it is, is only as an *instrumental* good, a vehicle or platform for a 'worthwhile' life, a life whose value resides in meeting a particular 'quality' threshold (howsoever defined). The lives of certain patients fall below this threshold, not least because of disease, injury, or disability. This valuation of human life grounds the principle that, because certain lives are not worth living, it is right intentionally to terminate them, whether by act or omission. A core principle, therefore, is: 'one may try to extinguish the life of a patient which is of such poor quality as to be not worth living'. (Many of those who adopt this approach also believe that only a sub-set of human beings, those who meet a criterion such as a particular level of intellectual ability, qualify as 'persons.')

(c) *The inviolability of life*

Human life is a *basic, intrinsic* good. All human beings possess, in virtue of their common humanity, an inherent, inalienable, and ineliminable dignity. The dignity of human beings inheres because of the radical capacities, such as for understanding, rational choice, and free will, inherent in human nature. Some human beings, such as infants, may not yet possess the ability to exercise these radical capacities. But radical capacities must not be confused with abilities. We may have the radical capacity to speak Swahili but not the ability to do so. All human beings possess the capacities inherent in their nature even though, because of infancy, disability, or senility, they may not yet, not now, or no longer have the ability to exercise them.[6]

---

[6] Gormally (1994: 118–119).

The right not to be killed is enjoyed regardless of inability or disability. Our dignity does not depend on our having a particular intellectual ability or having it to a particular degree. Any such distinctions are fundamentally arbitrary and inconsistent with a sound concept of justice:

> [E]very human being, however immature or mentally impaired, possesses a fundamental worth and dignity which are not lost as long as he or she is alive. Contrary to the view of some, human worth and dignity do not depend on acquiring and retaining some particular level of intellectual ability or capacity for choice or for communication. On that view of human worth and dignity, it turns out that the relevant level of intellectual ability (or whatever other characteristic is asserted to be morally decisive) always requires to be determined in an arbitrary fashion. In making the possession of human worth and dignity depend on an arbitrary discrimination between individuals, this view destroys the indispensable foundation of justice in society. For basic human rights belong to us precisely because of our worth and dignity, and if our possession of the latter is to be determined arbitrarily so will be our possession of the former. But there cannot be a framework conducive to just relationships in a society if *who are to count as the subjects of justice* is determined in an arbitrary fashion. That is why recognition of the fundamental worth and dignity of *every* human being is the indispensable foundation of justice in society.[7]

Human life is not, then, only an instrumental good, a necessary precondition of thinking or choosing or doing, but a basic good, a fundamental constituent of human flourishing. It is, in other words, not merely good as a means to an end but is, like other integral aspects of a flourishing human life, like friendship and the appreciation of beauty, something worthwhile in itself. Of course some people, like those who are pictures of health in the prime of life, participate in the good of life and health to a greater extent than others, such as the terminally ill, but even the sick and the dying participate in the good to the extent that they are able.

Although life is a basic good it is not an absolute good, a good to which all the other basic goods must be sacrificed in order to ensure its preservation. The IOL doctrine is not vitalistic. The core of the doctrine is the principle prohibiting intentional killing, not an injunction requiring the preservation of life at all costs. The core principle is: 'it is always wrong to try to extinguish a patient's life'. Although the doctrine denies that human life is an absolute good, the principle that it may never intentionally be taken is an absolute principle, that is, one which has no acceptable exceptions. Although the value of human life is not absolute, the prohibition on taking it is. The core principle prohibits trying to kill, but the IOL also prohibits exposing life to unreasonable risk. It is wrong to take life not only intentionally but also recklessly or negligently.

To sum up, the doctrine of the IOL holds that we all share, in virtue of our common humanity, an ineliminable dignity. This dignity grounds our 'right to life'. The principle of the IOL holds in essence that it is wrong to try to extinguish life.

---

[7] Keown and Gormally (1999) 4 *Web Journal of Current Legal Issues* Part II (emphasis in original) http://www.wjcli.ncl.ac.uk.

7.3 Main Features of the IOL and Their Influence on the Common Law

7.3.1 Ineliminable Dignity

The ineliminable equality-in-dignity of human beings has long been recognized by the common law and by international declarations on human rights. As the Preamble to the Universal Declaration of Human Rights proclaims: "recognition of the inherent dignity and of the equal and inalienable rights of all members of the human family is the foundation of freedom, justice and peace in the world."[8] Inherent human dignity is a core value of English law:

> The recognition and protection of human dignity is one of the core values——in truth *the* core value——of our society and, indeed, of all the societies which are part of the European family of nations and which have embraced the principles of the Convention. It is a core value of the common law, long pre-dating the Convention and the Charter [of Fundamental Rights of the European Union].[9]

Just as inherent dignity is a core value of English law, so is the principle of the IOL in which it is grounded. As Lord Goff observed in *Airedale NHS Trust v Bland*:

> [T]he fundamental principle [in this case] is the principle of the sanctity of human life——a principle long recognized not only in our own society but also in most, if not all, civilized societies throughout the modern world, as is indeed evidenced by its recognition both in article 2 of the European Convention for the Protection of Human Rights and Fundamental Freedoms 1953 … and in article 6 of the International Covenant of Civil and Political Rights 1966.[10]

Article 2(1) of the European Convention on Human Rights provides:

> Everyone's right to life shall be protected by law. No one shall be deprived of his life intentionally save in the execution of a sentence of a court following his conviction of a crime for which this penalty is provided by law.

The prohibition on intentional killing was aptly described by the House of Lords Select Committee on Medical Ethics in 1994 (the 'Walton Committee') as "the cornerstone of law and of social relationships" which "protects each one of us impartially, embodying the belief that all are equal."[11] The prohibition applies even if a patient is suffering, even if the doctor's motive is compassionate, even if the patient is close to death, and even if the patient autonomously requests a lethal injection. In *Bland* Lord Goff observed:

> [I]t is not lawful for a doctor to administer a drug to his patient to bring about his death, even though that course is prompted by a humanitarian desire to end his suffering, however

---

[8] See http://www.un.org/en/documents/udhr/.

[9] *R (A) v East Sussex County Council (No 2)* [2003] EWHC 167 (Admin) para 86, per Munby J (as he then was) (emphasis in original).

[10] [1993] AC 789, 863–864.

[11] *Report of the Select Committee on Medical Ethics* (HL Paper 21-I of 1993–4) para 237.

great that suffering may be ... So to act is to cross the Rubicon which runs between on the one hand the care of the living patient and on the other hand euthanasia——actively causing his death to avoid or to end his suffering. Euthanasia is not lawful at common law.[12]

Nor is the law concerned to prohibit only active intentional killing. Although there is generally no liability for an omission to preserve life, it is well established that it is murder to omit to discharge a duty to preserve life with intent to kill, as by deliberately starving to death a child in one's care.[13] Also reflecting the IOL, the law punishes assisting or encouraging another to commit suicide. Section 2(1) of the Suicide Act 1961 provides a maximum penalty of 14 years' imprisonment for aiding, abetting, counseling, or procuring suicide or an attempt to commit suicide. The prohibition has been updated by section 59(2) of the Coroners and Justice Act 2009 which, replacing section 2(1), provides that a person commits an offence if he does an act capable of encouraging or assisting the suicide or attempted suicide of another person and the act was intended to encourage or assist suicide or an attempt to commit suicide.

7.3.2   Intention and Foresight

The IOL draws an important distinction between intending death and merely foreseeing death as a side-effect of one's conduct. It adopts the principle of 'double effect', according to which it is permissible to bring about a foreseen bad consequence if the bad effect is not intended, whether as an end or as a means, and the foreseen or foreseeable causing of the side-effect does not violate other moral norms, especially fairness. It is therefore ethical and lawful to, for example, administer palliative drugs to the dying even if they will shorten life.

Foreseen causation should not be conflated with intention.[14] Intention, properly understood, always means purpose, not merely foresight plus causality and, despite occasional digression, the law (like common sense) always returns to this truth. One may intend and foresee a consequence of one's action (as when one deliberately decapitates another person). But one may intend a consequence without foreseeing that it will occur (as when one buys a lottery ticket to win a million-to-one jackpot). Conversely, one may not intend a consequence even though one foresees it as certain to occur (like the hangover after a bottle of port). As Lord Goff helpfully put it:

[T]here can be intention without foresight that the relevant consequence was likely to occur. Conversely, there can be foresight of consequences without intention. [W]hen Field Marshal Montgomery invaded France on D-Day, he foresaw that many of the troops under his command would be killed on that very day. Obviously, however, he did not intend that any of them should be killed. [I] cannot emphasise too strongly that, because foresight of the consequence of death resulting from your act does not necessarily connote an intention on your part to kill, it cannot, in my opinion, be right for a jury to be told that the former will, as a matter of law,

---

[12] *Bland* (n 10) 865.

[13] *R v Gibbins and Proctor* (1919) 13 Cr App R 134.

[14] See generally Finnis (2011) (Part Three).

of itself establish the necessary intent, however overwhelming the probability of the consequence may be——as witness the example of Field Marshal Montgomery and D-Day.[15]

Some jurists, like Professor Glanville Williams, have proposed that 'intention' should be stretched to include 'oblique' intent (as Bentham called it) so that killers who foresee death as virtually certain but who do not intend it can nevertheless be convicted of murder. Williams instanced the villain who places a bomb on a plane in order to claim the insurance on a parcel but not to kill the pilot. Lord Goff rejected this proposed extension of intention:

> Now I have to confess that, as soon as somebody starts using an expression like 'oblique intention', I become suspicious; because I suspect that it is only necessary to use the rather mysterious adjective 'oblique' to bring within "intention" something which is not intention at all. And that is exactly what is happening here. For the trouble with this kind of approach is that it has distorted the plain meaning of the word. To the question——did the defendant mean to destroy the parcel? The answer is, of course, yes, he did. But to the question—— did the defendant mean to kill the pilot? The answer is, no, he didn't. Indeed, if he saw the pilot safely descending by parachute, he would no doubt be delighted; and so it is absurd to say that he meant to kill him. Of course, if the pilot is killed by the explosion, I share Professor Glanville Williams' *feeling* that the defendant can properly be called a murderer; but I do not think that that result can be achieved by artificially expanding the meaning of the word "intention." Quite apart from anything else, it can only lead to difficulties in directing juries. In a jury system, it is far better, if you can, to use a word in its plain and ordinary meaning. And you do not intend something merely because you know that it is virtually certain to happen; see the example of Field Marshal Montgomery and D-Day.[16]

His Lordship added that the parcel bomber should be convicted of murder not by way of artificially stretching the ordinary meaning of intention but by expanding the *mens rea* of murder to include 'indifference to death':

> [T]he jurists have become imprisoned within their own favourite concept of intention, to such an extent that they have tried, illegitimately, to expand it to include other cases. By adopting the solution that the mental element of murder consists of either (1) an intention to kill, or (2) indifference to death, we can, I suggest, both satisfy the general sense of justice as evidenced in the cases, and avoid the trap of using words otherwise than in their ordinary meaning——a trap which it is especially important to avoid in systems in which judges have to direct juries.[17]

English law appears to agree with Lord Goff in thus rejecting "'oblique intent'". As Professor Peter Skegg has observed, English courts have "tended to say that

---

[15] Goff (1988); 104 (30): 45 (emphasis in original). The same example, with Eisenhower substituted for Montgomery, was later used by the judgment of the court in the leading US Supreme Court decision on physician-assisted suicide: *Vacco v Quill* 521 US 793 at 802–803 (1997), per Rehnquist CJ: "The law has long used actors' intent or purpose to distinguish between two acts that may have the same result. ... Put differently, the law distinguishes actions taken 'because of' a given end from actions taken 'in spite of' their unintended but foreseen consequences ... ('When General Eisenhower ordered American soldiers onto the beaches of Normandy, he knew that he was sending many American soldiers to certain death .... His purpose, though, was to ... liberate Europe from the Nazis')."

[16] Goff (1988); 104 (30): 46 (emphasis in original).

[17] ibid 45.

foresight of virtual certainty is something from which intention may be found or inferred, and … have stopped short of saying that such foresight is itself a form of intent …."[18]

Consistent with the law's rejection of oblique intent is its endorsement of double effect. Lord Goff has referred to:

> the established rule that a doctor may, when caring for a patient who is, for example, dying of cancer, lawfully administer painkilling drugs despite the fact that he knows that an incidental effect of that application will be to abbreviate the patient's life.[19]

Unfortunately, the law's rejection of oblique intent is by no means as clear as it could and should be. The reasoning or dicta of the single judgment in the House of Lords in *R v Woollin*[20] is ambiguous enough to be read as holding not only that foresight of virtual certainty can be *evidence of* intention but that it *is* intention. It was, indeed, so interpreted by the majority of the Court of Appeal in *Re A*, the 'Conjoined Twins' case, where the question was whether it would be lawful to separate the weaker twin (Mary) to save the stronger one (Jodie), even though it was foreseen that Mary would die. The presiding judge stated: "Unpalatable though it may be … to stigmatize the doctors with 'murderous intent', that is what in law they will have if they perform the operation and Mary dies as a result."[21] The majority's adoption of 'oblique intention', though understandable in view of the ambiguity in *Woollin*, deprived them of the most cogent and coherent way of resolving the tragic dilemma before them: the principle of double effect. According to that principle, the separation of conjoined twins is justified where the death of the doomed twin is not intended and is merely foreseen as a side-effect, and the foreseeable causing of that side-effect does not violate the norm of fairness. Given that both Mary and Jodie would have died without separation, and that Mary was doomed with or without separation, it was not unfair to separate her from Jodie who could, and did, survive. The majority explicitly rejected double effect on the ground that the good and bad effects did not affect the same individual, as is the case with the administration of palliative drugs to a dying patient. However, this limitation has never been a requirement of double effect. The principle could, for example, justify the allied bombing of Nazi headquarters even if it were foreseen that innocent civilians nearby would be killed as a side-effect of the raid. Fortunately, the core common-sense meaning of intention asserts itself at points in the judgments of the Court of Appeal in the Conjoined Twins case where *Woollin*'s authority in relation to the crime of murder is no longer in issue, but rather the issue as framed in civil and human rights law. One such point is the following statement by Robert Walker LJ in relation to the 'right to life' in Article 2 of the European Convention on Human Rights:

> The Convention is to be construed as an autonomous text, without regard to any special rules of English law, and the word "intentionally" in article 2(1) must be given its natural

---

[18] Skegg (2006): 505, 524.

[19] *Bland* (n 10) 867. See also *R v Cox* (1992) 12 BMLR 38, 41 (Ognall J).

[20] [1999] 1 AC 82.

[21] *Re A* (2001) Fam 147, 198–199, per Ward LJ. See also ibid 216, per Brooke LJ.

and ordinary meaning. In my judgment the word, construed in that way, applies only to cases where the purpose of the prohibited action is to cause death.[22]

That is the position to which English law, too, gravitates, as many cases—including those discussed in *Woollin*—demonstrate when properly analyzed.

7.3.3   Acts and Omissions

The IOL prohibits intentional killing by act or omission. It therefore prohibits withholding/withdrawing treatment with intent to shorten life. But it permits withholding/withdrawing a life-prolonging treatment which is not worthwhile because it is futile or too burdensome. The IOL is, therefore, not vitalist: it does not require doctors to try to preserve life at all costs. Just as the IOL is not vitalist, neither is English law:

> [I]t cannot be right that a doctor, who has under his care a patient suffering painfully from terminal cancer, should be under an absolute obligation to perform upon him major surgery to abate another condition which, if unabated, would or might shorten his life still further. The doctor who is caring for such a patient cannot, in my opinion, be under an absolute obligation to prolong his life by any means available to him, regardless of the quality of the patient's life. Common humanity requires otherwise, as do medical ethics and good medical practice accepted in this country and overseas.[23]

7.3.4   Worth of Treatment v Worth of Life: 'Quality of Life Benefits' v 'Beneficial Quality of Life'

It is always wrong to withhold/withdraw treatment because it is thought that the patient, rather than the treatment, is not worthwhile, because death is thought to be in the 'best interests' of the patient. The IOL distinguishes what we may call 'quality of life benefits' (used to judge whether a treatment would be worthwhile, comparing its benefits and burdens) from 'beneficial Quality of life' (QOL) (used to judge whether the patient's life is or will be 'worthwhile').

(a) 'Quality of life benefits' v 'beneficial Quality of life'

Given that the same phrase, 'quality of life', is used to refer to these two very different concepts, it is not surprising that judges and academics have sometimes confused the question whether a *treatment* would be worthwhile with the question whether a patient's *life* would be worthwhile. Examples of its usage in the latter, QOL sense (but without advertence to its use in the alternative, former sense), can

---

[22] ibid 256.

[23] *Bland* (n 10) 867, per Lord Goff.

be found in leading cases on non-treatment of children (such as *Re J*) and of incompetent adults (most notably *Bland*). In *Re J*, where the question was whether it would be in the best interests of a disabled, premature baby with a short life-expectancy to be ventilated, Taylor LJ stated:

> I consider the correct approach is for the court to judge the quality of life the child would have to endure if given the treatment and decide whether in all the circumstances *such a life would be so afflicted as to be intolerable to that child*. I say "to that child" because the test should not be whether the life would be tolerable to the decider. The test must be whether the child in question, if capable of exercising sound judgment, would consider the life tolerable.[24]

Similarly, in *Bland,* where the question was whether it would be lawful to withdraw tube-feeding from a patient in a persistent vegetative state even though he would die as a result, Lord Keith ruled:

> [A] medical practitioner is under no duty to continue to treat such a patient where a large body of informed and responsible medical opinion is to the effect that no benefit at all would be conferred by continuance. *Existence in a vegetative state with no prospect of recovery is by that opinion regarded as not being a benefit*, and that, if not unarguably correct, at least forms a proper basis for the decision to discontinue treatment: *Bolam v. Friern Hospital Management Committee* [1957] 1 W.L.R. 582.[25]

To hold, as in *Re J*, that life-prolonging treatment may be withheld/withdrawn from a child because the child's life would be 'intolerable' involves a judgment that the child no longer has a 'beneficial Quality of life'. This remains so irrespective of the rider that the judgment should made from the child's perspective. Even if adopting such a perspective were feasible, the judgment of 'intolerability' would remain a judgment that the child's life was no longer beneficial. Similarly, to judge that Tony Bland's existence was not beneficial (or, as one learned Lord Justice described it, a 'humiliation'[26]) is to judge that his life was no longer worth living. Indeed, a majority of the Law Lords judged that it would be lawful to withdraw his tube-feeding even though they thought that the doctor's intention was to kill.[27] Once the law endorses the judgment that certain patients have no 'beneficial quality of life', and even that patients may lawfully be killed by deliberate withdrawal of treatment or tube-feeding, it forfeits any principled objection to the taking of positive steps to end their lives. Lord Mustill aptly observed that *Bland* left the law in a 'morally and intellectually misshapen' state, prohibiting active intentional killing, but permitting intentional killing by omission.[28] The misshapenness resulted from the courts mistakenly thinking that the key moral distinction is between act and omission when, as the IOL holds, it is between intention and foresight.

---

[24] [1991] Fam 33, 55 (emphasis added). For the current status of the "intolerability" test see *W (by her litigation friend B) and M (by her litigation friend, the Official Solicitor) and S and A NHS Primary Care Trust* [2011] EWHC 2443 (Fam).

[25] *Bland* (n 10) 858–859 (emphasis added).

[26] *Bland* (n 10) 831, per Hoffmann LJ.

[27] ibid 876 (Lord Browne-Wilkinson); 877 (Lord Lowry); 887 (Lord Mustill).

[28] ibid 887.

Some judges appear to believe that the IOL is consistent with the QOL view that some lives are not beneficial. For example, Lord Keith said in *Bland* that although it was the duty of the state, and the judiciary as one of the arms of the state, to uphold the sanctity of life, the principle was not 'absolute'. While the principle forbade the taking of active measures to cut short life, it did not, for example, "compel the temporary keeping alive of patients who are terminally ill where to do so would merely prolong their suffering."[29] But once the principle is clarified, and clearly distinguished from vitalism, then we should say, with respect, that it *is* absolute. It endorses allowing terminally ill patients to die but never endorses judging that their lives lack worth, and treating oneself or anyone else as free to *try* to hasten their death. Allowing the terminally ill to die is not an exception to the principle but an application of it. In short, although the value of human life is not absolute, the prohibition on trying to extinguish it, by act or omission, is.

Bland raised ethical and legal issues scarcely less complex and profound than the Conjoined Twins case. But just as the principle of double effect offered a sound way through the thicket of questions raised by separating conjoined twins, it also offered a sound resolution to the question of withdrawing tube-feeding from a patient in a persistent vegetative state. Had their Lordships in *Bland* held that the tube-feeding could be withdrawn on the ground that it was a futile medical treatment, because it could do nothing to improve Tony Bland's medical condition (or quality of life), their reasoning would have left the law in much more reasonable moral and intellectual shape. As the IOL is not vitalist it does not require life to be preserved at all costs. It regards the core purposes of medicine as the restoration to health and well-functioning and, if that cannot be achieved, the alleviation of symptoms. As Sir Thomas Bingham MR (as he then was) noted in the Court of Appeal in *Bland*, the objects of medical care have traditionally been understood as:

(1) to prevent the occurrence of illness, injury or deformity ... before they occur;
(2) to cure illness when it does occur;
(3) where illness cannot be cured, to prevent or retard deterioration of the patient's condition;
(4) to relieve pain and suffering in body and mind.[30]

As the tube-feeding could do nothing to restore Tony Bland to health and well-functioning, its removal could (at least arguably) have been justified on the ground that it was a futile medical treatment. This was in essence the approach taken by Lord Goff, who drew an analogy between the tube-feeding and a ventilator.[31]

---

[29] ibid 859.

[30] *Bland* (n 10) 809.

[31] Bland (n 10) 870. Whether tube-feeding *is* a medical treatment, as opposed to basic care which should be provided to all patients, is a matter for reasonable ethical debate, but at least an approach which considers whether a treatment is beneficial involves no judgment that the patient's life is no longer beneficial.

In the Conjoined Twins case, the presiding Lord Justice delivered a welcome reaffirmation of the key distinction between judging that a treatment is not worthwhile and that the patient's life is not worthwhile. His Lordship stated:

> Given the international conventions protecting "the right to life" … I conclude that it is impermissible to deny that every life has an equal inherent value. Life is worthwhile in itself whatever the diminution in one's capacity to enjoy it and however gravely impaired some of one's vital functions of speech, deliberation and choice may be.[32]

Moreover, it appears that Parliament has restored the prohibition on intentionally withholding/withdrawing treatment or tube-feeding with intent to kill. In relation to the determination of the 'best interests' of a mentally incapacitated adult, section 4(5) of the Mental Capacity Act 2005 provides that where the determination relates to life-sustaining treatment the person making the determination must not "be motivated by a desire to bring about his death." As Professor Finnis has pointed out, this should be interpreted as prohibiting any intent that death be brought about, either as an end or as a means:

> The phrase 'motivated by a desire' has been used in the courts … as equivalent to the phrase 'influenced by a desire', which is found in the Insolvency Act 1986, s 239(5). These judgments show that the courts treat the motivating desire … as including … all purposes which affect the decision-maker's deliberations and shape or enter into its conclusions——that is, all the kinds of purpose which are referred to when one says that in carrying out one's decision one has an intent to … or a purpose of …. And all this is reinforced by the way courts have spoken of intent and motivating desire in the context of Art.81 of the EC Treaty.[33]

Moreover, the alternative interpretation, which would allow a carer to withdraw treatment as a means of bringing about death provided he or she was motivated by a desire to achieve some other end, would gut the obvious protective function of the provision. Such an interpretation would allow a doctor to shorten life if motivated by a desire to get away early for the weekend.

(b) 'Best interests': subjective or objective?

Though section 4(5) of the Mental Capacity Act 2005 is welcome, the definition of 'best interests' in section 4(6) and (7) is less so, for they define 'best interests' largely in terms of subjective opinions rather than objective criteria. Section 4(6) provides that the person making the determination must take into account, so far as is reasonably ascertainable:

(1) the person's past and present *wishes and feelings* (and, in particular, any relevant written statement made by him when he had capacity),
(2) the *beliefs and values* that would be likely to influence his decision if he had capacity, and
(3) the *other factors that he would be likely to consider* if he were able to do so.[34]

---

[32] *Re A* (n 2) 187–188, per Ward LJ.

[33] Finnis (2009); 95: 101–102 (footnotes omitted), citing *Re MC Bacon Ltd* [1990] BCC 78, 86; *Re Hawkes Hill Publishing* [2007] BCC 937, para 33 and, in another context, *R v Greenwich LBC* [1991] 1 WLR 506, 508.

[34] Emphases added.

Section 4(7) adds that the person making the determination must take into account, if it is practicable and appropriate to consult them, the *views* of:

(1) anyone named by the person as someone to be consulted on the matter in question or on matters of that kind,
(2) anyone engaged in caring for the person or interested in his welfare,
(3) any donee of a lasting power of attorney granted by the person, and
(4) any deputy appointed for the person by the court,
  as to what would be in the person's best interests and, in particular, as to the matters mentioned in subsection (6).[35]

As Finnis comments:

> This appearance of unrooted subjectivity remains a deep weakness in the Act's treatment of best interests, and it is important that commentaries on the Act encourage carers to feel confident that they have the right, indeed the duty, to consider the *real* true interests of the person and not *simply* the wishes and feelings of someone who may be incapable of sound judgment, or be in the grip of wrong-headed views about his or her own worth, or human worth in general; nor *simply* the views of others involved in the case.[36]

One way of denying worth to incompetent patients is to adopt the judgment that the value of life depends wholly on the value people *give* to their life through their choices, and that the loss of one's capacity to choose means that the only value in one's continued existence depends on the value one had chosen to attach to one's life when competent. Such an approach is inconsistent with the ineliminable dignity which we all share whether or not we are competent:

> [E]xercises of autonomy … are *not* the fundamental source of worth and value in a person's life. Human beings possess an ineradicable value prior and subsequent to the possibility of exercising autonomy. Autonomy itself as a capacity is to be valued *precisely in so far as its exercise makes for the well-being and flourishing of the human beings who possess it.* But it is plain that many exercises of the capacity, that is, many self-determining choices, are destructive of human well-being——both in the life of the chooser and in the lives of others affected by his or her choices. The mere fact that someone has *chosen* to act or to be treated in a certain way establishes no title to moral respect for what has been chosen. The character of the choice must satisfy certain criteria in order to warrant our respect. The most basic criterion is that a choice should be consistent with respect for the fundamental dignity both of the chooser and of others.[37]

In the leading case on the treatment of mentally incapacitated adults at common law, Lord Brandon observed: "The operation or other treatment will be in their best interests if, but only if, it is carried out in order either to save their lives, or to ensure improvement or prevent deterioration in their physical or mental health."[38]

---

[35] Emphases added.

[36] Finnis (n 33) 100 (emphases in original).

[37] Keown and Gormally (n 7) (emphases in original).

[38] *Re F* [1990] 2 AC 1, 55.

In relation to health care, 'best interests' should be understood to include the standard objectives of health care practice:

> the restoration and maintenance of health, or of whatever degree of well-functioning can be achieved; the prolongation of life; and the control of symptoms when cure cannot be achieved. It is in serving these ends that doctors serve the good——and, therefore, the best interests——of their patients. And, in the absence of these criteria, how can the courts hope to resolve disputes? If the understanding of 'best interests' fails to include objective, substantive requirements there will be no non-arbitrary way of judging whether the testimony of relatives and others about a patient's 'preferences' is self-serving; no non-arbitrary way of settling differences of opinion; and no objective criteria for determining whether a regulatory system is in fact operating to protect patients.[39]

In short, just as doctors and relatives can lose sight of the inherent dignity of a mentally incapacitated patient, so can the patient himself or herself. Misguided subjective views about the patient's worth should never be allowed to obscure what is truly and objectively in the best interests of the patient.

Further, section 4's vaguely defined criterion of 'best interests', which guides those making decisions in relation to incompetent adults, does not apply to 'advance decisions' made by adults themselves while still competent. There is a real risk, therefore, that some patients will make advance refusals of treatment based on a misguided opinion that in such-and-such a condition, their life would not be worth living, and perhaps refuse treatment in advance of incompetence with intent to put an end to their life. It will now be suggested that the courts should make it clear that, while there is a right to refuse treatment, there is no right to commit suicide such as could impose a duty on others to facilitate death for that purpose, even by omission.

7.3.5 Autonomy

Autonomy is a valuable capacity, and part of human dignity, but its contribution to dignity is conditional, not absolute. Exercising one's autonomy to destroy one's (or another's) life is always wrong because it is always disrespectful of human dignity. So: it is always wrong intentionally to assist/encourage a patient to commit suicide and, equally, there is no 'right to commit suicide', let alone a right to be assisted to commit suicide, either by act or omission.

The principle of 'respect for autonomy' has in recent years become for many a core if not dominant principle of biomedical ethics and law. It is not, however, unproblematic. Its advocates often fail to agree on precisely what constitutes an 'autonomous' choice or to offer any convincing account of why respect for someone else's choice as such should be regarded as a moral principle at all, let alone a core

---

[39] Keown and Gormally (n 7).

or dominant moral principle.[40] Our capacity for choice is undoubtedly very important, for it is through our choices that we shape our lives and influence the lives of those around us, for good or for ill. But we should exercise our autonomy responsibly, choosing for good, not ill. Neither the common law nor professional medical ethics has ever held that the mere fact *that* I have chosen justifies *what* I have chosen. Consequently, the law refuses to respect various choices, however autonomous. It disallows choices to be owned, eaten, or executed, to be the victim of actual bodily harm,[41] to possess illicit drugs, or to drive while not wearing a seat-belt. In the medical context patients have no right to demand whatever treatment or drugs they may want, including palliative sedation. A doctor may not amputate a healthy limb even on request, and female genital mutilation is prohibited by section 1 of the Female Genital Mutilation Act 2003, regardless of the woman's consent. The Mental Health Act 1983 allows treatment for mental disorder to be imposed on even a competent patient who chooses not to have it.[42] None of these autonomous choices need involve a risk of harm to anyone but the person making them but they are, nevertheless, disallowed by the law. Other autonomous choices do involve a risk of harm to others, which helps explain why they too are rejected by the law even when, as with dueling, the risk of harm may be entirely consensual. Choices which undermine human flourishing or well-being, such as choices to kill or mutilate (whether oneself or another), simply lack moral justification. A patient's demand for palliative sedation in order to hasten death is not a demand which a doctor either must or should respect.

It is occasionally suggested that the decriminalization of suicide by the Suicide Act 1961 recognized a right to commit suicide.[43] However, the legislative history of the Suicide Act demonstrates that it was not the intention of Parliament to condone suicide, let alone establish a "'right to suicide."'[44] Far from it. The government made clear its hope that decriminalization would not give the impression that it regarded what it described as 'self-murder' at all lightly.[45] As Lord Bingham explained in *R (Pretty) v Director of Public Prosecutions*:

> The law confers no right to commit suicide .... Suicide itself (and with it attempted suicide) was decriminalized because recognition of the common law offence was not thought to act as a deterrent, because it cast an unwarranted stigma on innocent members of the suicide's family and because it led to the distasteful result that patients recovering in hospital from a failed suicide attempt were prosecuted, in effect, for their lack of success. But while the 1961 Act abrogated the rule of law whereby it was a crime for a person to commit (or attempt to commit) suicide, it conferred no right on anyone to do so. Had that been its object there would have been no justification for penalizing by a potentially very long term

---

[40] For valuable contributions to the growing debate about the proper role of autonomy see: McCall Smith (1997); 14: 23; O'Neill (2002); Foster (2009).

[41] *R v Brown* [1994] 1 AC 212.

[42] Section 62.

[43] eg *Bland* (n 10) 826–827, per Hoffmann LJ.

[44] *Hansard*, HC vol 645, cols 822–823 (1960–1961).

[45] *Hansard*, HC vol 644, cols 1425–1426 (1960–1961).

of imprisonment one who aided, abetted, counseled or procured the exercise or attempted exercise by another of that right. The policy of the law remained firmly adverse to suicide, as section 2(1) makes clear.[46]

Further, as Professor Skegg has observed, even since the Suicide Act 1961 "it has continued to be accepted that doctors are sometimes free—sometimes, indeed, under a duty—to prevent patients from committing suicide."[47] In *Reeves v Commissioner of Police of the Metropolis*[48] the House of Lords held that police and prison authorities owe even competent prisoners a duty to take care to prevent them from committing suicide. Suicide may, moreover, be committed by omission, such as a refusal to eat, just as it may be committed by an act. In *R v Collins and Ashworth Hospital Authority, ex p Brady* Maurice Kay J (as he then was) observed that there should be circumstances in which public interests such as the preservation of life, the prevention of suicide, the maintenance of the integrity of the medical profession, and the preservation of institutional discipline "would properly prevail over a self-determined hunger strike so as to enable, even if not to require, intervention." His Lordship observed:

> It would be somewhat odd if there is a duty to prevent suicide by an act (for example, the use of a knife left in the cell) but not even a power to intervene to prevent self-destruction by starvation. I can see no moral justification for the law indulging its fascination with the difference between acts and omissions in a context such as this and no logical need for it to do so.[49]

In *Bland* Lord Goff said that when a patient refuses life-saving treatment "there is no question of the patient having committed suicide, nor therefore of the doctor having aided or abetted him in doing so": it was simply that the patient had declined to consent to treatment which might or would have the effect of prolonging his life, and the doctor had, in accordance with his duty, complied with his patient's wishes.[50] While this is no doubt generally the case, his Lordship did not appear to have considered the scenario where a patient's refusal of treatment is clearly designed to kill himself and where he demands that doctors assist him to carry out his suicidal enterprise. Imagine an otherwise healthy diabetic who refuses his regular insulin shot in order to end his life and who demands to be kept comfortable in hospital while he dies, perhaps as part of a campaign to undermine the law against assisting suicide. If the courts were to hold that doctors were under a duty to comply with his demands (and could not for example discharge him), then the law against assisted suicide would indeed be undermined. If the law were to require, or even permit, doctors *intentionally* to help him kill himself by withholding treatment, how could the law, without inconsistency, prohibit doctors from providing him with active assistance? The courts need to be wary of the right to refuse treatment being manipulated to

---

[46] *R (Pretty) v DPP* [2001] UKHL 61 at [35].

[47] Skegg (1988) 111 and authorities there cited.

[48] [2000] 1 AC 360.

[49] [2000] 8 Lloyd's Rep Med 355, 367.

[50] *Bland* (n 10) 864.

undermine the law against assisting suicide. It is one thing for doctors to withhold/withdraw treatment with the intention of respecting the patient's legal right to refuse treatment (even if they feel sure that the patient's refusal is suicidal). It is quite another for doctors *intentionally to assist*—try to assist—suicidal refusals and for the courts to endorse such intentional assistance. Just as a patient could try to commit suicide by refusing an insulin injection, a patient could equally try to commit suicide by demanding palliative sedation accompanied by the withholding or withdrawal of tube-feeding.

Surprisingly, the European Court indicated in *Pretty*,[51] albeit cryptically, that the UK's blanket ban on assisting suicide engaged the respect for 'private and family life' guaranteed by Article 8(1) of the Convention, although the ban was saved by Article 8(2). The Court's interpretation of Article 8(1) was mistaken. The Court should have followed Lord Bingham's opinion in that case that Article 8(1) sought to protect certain choices while people are living their lives, not the choice to live no longer.

Unfortunately, the Law Lords in the *Purdy* case went even further than the European Court when they ordered the Director of Public Prosecutions (DPP) to issue guidance spelling out the factors he would take into account in deciding whether to prosecute Debbie Purdy's husband should he assist her to commit suicide.[52] As the Lord Chief Justice rightly observed in that case, delivering the judgment of the Court of Appeal, such an order would in effect create exceptions to the crime, exceptions which Parliament had not chosen to enact.

7.4 Conclusions

The IOL has long been a foundational principle of the common law. This has not saved it from being widely misunderstood, in the academy, at the Bar, and on the Bench. The root cause of the misunderstanding is the tendency to confuse it with one (and sometimes both) of the two alternative approaches to the value of life: "vitalism" and "QOL." The confusion has, inevitably, impaired the law's moral and intellectual coherence. The law would regain its coherence if it:

- clearly denied that 'oblique intent' is intent;
- clearly distinguished between 'quality of life benefits' and 'beneficial Quality of life';
- adopted a definition of 'best interests' tied to the objective good of the patient, not least to the patient's life and health;
- clearly ruled out any intent to shorten life, whether by act or by omission, and as a means or as an end;

---

[51] *Pretty v United Kingdom* (2002) 35 EHRR 1.
[52] *R (Purdy) v Director of Public Prosecutions* [2009] UKHL 45.

- recognized that the exercise of autonomy is to be valued to the extent that it serves the good of the patient, and that choices which are inconsistent with that good, not least choices to extinguish life, have no right to be endorsed;
- clearly denied that the right to refuse treatment involves a right to commit suicide and to be intentionally assisted to commit suicide.

As we noted in the Introduction, this chapter has not sought directly to address the many ethical and legal questions raised by 'palliative' or 'terminal' sedation: that would involve an analysis of many different scenarios. Suffice it to say that, depending on the particular circumstances of each case, not least the doctor's intention, 'palliative' or 'terminal' sedation may be ethical and lawful or may be unethical and unlawful. Much work remains to be done unpacking the ethical and legal implications of the many different possible scenarios.[53] Two contrasting scenarios can be touched on here. If sedating a patient (who is close to death) into unconsciousness is the only way of relieving the patient's refractory symptoms; if the doctor acts with the patient's informed consent, and if there is no shortening of life, then it is difficult to see why the doctor should incur ethical or legal censure. (Indeed, a failure to provide sedation in such circumstances could expose the doctor to a civil action in negligence for failing to discharge the doctor's duty to take reasonable steps to prevent reasonably avoidable suffering.) Even if the patient's life is shortened by hours or perhaps even days, then provided this is no part of the doctor's purpose, and there is a proportionate reason for allowing the shortening of life, the doctor's actions would appear satisfy the principle of 'double effect' (though the greater the shortening of life, the more difficult it will be to satisfy the requirement of proportionality). If, by contrast, the doctor sedates the patient in order to shorten the patient's life (even at the patient's request) then the doctor breaches the cardinal ethical and legal principle of the inviolability of life and risks prosecution for homicide. There are many other scenarios in between which will require ethical and legal analysis. The modest but not unimportant goal of this chapter has been to help lay a sound ethical and legal foundation for that project.

References

Finnis, J. 2009. The Mental Capacity Act 2005: Some ethical and legal issues. In *Incapacity and care*, ed. H. Watt. London: The Linacre Centre.

Finnis, J. 2011. *Intention and identity: Part three*. Oxford: Oxford University Press.

Foster, C. 2009. *Choosing life, choosing death: The tyranny of autonomy in medical ethics and law*. Oxford: Hart Publishing.

Goff, R. 1988. The mental element in the crime of murder. *Law Quarterly Review* 104: 30.

Gormally, L. (ed.). 1994. *Euthanasia, clinical practice and the law*. London: The Linacre Centre.

Jones, D.A. 2013. Death by equivocation: A manifold definition of terminal sedation. In *Continuous sedation at the end of life: Ethical perspectives*, ed. S. Sterckx et al. Cambridge: Cambridge University Press.

---

[53] For a valuable overview of various possible scenarios see Jones (2013).

Keown, D. 1995. *Buddhism and bioethics*. Basingstoke: Macmillan/St Martins Press.
Keown, J. 2012. 'The sanctity of life', 'best interests' and 'autonomy': An overview. In *The law and ethics of medicine: Essays on the inviolability of human life*, ed. J. Keown. Oxford: Oxford University Press.
Keown, J., and L. Gormally. 1999. Human dignity, autonomy and mentally-incapacitated patients: A critique of who decides? *Journal of Current Legal Issues*. 4 web Available at: http://www.wjcli.ncl.ac.uk
Mason, J.K., and R.A. McCall Smith. 1994. *Law and medical ethics*, 4th ed. Oxford: Oxford University Press.
McCall Smith, A. 1997. Beyond autonomy. *Journal of Contemporary Health Law and Policy* 14: 23.
O'Neill, O. 2002. *Autonomy and trust in bioethics*. Cambridge: Cambridge University Press.
Re, A. 2001. *Fam.* 147, 211.
Report of the Select Committee on Medical Ethics. 1994. (HL Paper 21-I of 1993–4). London: HMSO.
Skegg, P.D.G. 1988. *Law, ethics and medicine*, Rev. ed. Oxford: Clarendon Press.
Skegg, P.D.G. 2006. Medical acts hastening death. In *Medical law in New Zealand*, ed. P.D.G. Skegg et al., 505. Wellington: Thomson Brookers.

Chapter 8
Palliative Sedation: Some Legal Precautions in the Case of Chile

Angela Vivanco

8.1 Palliative Sedation: The Need for a Legal Analysis

Sedation, understood from the medical perspective as: the administration of drugs to lessen the patient's level of consciousness, with the objective of controlling some of the symptoms or to prepare the patient for a diagnostic or therapeutic intervention that could be stressful or painful (Comité de Ética 2002). It is described as "palliative" when such an administration is done to "lessen the patient's level of consciousness with the objective of controlling physical or psychical symptoms or both", which can equate to a *primary sedation*: to reduce the level of consciousness in a patient with an advanced or terminal illness, as much as it is necessary to adequately alleviate one or more refractory symptoms and according to the patient's explicit, implicit or delegated consent; or *terminal sedation,* which implies the: deliberate administration of drugs to achieve relief, unachievable in any other way, of a physical or psychic pain, or both, through the sufficiently deep and foreseeably irreversible lessening of consciousness in a patient close to death and with the patient's explicit, implicit or delegated consent (Santos et al. 2009).

Although medical literature has expounded considerably on this subject, the need for a legal assessment of the concept which has generated some controversy should not be overlooked. Indeed, even though palliative care is a tool used around the world as part of good medical practice, developed to benefit the patient suffering psychological and physical effects of specially complex situations such as prostration, chronic illness, pain and proximity of death, etc. and in relation to which, healing medicine has few possibilities for application, the alternative of palliative sedation has some unique aspects which have been a matter of debate: The first

A. Vivanco (✉)
Faculty of Law, Pontificia Universidad Católica de Chile,
Alameda 340, Santiago, Chile

Universidad Santo Tomás, Chile, Ejército 156, Santiago, Chile
e-mail: avivanco@santotomas.cl

P. Taboada (ed.), *Sedation at the End-of-life: An Interdisciplinary Approach*, 111
Philosophy and Medicine 116, DOI 10.1007/978-94-017-9106-9_8,
© Springer Science+Business Media Dordrecht 2015

aspect, the deliberate lessening of the patient's consciousness, an effect that intensifies at the stage of terminal sedation, and which for some critics could mean an escape option for the patient which will bring him dangerously close to the decision to die (Clark 2002); the second aspect, the difficulties of external control in relation to the use of a measure regarding real *refractory* symptoms (Cherny and Portenoy 1994) and, the third, the eventual effect of shortening the patient's life as a consequence of the administration of certain drugs, which would become an unwanted result of certain forms of sedation (Kris et al. 2007).

This controversy, which evidently also involves the legal sphere, requires certain definitions on the part of the current Law, in particular with three objectives:

(a) To establish if the application of palliative sedation is a conduct considered lawful in juridical terms, within the exercise of the medical profession.
(b) To determine if it is one of the patient's rights, from which guarantees peculiar to its exercise are derived.
(c) To distinguish this practice from other conducts which may be considered inadmissible by the local legal system, as can be the case of euthanasia?

8.2 The Constitutional Code Regarding This Subject in Chilean Law

Palliative sedation is not a concept directly covered by the Chilean legal system, although the constitutional foundations on the right to life, autonomy and health protection give us important references for establishing an applicable framework in this matter.

Indeed, the Chilean Constitution in Article 19, No. 1, guarantees that all persons have the right to life, and physical and psychical integrity. This comes from the constitutional statement of the 1st Article of the Constitution: All persons are born free and equal in dignity and rights. Similarly, in Article 19, No. 9 the fundamental right to health protection is recognized, which, understood in the terms expressed by the WHO, does not only represent the absence of illness but also the subject's complete wellbeing,[1] and in its Article 19, N° 7 recognizes personal freedom as a constitutional right, which not only comprises the physical protection of the subject in relation to imprisonment and other illegal or arbitrary detentions and the respect for their autonomy:… it is the right of every person, without interference in the sphere of personal autonomy by public institutions or third parties, to self-determination and to act according to his/her will without limitations other than those imposed by the natural environment, the rights of others or the regulations of the constitution (Nogueira 2002).

---

[1] «Health is a state of complete physical, mental and social well-being and not merely the absence of disease or infirmity. »: Preamble to the Constitution of the World Health Organization, adopted by the International Health Conference, New York, 19th June to 22nd July, and entered into force on the 7th April 1948.

From that perspective, palliative sedation, as a form of reducing the suffering of the person and the physical and mental pain which are produced in the patient by both the disease and the proximity of death, is incorporated in a model which protects life, but recognizes the person's own decision taking sphere and in a health environment increasingly marked by respect for the quality of life.[2]

8.3   The Rights of Patients in Chile

In this country, many areas unique to Bio-Law have had a slow development, therefore the legal codes for important topics can often be found more in administrative regulations and in an increasing jurisprudential development, than in the body of the Law.

(a) **References in administrative regulations**

It is important to mention Decree No. 40 from the Ministerio de Salud [Ministry of Health] published on the 21st April 2005, Reglamento Orgánico de los Servicios de Salud [Organizational Regulations for Health Services], whose latest modification is dated October 2006, which says: the right of patients, or those who represent them, to deny or reject diagnostic or therapeutic procedures, this having to be recorded in an official document of the Service.

This aspect, belonging to the theory of informed consent, is not marginal in terms of material recognition, because often the possibility that the patient could reject certain therapies or interventions is forgotten, considering, erroneously, that their right is purely to agree: "The patient has the right to self-determination and to take free decisions regarding himself/herself. The physician will inform the patient of the consequences of his/her decision. A mentally competent adult patient has the right to give or withhold consent for any diagnostic procedure or therapy. The patient has the right to the information necessary to make his/her decisions. The patient should understand clearly what is the purpose of any test or treatment, what the results would imply, and what would be the implications of withholding consent" (Vivanco 2009).[3]

(b) **Jurisprudential interpretation**

Jurisprudence, both from the Courts as from the constitutional judgments in our continent has evolved gradually concerning the importance of the patient's informed consent in its negative aspect, that is to say, that which implies for example opting for a palliative measure rather than for an aggressive treatment,

---

[2] This implies, for example, to recognize "an equitable access to palliative care for all terminally ill or dying persons" (Recommendation 1418 (1999), of the 25th June, European Council Parliamentary Assembly, on the Protection of the human rights and dignity of the terminally ill and the dying, Section 9.A.II).

[3] It has to be taken into account that our jurisprudence has also considered the appropriateness of the withholding of treatment in the case of patients under age (Vivanco 2002).

or directly to reject a particular therapy, despite the doctor's recommendation to accept it. However, this recognition has happened slowly, both in comparative instances and nationally.[4]

The legal consideration of the patient's right to accept or reject, being well informed, a measure or intervention, has several consequences for the development of these jurisprudential theses:

---

[4] In the case of Chile, from the middle of the nineteen nineties there are the beginnings of jurisprudence, in the sense that the patient cannot be forced to accept a therapeutic measure on the basis that no-one can be forced to defend his/her own rights, v.g. The judgment from the Corte de Apelaciones de Santiago [Court of Appeal in Santiago] in Autos Rol N° 806-96 [Record number 806-96] Hospital San José against J.C. rejected the protective injunction lodged by that Hospital to force the patient to have a transfusion saying that the lodged injunction has to protect the life of a person who is disturbed or threatened by the action of a third party, but cannot pursue the protection against the voluntary omission of a person to save their life, because no-one can be forced to defend his/her own right. In the same way, in 2001 the Corte de Apelaciones de Talca [Court of Appeal in Talca] in Autos Rol N° 60069-01, declared inadmissible the protective injunction in the same vein, considering that taking into account the background it can be implied that the person in favor and against is the same one, therefore, the injunction is declared inadmissible. Later, the court recognized the right to reject medical treatments on the part of a competent patient, when a statement is filed of such decision: v.g. Sentencia de la Corte de Apelaciones de San Miguel en Autos Rol N° 104 2008: [the Appeal Court in San Miguel, Record Number 104-2008] [Fourteenth]: that as a consequence, in the cases of prescription of therapeutic treatments on the part of a medical doctor regarding a patient, who in a fully competent state of physical and mental faculties, resolves to reject the treatment, whether because they believe it will produce a therapeutic deterioration or because the patient considers that they will be deprived of the conditions of life that they consider essential and minimal, the affected guarantee would not necessarily be the right to life. Indeed, in this situation two different opposing interests will be in conflict over the same fundamental right. From the perspective of the sentencing tribunals, the freedom of conscience between two subjects becomes contradictory, first the right of the patient required to have a curative procedure, and secondly, the freedom of conscience of the medical doctors who offer that procedure and who in carrying it out are fulfilling their duty of looking after the health and life of the persons in their charge. Fifteenth: that when facing a bioethical conflict of this nature, the doctrine has orientated in the sense to recognize that in the adult individual, in full possession of his physical and mental faculties, the prerogative of opposing therapeutic treatment when considered extreme or unbearable, or because it can damage, in that individual's appreciation, aspects that constitute essential elements of life and of its quality.../ Sixteenth : that in the terms described, it is important to analyze the degree of freedom and independence in the decision adopted by Mr. L.S.G. – if in reality there has been – and if when it was adopted, he/she acted in full knowledge of it, and in particular of its consequences. Nineteenth: that as a consequence the sentencing tribunals have not acquired the indispensable and essential conviction that Mr. L.S.G., in full use and exercise of his physical and mental faculties, has rejected the prescribed therapeutic treatment./ Twentieth: that, on the other hand, according to the medical records attached to the appeal, there is certainty, that without the recommended surgical operation, Mr. L.S.G. will die in a short period of time./ Twenty-first: that the conflict between the protected right to freedom of conscience and the right to life, having been elucidated as has been done in the preceding reasoning, these sentencing tribunals will opt to protect the constitutional guarantee of the right to life as it is protected in Article 19, No.1 of the Chilean State Constitution, in the terms that are allowed by Article 20 of the same document … and therefore, the medical doctors of this health service are authorized to carry out the necessary procedures to preserve his life and prompt recovery, including surgical operations required for such effect.

1. The accepting of therapies or procedures, even when disproportionate, by the competent patient is a declaration of his/her will, but it compromises the responsibility of the person proposing them (Vivanco 2002).[5]
2. The rejection of or the request for withdrawal or suspension of disproportionate measures, is part of the rejection that the competent patient can ethically and legally take and it would generate responsibility on the part of the person imposing treatment or not accepting the expressed wish.[6]
3. To supply the suffering individual with medications that could shorten his/her life expectancy, in as far as the aim is to palliate the suffering, implies a wish to dignify treatment and not the disposition of his/her life: ... death caused as a secondary effect of the medications applied with the objective of alleviating pain or other symptoms in the patient... death considered as a foreseeable but undesirable effect (Comisión Nacional de Bioética de México).

(c) **The introduction of legal regulations**

The law which regulates the rights and obligations of people regarding actions related to their health care, Act number 20.584, published on October 12th, 2012[7] regulate the so called rights of the patients, even though it does not directly refer to palliative sedation, has several rulings referring to the patient's informed consent and to the prospective possibility of rejecting treatments or therapies, which we transcribe:

1. Artículo 10 inciso 1°: [Article 10 section 1]: Every person has the right to be informed, promptly and understandably, by the medical doctor or another treating professional, about the state of his/her health, of the possible diagnosis of the illness, of the alternative treatments available for curing it and the risks involved, **as well as the expected prognosis**,[8] and the foreseeable postoperative process, when that goes forward, according to their age, and personal and emotional condition.

---

[5]...the faculty that a competent person has to reject medical treatment, even when they are vital, has to be clearly distinguished from direct collaboration in causing death, because in one case, it is about a decision proper to the parity currently recognized in the medical doctor-patient relationship and of the value of the principle of quality of life when the treatments are onerous, out of proportion or useless, while in the other case, there is an action directly taken to cause death in the individual (Vivanco 2002).

[6]In some legal systems, it has been recognized as a medical doctor's obligation to respect the patient's decisions and avoid forced treatment: in Article 2.6 of the Law 41/2002, of the 14th November, basic regulator of the patient's autonomy and the rights and obligations in terms of information and clinical documentation (BOE No. 274, dated 15.11.2002) in Spain, expresses: Any professional who intervenes in the assistant activity is obliged not only to the correct rendering of his technical capacities, but also to fulfill the duties of information and clinical documentation, and to respect the free and voluntary decisions adopted by the patient.

[7]The law obtained the approval of Tribunal Constitucional (Constitucional Court) on year 2012 for it to be enacted as law for the República de Chile [Republic of Chile].

[8]Bold characters are ours.

2. Artículo 14 incisos 1°, 2° y 3°: [Article 14 sections 1, 2 and 3]: Every person has the right to grant or deny his/her will to undergo any procedure or treatment related to his/her health care, within the limitations established by Article 16./ This right must be exercised in a free, voluntary, expressed and informed way, for which it is necessary that the treating professional gives adequate, sufficient, and comprehensible information, in accordance with Article 10./**In no case, the rejection of treatments may have as its objective the artificial acceleration of death, the carrying out of practices of euthanasia or assistance to suicide.**[9]

3. Article 16: The person who is informed that his/her state of health is terminal, has the right to grant or deny his/her wish to submit him/herself to any treatment which would have the effect of artificially prolonging his/her life, without prejudice to the maintenance of normal support. In no case, **can the rejection of treatment imply as its objective the artificial acceleration of the process of death**./ This right to choose is not applicable when as a result of the absence of this intervention, procedure or treatment, public health is placed at risk, in the terms established by the Health Code. This circumstance should be formally recorded by the treating physician in the clinical file of the person. / For the correct exercise of the right established in the first section, the professionals treating the case are obliged to provide complete and understandable information. / Those who find themselves in this condition will have the right to live in dignity up to the moment of their death. As a consequence, **they have the right to palliative care which enables the effects of their illness to be rendered more supportable,**[10] in the presence of their families and of those in whose care they may be, and to receive, when they ask for it, spiritual support./Voluntary discharge can always be requested by the patient, by the person empowered as designated by the patient or by the relatives as defined in Article 42 of the Civil Code, in the preferential and exclusive order established by the said article.

If we revise this legal regulation, concerning the characteristics of palliative sedation, we may note the following:

(a) The right of the patient to agree to or reject medical treatment is recognized, therefore, both decisions are given equal value. That, obviously, implies also the selection of such therapy or procedure that the patient prefers, which could mean to opt for a palliative measure instead of a treatment with little expectation of success and very damaging for the person receiving it. If palliative sedation is a legally suitable measure within the legal system, the patient has the right to opt for it, according to his/her autonomy and ethical views: Greater anticipation in planning the taking of decisions by patients with advanced illnesses, will improve the involvement of the patient-family unit and result in a better control of the symptoms, avoiding conflictive situations at important moments in the patient's life. / The perception of death as a medical failure and

---

[9] Idem.
[10] Idem.

clinging on to the maintenance of certain therapeutic attitudes as an escape mechanism so as not to face the inevitable, are two attitudes that need to be modified (Navarro and Lopez 2008).

(b) The effects of rejection are, however, limited by law: the rejection of treatment may entail as an objective the artificial acceleration of the death process. Note that this limitation does not affect the patient's choice of a terminal sedation, because the latter constitutes a choice and not a rejection, notwithstanding that choosing one measure means rejecting the other. However, even though the rejected measure could have had a beneficial effect on the prolongation of life, the patients who opts for palliative care does not do so because the objective is to die, it is because they consider that such care is the most suitable in their situation of sickness, their vision of quality of life, their values and their right to receive a dignified treatment. Additionally, if the death process is accelerated the rejection would not be given artificially, but naturally and as a result of the illness which follows its natural course.

(c) The patient's rights to palliative care are recognized expressly. Even though a distinction has been made between terminal sedation and the use of analgesic drugs, which would produce a respiratory deprivation with an unwanted result of acceleration of death, could it be lawfully expected that palliative sedation exceeds the boundaries of this right, as an option for the patient? In our view, if effectively it is about the measure as described in this document, and not about the carrying out of a hidden euthanasia (Porta 2000), as we will discuss in the following paragraph, there are no bases within the revised regulations which could be considered as impediments to the application of this measure within the concept of palliative care.

8.4   Treatment of Euthanasia: Differences with Palliative Sedation

Euthanasia, in Chilean Law, is treated as a form of homicide, conduct characterized as: to kill someone. Even though there have been some attempts to modify it, in the sense of creating a special criminal type for this conduct, these attempts have not succeeded, and there are no grounds for exception or legal justification based on the consent of the alleged victim or the pious character of the agent.

Figure 8.1 shows the main features of this conduct.

Euthanasia, thus characterized, as a killing conduct, be it by action or omission is carried out by a different person to the patient, with a humanitarian or pious motivation stemming from the suffering condition or the seriousness of the state of the patient, acting at the request of the latter or even without their expressed wish, but never against it (Vivanco 2006).

The fact that euthanasia, in the countries that legally accept it, is applied by medical doctors and in relation to patients with high levels of suffering or qualified

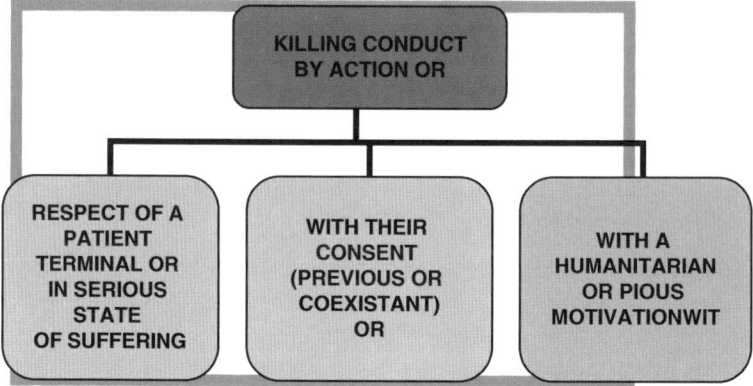

Fig. 8.1 Euthanasia

as terminal, brings the conduct closer to the sphere of palliative sedation, but it should not be confused:

1. Palliative sedation, as has already been explained, is immersed in the concept of palliative care, that is to say, those measures that seek: to alleviate the patients' symptoms of pain and suffering when they suffer a chronic-degenerative illness or are in the terminal phase; the patient is treated as an overall complete being by seeking to improve their quality of life (Pessini and Bertachini 2006). From this perspective, the intention of the person applying palliative sedation is this: the medical doctor prescribes the sedative drugs with the intention of alleviating the patient's suffering in the face of certain defined symptom(s). In the case of euthanasia, the objective is to cause the death of the patients to free them from their sufferings. The sedation alters the patient's consciousness in a way which seeks a state of indifference to the suffering or to the threat arising from the symptom. When the sedation is deep, conscious life is lost. Euthanasia, however, eliminates physical life (Casas 2005).

2. The consent of the patients, or of those who represent them, to apply a palliative measure of sedation is not intended to terminate life, but only to avoid suffering. This differs from the request for euthanasia, which means death at the hands of a third party, not the choice of a palliative measure. Precisely for that reason, the reproachable aspect of carrying out euthanasia is not the humanitarian intention, but the inability of the medical doctor to put himself in the patient's place and to procure a solution that is not homicide.

3. The procedure is also a source of distinguishing between both conducts: in palliative sedation, the objective is the fine adjustment of sedative drugs, in euthanasia the objective is to administer lethal drugs.(16) It may mean different concentrations of the same drug, but precisely that indicates what they are being used for, and, if that were the case, distinguishes a killing conduct from a collateral result of shortening life.

4. With regards to the result, both types of conduct also differ: in sedation, the responding measurement (of success) is the relief of pain, which can and must be

differentiated through an assessment system.(17) However, in euthanasia the responding measurement (of success) is death.(18)

In this way, even though neither euthanasia nor palliative sedation are specifically regulated in the Chilean legal system, clearly both conducts are diametrically opposite, with the result that the first is a punishable conduct, which is contrary to the constitutional framework which protects life and the person's integrity, and the second a measure that can be identified with the patients' rights in using their lawful autonomy.

This, evidently, does not imply ignoring that sedation can be used invoking palliative objectives, when the reality is to seek to cover up a conduct of euthanasia, but such a possibility is one of the many possibilities that exist, in every country and legal system, to circumvent the law and to disguise criminal conducts as lawful: The keys to avoiding such excesses are, on the one hand, the ethics of the health professional, and on the other, the information due to the patient, the verification of his/her true wishes and the formal and substantial controls of the actions taken, with the objective of checking them with the current legal system.

References

Casas, M.L. 2005. *Sedación terminal, eutanasia y bioética*. Available at: http://scielo.sld.cu/scielo.php?script=sci_arttext&pid=S0034-75232005000500013&nrm=iso.

Cherny, N.I., and R.K. Portenoy. 1994. Sedation in the management of refractory symptoms: Guidelines for evaluation and treatment. *Journal of Palliative Care* 10: 31–38.

Clark, D. 2002. Between hope and acceptance: The medicalization of dying. *BMJ* 324: 905–907.

Comisión Nacional de Bioética de México. Eutanasia. Algunos elementos para el debate. Available at: http://cnb-mexico.salud.gob.mx/descargas/pdf/eutanasia.pdf.

Comité de Ética. 2002. *Sociedad Española de Cuidados Paliativos (SECPAL)*. Aspectos Éticos de la Sedación en Cuidados Paliativos. www.diariomedico.com, 24th Apr 2002. Available at: http://www.federaciocristians.org/metges/Buscar/10_eutanasia/05.05_sedacio_porta.pdf

Kris, Vissers C.P., J. Hasselaar, and S. Verhagen. 2007. Sedation in palliative care. *Current Opinion in Anaesthesiology* 20: 137–142.

Navarro, R., and C. Lopez. 2008. Aproximación a los Cuidados Paliativos en las enfermedades avanzadas no malignas. *Anales de Medicina Interna (Madrid)* [online]. 25(4): 187–191. http://dx.doi.org/10.4321/S0212-71992008000400009. Available at: http://scielo.isciii.es/scielo.php?script=sci_arttext&pid=S0212-1992008000400009&lng=es&nrm=iso. ISSN 0212-7199.

Nogueira, H. 2002. La libertad personal y las dos caras de Jano en el ordenamiento jurídico Chileno. *Revista de Derecho (Valdivia)* [online] 13: 161–186. Available at: http://mingaon-line.uach.cl/scielo.php?script=sci_arttext&pid=S071809502002000100011&lng=es&nrm=iso. ISSN 0718-0950.

Pessini, L., and L. Bertachini. 2006. Nuevas perspectivas en cuidados paliativos. *Acta Bioethica* [online] 12(2): 231–242. doi:10.4067/S1726-569X2006000200012. Available at: http://www.scielo.cl/scielo.php?script=sci_arttext&pid=S1726-569X2006000200012&lng=en&nrm=iso&ignore=.html. ISSN 1726-569X.

Porta, J. 2000. Sedación en cuidados paliativos: reflexiones éticas. *Acta Bioethica* [online]. 6(1): 77–87. doi:10.4067/S1726-569X2000000100006. Available at: http://www.scielo.cl/scielo.php?script=sci_arttext&pid=S1726-569X2000000100006&lng=es&nrm=iso. ISSN 1726-569X.

Santos, D., et al. 2009. Sedación paliativa: experiencia en una unidad de cuidados paliativos de Montevideo. *Revista Médica del Uruguay* [online] 25(2): 78–83. Available at: http://www.scielo.edu.uy/scielo.php?script=sci_arttext&pid=S0303-32952009000200002&lng=es&nrm=iso. ISSN 0303-3295.

Vivanco, A. 2002. La autonomía de la persona frente al derecho a la vida no incluye el derecho a ser muerto por un tercero: la solicitud de asistencia al suicidio y el caso de Diane Pretty. *Acta Bioethica* [online] 8(2): 299–313. doi: 10.4067/S1726-569X2002000200010. Available at: http://www.scielo.cl/scielo.php?script=sci_arttext&pid=S1726-569X2002000200010&lng=es.

Vivanco, Á. 2006. La Eutanasia ante el Derecho: Definición y penalización de la conducta eutanásica. [Euthanasia before the Law: Definition and sanctioning of the conduct of euthanasia] *Ars Médica* 12: 53–92.

Vivanco, A. 2009. Negativa de un menor de edad y de su familia a que este reciba una terapia desproporcionada o con pocas garantías de efectividad: Apelación de medida de protección otorgada por la Jueza de Familia de Valdivia. *Revista-Chilena derecho* [online] 36(2): 399–440. doi: 10.4067/S0718-34372009000200008. Available at: http://www.scielo.cl/scielo.php?script=sci_arttext&pid=S0718-34372009000200008&lng=es&nrm=iso. ISSN 0718-3437.

World Medical Association (WMA). *Lisbon declaration on the rights of the patient*. Adopted by the 34th World Medical Assembly, Lisbon, Portugal, September/October 1981, amended by the 47th WMA General Assembly, Bali, Indonesia, September 1995, and editorially revised by the 171st WMA Council Session, Santiago, Chile, October 2005.

Chapter 9
Clinical Guidelines for the Use of Palliative Sedation: Moving from Contention to Consensus

Blair Henry

Our patients come to us complaining not of disease, but of their subjective experience of illness. (Mount 2003)

9.1 Introduction

At its core, medicine strives for a compassionate and skilled response to all patients experiencing pain and suffering. Through the concurrent growth of palliative care as a medical specialty and an enhanced pharmaceutical armamentarium available to clinicians working with patients at the end of life, this core aim can be realized. Evidence-based data demonstrates that the range of refractory or intolerable symptomatology is constantly being reduced. Nonetheless, the clinical presentation of disease, particularly at the end of life, can be such a distressing experience that induced sedation may be the most appropriate and clinically beneficial treatment. This chapter will attempt to present a case for the utility of establishing clinical guidelines to support the practice of palliative sedation by exploring the contextual history of end-of-life care, particularly as it relates to the contentious advent of sedation as a therapy of choice for the palliation of refractory and intolerable symptoms in a subset of terminally ill patients.

B. Henry (✉)
Ethics Centre, Sunnybrook Health Sciences Centre, Room H 2 39, 2075 Bayview Ave, Toronto, ON M4N 3M5, Canada

Joint Center for Bioethics, University of Toronto, Toronto, ON, Canada
e-mail: Blair.henry@sunnybrook.ca

P. Taboada (ed.), *Sedation at the End-of-life: An Interdisciplinary Approach*, Philosophy and Medicine 116, DOI 10.1007/978-94-017-9106-9_9, © Springer Science+Business Media Dordrecht 2015

9.2 Historical Perspective

Pharmacological agents with sedative properties (bromide and chloral hydrate) were first introduced into medicine in the early part of the nineteenth century. Central nervous system depressants such as barbiturates were made available in 1903, and psychoactive drugs such as benzodiazepines have been a mainstay since 1959 (Hauser and Walsh 2009). These medications were routinely used to help patients endure the distressing pain and anxiety commonly associated with noxious procedures in medicine, but their use in the context of end-of-life care was seldom mentioned in the medical literature (Cherney and Portenoy 1994).

The use of sedation for sleep induction, as a means to control symptoms in advanced disease, was first discussed by Dr. Robert Enck in 1990 (Enck 1991). In fact, Enck's article was the first in the literature to use the phrase 'terminal sedation' – and he did so in the context of it being an already existing practice, however, in reality little was known of its practice prior to this time (Veterans Health Administration National Ethics Committee 2006; Ventafridda et al. 1990).

Figure 9.1 presents a historical timeline and broad overview of key events surrounding the introduction and practice of palliative sedation over the past 20 years. This timeline has been deliberately set against activities surrounding the larger national and international end-of-life movement to provide a fuller context of the formal origins of palliative sedation into hospice and palliative care. Understanding the concurrent societal issues facilitates realization of why the use of palliative sedation was steeped with controversy and concern; a contentious history that still exists in the current practice of palliative medicine.

The modern history of palliative sedation spans two unique decades: 1990 to 2000 and 2000 to 2010. For the purposes of this article, the first period could be considered a decade of differentiation wherein palliative sedation attempted to differentiate itself from the growing choice in dying movement. In particular, the growing calls for acceptance of physician assisted suicide (PAS). During this period, the practice of sedation was suspected of being a form of 'slow euthanasia' and questions regarding its ethical and legal status were discussed in the academic literature. This decade is also remarkable for the legal and legislative activity taking place particularly in the United States. In 1990, the Nancy Cruzan case was a striking victory for the 'right to die' movement. The court held that if the evidentiary threshold is met (prior wishes expressed by) a capable person's request to refuse medical treatment should be honoured, even when the treatment refusal can result in death. By 1994, the state of Oregon had passed its Death with Dignity Act, legalizing PAS. During the decade other U.S. states attempted unsuccessfully to pass similar legislation: New York (1996), Florida (1997), Michigan (1998), Maine (2000) and Colorado (2000) (Behuniak 2003).

It would be against this backdrop that discussions of the utility, merit, and practice of palliative sedation were initiated. In both national and international forums, medical professionals, primarily nurses and physicians, were frequently polled on their attitudes and practice relating to euthanasia, PAS, and palliative sedation. In its

Decade of differentiation

1990	Enck's original article identifying "Terminal Sedation" as a therapy for symptom control
1990	*Cruzan v. Director, Missouri Dept. of Health* (1990) Decision conferring a "right to die"
1994	Cherny & Portenoy publish first "guidelines for sedation in the management of refractory symptoms"
1994	Oregon Death with Dignity Act passed-legalizing Physician Assisted Suicide
1997	*Vacco v. Quill*, 117 S. Ct. 2293 (U.S. 1997) landmark decision regarding the right to die, upholding a New York ban on physician assisted suicide and outlining there is no constitutional guarantee to a "right to die"
1997	*Washington v. Glucksberg*, 521 U.S. 702 (1997) the Supreme Court of the United States unanimously held that a right to assistance in committing suicide was not protected by the Due Process Clause.

Decade of standardization

2001	Netherlands pass legislation making euthanasia legal
2001	The American College of Physician's Ethics and Human Rights Commission issue a position on Physician Assisted Suicide, drawing a clear distinction between this practice and palliative sedation.
2005	A notable shift in the academic literature away from using the term "terminal sedation" to the use of "palliative sedation"
2002/ 2010	Publication of 9 National and International Guidelines/Framework/Position Statements outlining the use of palliative sedation as an accepted therapy (with conditions) for EOL care

Fig. 9.1 Historical timeline

rather unfortunate introduction in the academic literature, sedation was labelled a treatment of 'last resort' and often referred to as 'terminal sedation'- a rather ambiguous term which was open to different interpretations: Did the word 'terminal' refer to the patient or to the proposed purpose of the sedation? (Chater et al. 1998; Bloche 2006) This ambiguity resulted in palliative sedation being viewed suspiciously by some physicians as well as large sections of the population who advocated to restrict choices in dying.

The 1994 article: *Sedation in the management of refractory symptoms: Guidelines for evaluation and treatment*, by N Cherny and K Portenoy was an essential forerunner to the future development of clinical guidelines for palliative sedation. They provided a very important clinical criterion to determine symptom refractoriness to aid in the standardization of how patients should be evaluated when considering the use of palliative sedation (Cherney and Portenoy 1994).

By the end of the decade, two key legal decisions by the United States Supreme Court (*Vacco v. Quill* and *Washington v. Glucksberg*) (Chater et al. 1998; Bloche 2006; King 2000–2001; McStay 2003) would result in a much clearer demarcation of the 'right to die' movement. In these two landmark cases, the courts outlined that there was no constitutional guarantee to support assisted suicide, and that the legalization of PAS or euthanasia would require individual state legislation. Additionally, the Supreme Court established that allowing death (e.g. withdrawing life support) to occur was to be considered an event clearly differentiated from the act or the intention of causing death.

The second formative decade: identified here as the period between 2000 and 2010 can be considered as the decade of standardization. During this decade, attempts were made to standardize the practice of palliative sedation. The American College of Physician's position paper clearly articulated that palliative sedation was distinct from PAS, and also that it was an ethical and valid form of therapy in the provision of palliative care (American Academy of Hospice and Palliative Medicine 2006). By 2005, the frequency in which the use of the term 'terminal sedation' was cited had significantly dropped in the literature, and at the end of the decade a total of 11 policy-directed documents had been published. It should be noted that though significant progress was made over this decade, as seen in the publication of policies attempting to regulate the use of palliative sedation, regrettably it would be inaccurate to suggest that the actual practice of palliative sedation does not remain open to potential misuse and abuse. In fact, in Chap. 10, Dr. Scott presents a compelling case for ongoing concerns over the use and practice of palliative sedation at the end of life.

9.3   The Prevalence of Palliative Sedation Use in End-of-Life Care

The data in Table 9.1 represents a detailed literature review (spanning 20 years) describing the frequency that sedation is reportedly used at the end of life. Most of the available data comes from either case reports or retrospective studies. However, the first prospective study was reported in 1990 by Ventafridda et al. (1990) In their report, the authors followed 120 home-based palliative patients and they observed that in 52 % of these patients, the level and degree of physical suffering (typically arising in the last 2 days of life) was such that palliation could only be achieved through sedation. The remainder of the data reported in the literature suggests an extreme level of variability in practice with a reported range of prevalence noted between 0.21 and 88 %. Of the cases reported, 62 % fall within a reported 5–30 % (patients requiring sedation) frequency range, 15 % of reported cases had a frequency rate less than 5 and 20 % had a reported frequency rate in excess of 40 %.

The major impediment to compare national or international data can be explained in part by the lack of a standard definition for sedation being used: in some articles the reported frequency referred only to sedation that was deep (rendered patient

Table 9.1 Reported prevalence rates of PST at the end of life

Item	Year	Country	% PS utilization	Special considerations
1	1990	Italy	52	63/120 home based palliative patients (Ventafridda et al. 1990)
2	1990–2005	Sweden	40 %	(Engstrom et al. 2007; Cunningham 2008)
3	1991	Canada	16	N = 100 (Fainsinger et al. 1991)
4	1991	Australia	20	(Cunningham 2008)
5	1994	USA	25	N = 20 (McIver et al. 1994)
6	1994–1995	Canada	1	N = 87 "terminal sedation" (Fainsinger 1998)
7	1995	Germany	7	Sedation increased continuously from 7 % in 1995 to 19 % in 2002 (Devulder et al. 2004)
8	1995	Italy	25	N = 401 (Peruselli et al. 1999)
9	1996	Japan	48	N = 143 (Morita et al. 1996)
10	1996	Australia	88	N = 50 (Turner et al. 1996)
11	1997	UK	26	N = 115 (Stone et al. 1997)
12	1998	Japan	45	N = 157 (Morita et al. 1999)
13	1998	South Africa	28	(Fainsinger et al. 1998)
14	1998–1999	Taiwan	27.9	N = 251 (Levisman et al. 1975)
15	1999	Belgium	7	(Claessens et al. 2007)
16	2000	Japan	8	N = 248 (Morita et al. 2000)
17	2000	Israel, South Africa and Spain	15–36	N = 287 (Fainsinger et al. 2000b)
18	2000	Canada	4–10 %	4 % in hospice 10 % tertiary PCU N = 150 (Fainsinger et al. 2000a)
19	2000	Italy	14.2	N = 331 Continuous deep sedation (Bulli et al. 2007)
20	2000–2001	Netherlands	10	Based on survey of 410 physicians (Rietjens et al. 2005)
21	2001	Netherlands	5.6	(van der Heide et al. 2007)
22	2001	USA	20-30	(Cowan and Walsh 2001)
23	2001	Japan	60	N = 209 (Fainsinger et al. 1991)
24	2001–2005	Netherlands	43 %	CPST in N = 157 (Rietjens et al. 2008)
25	2002	Germany	19	The annual frequency to apply sedation increased continuously from 7 % in 1995 to 19 % in 2002
26	2003	UK	48 %	N = 237 in specialist PCU (Sykes and Thorns 2003a)
27	2003–2004	Italy	12	N = 744 continuous deep sedation (Bulli et al. 2007)
28	2003–2004	Germany	3.1	N = 160 deep and continuous in PCU (Stiel et al. 2008)
29	2004	Japan	1	Outlier: 90/9000 used PST for existential distress (Morita 2004)
30	2004	Belgium	5.5	(Devulder et al. 2004)
31	2004	Spain	17	N = 259 (Gilbert et al. 2004)

(continued)

Table 9.1 (continued)

Item	Year	Country	% PS utilization	Special considerations
32	2005	Belgium	5	(Claessens et al. 2007)
33	2005	Netherlands	7	The use of continuous deep sedation increased from 5.6 % of deaths in 2001 to 7.1 % in 2005 (van der Heide et al. 2007)
34	2005	Netherlands	7.1	(van der Heide et al. 2007)
35	2005	Netherlands	12	(Rietjens et al. 2005)
36	2006	USA	2.3	28 out of N = 1200 (Cowan et al. 2006)
37	2004–2005	USA	15	Admission to PCU N = 1207 (Elsayem et al. 2009)
38	2006–2008	Italy	36.4	16 out of 44 (Porzio et al. 2010)
39	2008	Spain	78 %	Referred to as terminal sedation 311 out of N = 401 (Vila Santasuana et al. 2008)
40	2008-09	Korea	56.6	Administered sedative for distressful symptoms (Ashby 2010)
41	2009	Spain	.21	2 cases in 995 patients over 2 years (Guell et al. 2009)
42	2009	Italy	25.1	N = 518 (Alonso-Babarro et al. 2010)
43	2010	Spain	12	N = 245 at home patients (Alonso-Babarro et al. 2010)
44	2010	Italy	3.3	Based on N = 182 all ALS patients (Sparato et al. 2010)
45	2010	Belgium	7.5	N = 266 (Claessens et al. 2007)

unresponsive to verbal commands) and continuous (intended use until death), whereas in others, the reported frequency may have included sedation that was light (where the patient is in a state of rest, but verbal contact is easily maintained) and temporary (intended for short term use only) or in some cases the reported frequency may have included sedation that was a secondary but unintended consequence of a more specific treatment. For example, many physicians misinterpret the somnolence of dying patients being treated with opioids as palliative sedation (Worthington 2005). Regrettably much of the earlier reported history of palliative sedation teaches us very little about palliative sedation in the context of how it has been developed and practiced, its necessity for or in some cases its avoidability, the appropriate types of medication to use and the required or appropriate depth and length of palliative sedation recommended (Broeckaert et al. 2011).

9.4 Ethical Considerations

Many of the recurrent ethical questions related to palliative sedation therapy have stemmed from disagreement and a lack of conceptual clarity pertaining to intention, justification, application, consequences, and use of this therapy. It is towards this

Table 9.2 Ethical issues central to the use of PST

Why is PST not a form of euthanasia?

Can a patient's free and informed consent ever be obtained in the context of intolerable suffering?

Is the use of PST for refractory and intolerable existential distress ethically justified?

Is a treatment that relies on the decrease/absence of consciousness a means to remove suffering by removing the sufferer?

In what stage of the illness is it appropriate to use PST?

In what circumstances is the withholding or withdrawing of treatments such as nutrition and hydration in PST ethical?

Can policy related to PST incorporate sufficient safeguards to prevent abuse?

Table 9.3 Application of key ethical principles to PST

Principle	Consideration in PST
Intentionality	What is the intention of the medical team?
	What are the unintended consequences of an act?
Proportionality	The titration of sedating medications.
	Accepting risks that are in proportion to the gravity of the clinical indications.
Autonomy	Informed consent
	Advance directives
Beneficence and Non-maleficence	Rubric of balance such that PST lies within the usual accepted medical guidelines of beneficence and non malfeasance

primary concern that the development of clinical guidelines and policies should be directed. Traditionally, the ethical authority for the use of palliative sedation comes from the moral imperative of medicine: relieve human suffering (Roy 1990; de Graeff and Dean 2007). However, to sufficiently address this complex topic a more nuanced understanding of the ethical issues is required.

In its work on the creation of a policy framework, the Canadian Palliative Sedation Task Force (Dean et al. 2012) identified several key ethical concerns most often cited in relationship to the practice of palliative sedation (see Table 9.2).

In part, policy statements or clinical guidelines should attempt to address each of the key ethical issues cited in Table 9.2, by providing (where possible) clear evidence and experience to redress any conflict or misunderstanding based on insufficient data or unexamined assumptions (Roy et al. 1994).

Table 9.3 outlines some of the central ethical principles commonly used in addressing the issues identified in Table 9.2. In spite of the challenge in ascertaining intentions and of distinguishing intended from foreseen consequences the differentiation between intended and unintended consequences of an act remains the basis for most of our moral censuring in medicine. From a legal perspective, two previously cited U.S. Supreme Court cases (Quill and Glucksberg) (Kawamura 1998) relied on the principle of double effect to justify and sanction the practice of palliative sedation.

Traditionally, applying the principle of double effect in the case of palliative sedation one asks: When is sedation, which results in both the relief of suffering and the possible hastening of death, ethically permissible? Though an important question for consideration, the limited data published to date (Maltoni et al. 2009; Sykes and Thorns 2003b; Muller-Busch et al. 2003) has indicated that when good palliative care is provided to patients, the appropriate use of palliative sedation does not shorten life. It should be noted that the level of evidence presented for this conclusion is limited in scope, and that clinicians continue to dispute the relationship between palliative sedation and the hastening of death. The principle of double effect does provide a clear ethical, legal and medical ground to proceed. The principle of double effect directs moral reasoning that if a contemplated action has a good and bad effect, the act can be considered permissible if the following five conditions are satisfied: the act in and of itself is either morally good or neutral; the foreseen yet undesired results are not intended; the good effect is not a direct result of the bad; the good effect is proportionate to the bad; and finally, that one is convinced that no other way exists to achieve the desired ends (Latimer 1991).

The concern for potential abuse or misuse of palliative sedation drives home the importance of autonomy, informed consent and shared decision-making. This is particularly evident in situations where intolerable pain could impact decision-making. Discussions with patients and families should occur when palliative sedation becomes a possibility. Particular attention to the collective patient-family-team perspectives in reaching consensus on palliative sedation helps to ensure due process.

The moral imperative to address human suffering is often accompanied in the ethics literature by the principles of respect for human dignity, beneficence, non-malfeasance, and non-abandonment. The understanding that pain is a subjective experience that extends beyond the mere physical dimension to include emotional, spiritual and psychological issues is well accepted in palliative care. However, in the context of addressing suffering by the use of palliative sedation the perceived practice of "ending the sufferer as a means to ending the suffering" resurfaces in the contemporary literature on palliative sedation. This emphasizes the necessity for vigilance in the form of thorough multi-disciplinary assessments of patients and adherence to clear policies and guidelines in the use of palliative sedation. Corresponding documentation that symptoms are refractory and intolerable should be demonstrated through systematic assessment and continued monitoring prior to and during palliative sedation.

The implication of a decision to use palliative sedation is that symptom relief could not be obtained without intentionally clouding consciousness. To assist in understanding the appropriate and ethical use of palliative sedation the principles of proportionality and intentionality play a key role. This calls for demonstrated prudence and transparency throughout the decision-making process (Simon et al. 2007), with agreement on a clear treatment goal i.e. relief of suffering, and the proportional use of sedative medication to adequately relieve suffering without overshooting that goal i.e. only enough sedation to relieve the suffering.

Offering palliative sedation in the last weeks of life has not traditionally been identified as a distinct ethical problem (Gevers 2003). Understanding that precise prognostic certainty is rarely possible in this context the condition of 'imminence' (Cellarius 2008) remains to be acceptably defined clinically. The major shift in re-addressing this issue is the appreciation that a narrowing of palliative sedation to only deep and continuous applications does threaten the notion of proportionality (titration to the relief of symptoms only) (Claessens et al. 2008). For these reasons, the practice of palliative sedation should be regarded as a proportionate procedure that is benchmarked against assessed and documented clinical conditions.

The inevitable linkage of palliative sedation with presumed life-shortening effects, such as the withholding of hydration and nutrition (Jansen and Sulmasy 2002) continues to cause concern. Decision-making regarding the use of nutrition and hydration (N&H) needs to be made independently of a decision for palliative sedation and clear reasons for the use or not of N&H should be documented to justify this decision (Broeckaert et al. 2011; Rietjens et al. 2005). An institution involved in the provision of end-of-life care should have in place policies and/or practice guidelines to assist decision-making involving the withholding and/or removal of life supportive therapies (e.g. ventilatory support, N&H) and these guidelines should be kept in mind whenever considering the use of palliative sedation.

Ultimately, agreeing to use the principle of proportionality entails accepting risks that are commensurate with the gravity of the clinical indication (Cherny 2006). In doing so we need to acknowledge that the potential for abuse does exist in palliative sedation, and establish guidelines and policy safeguards that ensure that care is delivered within accepted medical guidelines (Quill et al. 2009).

9.5 Overview of Current Position Statements, Frameworks and Guidelines for PST

In the face of widespread medical practice variance; as evidenced in the large range of reported prevalence use for palliative sedation (see Table 9.1), and given the absence of good research data to guide practice – the use of either position statements typically issued by professional associations, or medical/clinical guidelines and frameworks supported by appropriate professional groups can provide the necessary vehicle for enhanced standardization of practice (Rosalki and Karp 1999).

At present there are a limited number of official guidelines and recommendations to guide clinical practice (de Graeff and Dean 2007). As shown in Table 9.4, between 2000 and 2010 a total of 11 official policy-directed documents on palliative sedation, in the form of position statements, clinical guidelines or frameworks, had been developed and published. Of these, the Belgium Guideline (2010) was only available in Dutch and plans for its translation into English had not yet been announced (Broeckaert et al. 2011). In addition to these formal reports, three key publications by de Graeff and Dean (2007), Rousseau (2002), and Byock and Quill

Table 9.4 PST- guidelines, frameworks and consensus statements

	Name	Type	Original date/Rev.	Originator
1	Continuous PST (Dean et al. 2012)	Framework	2012	Canada- sponsored by Canadian Society of Palliative Care Physicians
2	Palliative Sedation Guidelines (Broeckaert et al. 2011)	Guideline	2010	Federation of Palliative Care Flanders [in Dutch]
3	Use of Palliative Sedation in Imminently Dying Terminally Ill Patients (Kirk and Mahon 2010)	Position statement	2010	National Hospice and Palliative Care Organization (NHPCO)
4	European Association for Palliative Care recommended framework for the use of sedation in palliative care (Cherny et al. 2009 Oct)	Framework	2009	European Association for Palliative Care (EAPC) Cherny et al.
5	Report of the Council on Ethical and Judicial Affairs. Report 5-A-08 Subject: Sedation to Unconsciousness in End-of-Life Care (American Academy of Hospice and Palliative Medicine 2007)	Special report	2008	American Medical Association
6	Guidelines for Palliative Sedation (Verkerk et al. 2007)	Clinical practice guideline (CPG)	Dec 2005 (Revised 2010)	Royal Dutch Medical Association
7	Clinical Practice Guidelines for Palliative Sedation (Alberta Health Services 2011)	Clinical Guideline	2005 (Revised 2009)	Alberta Health Services (Calgary Regional Health Authority CPG 1999)
8	Clinical Guideline for PST (Morita et al. 2005)	Clinical guideline	2005	Sedation Guideline Task Force in Japan (Morita et al.)
9	Position Statement on Palliative Sedation (American Academy of Hospice and Palliative Medicine 2006)	Position statement	2002 (Revised Sept 2006)	American Academy of Hospice and Palliative Medicine
10	Guidelines on Palliative Sedation (Forde et al. 2001)	Guidelines	2001	Norwegian Medical Association
11	Sedation in the management of refractory symptoms: Guidelines for evaluation and treatment (Cherney and Portenoy 1994)	General guidelines	1994	N.I. Cherny and R.K. Portenoy

(continued)

Table 9.4 (continued)

Name	Type	Original date/Rev.	Originator
PST: Therapy in the last weeks of life: A literature review and recommendations for standards (de Graeff and Dean 2007)	Formative review	2007	De Graeff and Dean
Existential Suffering and palliative sedation: A brief commentary with a proposal for clinical guidelines (Rousseau 2003)	Formative article	2001	P. Rousseau
Responding to Intractable Suffering: The Role of Terminal Sedation and Voluntary Refusal of Food and Fluids (Quill and Byock 2000)	Formative paper	2000	American Society of Internal Medicine EOL Consensus Panel (I Byock and T Quill authors)

(2000), were added to the table given their impact and influence in establishing requirements for consideration into the guideline development process used by many of the published sources outlined in the table.

Typically position statements or medical/clinical guidelines (inclusive of frameworks) are systematically developed statements designed to assist clinical staff in decision making about the appropriate healthcare (therapy, service) needed for specific clinical conditions (Rosalki and Karp 1999) Guidelines are not intended to prescribe the detailed management of individual patients. In fact many guidelines are typically based on literature reviews, where best treatments are deduced from the published data which in turn informs the creation of a guideline. However, well designed guidelines can define the most important questions related to clinical practice and identify all possible decision options and their outcomes (Field and Lohr 1990). The key to good guideline development is to identify the processes of care through which a patient may pass (irrespective of judgment that might be made about them) and to identify decisional nodes or branch points between them and to outline the range of possible decisions that might be taken- some guidelines use decisional algorithms as a tool to represent the process in clear stages. Ultimately, clinical guidelines address generic recommendations, which, should then be transitioned into institutionally specific protocols and clinical pathways/care plans that are meant to affect practice (Woolf 1992).

It is interesting to note that of the 11 policy-directed documents available in the literature, the only one formally listed with the National Guideline Clearinghouse repository (Agency for Healthcare Research and Quality) is the 2006 version of Royal Dutch Medical Association Palliative Sedation CPG (Verkerk et al. 2007).

9.6   Contention and Consensus

Table 9.5 outlines a comparative summary of the key issues involved in the use of palliative sedation – as identified from a review of the various published statements, guidelines and frameworks presented in Table 9.4. The recommendation to use a proportionate/titration ('just enough') approach to sedation for the palliation of both refractory and intolerable suffering can be considered an area of widespread consensus based on it being a recommendation advocated in 9 of the 11 statements reviewed. However, contention remains over the issue of existential distress: in terms of how it is understood in practice (definition/diagnosis), on how to treat and ultimately determine if it is refractory in nature, and that if- as a symptom on its own, it should stand as a sufficient indicator for the initiation of palliative sedation. Five of the current guidelines acknowledge that existential distress, deemed to be both refractory and intolerable to a patient, should be considered permissible to be palliated with sedation. However, one of these guidelines made the point that existential distress called for a 'special provision' prior to its consideration. Three of the guidelines clearly stated that existential distress alone would not be sufficient cause to employ palliative sedation, and the remaining three guidelines were undecided and did not provide a clear recommendation for this application. The prevalence of refractory and intolerable existential distress in a palliative care setting is under studied, however one informative study by Morita et al. in Japan, where sedation for existential distress is allowed, reported that only 90 out of 9,000 patients (1 %) who received palliative sedation did so for an indication of existential distress alone (Morita 2004). In regard to the recommended prognosis wherein palliative sedation could be used, all of the published guidelines and statements agreed that its use should be limited to only the last stages of life. However, consensus on an exact timeframe remains to be achieved. Five of the documents recommend that palliative sedation should only be used in patients with a prognosis no greater than 1 and 3 weeks of life (of which the majority specified less than 2 weeks). Three documents stipulated a much tighter prognosis in terms of hours to days of life, and the final three documents employed ambiguous criteria, such as: end of life; very advanced; and, final stages.

9.7   Guideline Development

An exploration and development of the contentious ethical, religious and legal issues at the core of palliative sedation are well represented in other chapters of this book. However a noteworthy and fortunate effect of having various position statements, frameworks, and guidelines for palliative sedation, has resulted in the creation of a rather robust and established structure for guideline development. A structure that is sensitive to and addresses the procedural aspects of the key decision-making nodes and processes that should be followed when palliative sedation

Table 9.5 Comparison of PST- guidelines, frameworks and consensus statements

	Name	Recommended prognosis	Consideration for existential distress	Proportionate sedation
1	Canadian Continuous PST Framework (2011)	<2 weeks	Yes	Yes
2	Palliative Sedation Guidelines Belgium (2010)	<1 week	Yes	Yes
3	National Hospice and Palliative Care Organization (NHPCO) Position Statement on Use of Palliative Sedation in Imminently Dying Terminally Ill Patients (2010)	<2 weeks	Unable to recommend	Yes
4	Dutch Guidelines for Palliative Sedation (2010)	1–2 weeks	Inclusive but never just for existential distress	Yes
5	European Association for Palliative Care recommended framework for the use of sedation in palliative care (2009)	Hours/days	Special consideration	Yes
6	Alberta Health Services- Clinical Practice Guidelines for Palliative Sedation (2009)	Few days	Controversial	Induce, maintain deep sleep
7	AMA Special Report of the Council on Ethical and Judicial Affairs. Report 5-A-08 Subject: Sedation to Unconsciousness in End-of-Life Care (2008)	Final stages	Not appropriate only for existential distress	Sedation to unconsciousness
8	AAHPM Position Statement on Palliative Sedation (2006)	Very advanced (would not alter time of death)	Not mentioned	Yes
9	Japan CPG for PST (2005)	2–3 weeks	Yes	Yes
10	Norwegian Medical Association Guidelines on Palliative Sedation (2008)	Few days	Not appropriate for only existential distress	Yes
11	Sedation in the management of refractory symptoms: Guidelines for evaluation and treatment (1994)	Not specified- "end of life"	Yes	Yes

Fig. 9.2 Key components
of a PST guideline

1) Terminology and Definitions
2) Aim statement
3) Indicators and Conditions
4) Communications
5) Decision-making and Informed Consent
6) Cultural considerations
7) Type of sedation
8) Drug selection, dosing and titration
9) Hydration, nutrition and concurrent medications
10) Ethical considerations
11) Outcome and monitoring
12) Family Supports
13) Staff Supports

is being considered. Based on a review and summary of the literature, Fig. 9.2 out-lines a recommended clinical guideline structure for consideration and use, which if properly applied, would ensure adequate attention is given to each of the critical composite stages of the clinical decision-making processes that are involved in the use of sedation at the end of life (Cherney and Portenoy 1994; de Graeff and Dean 2007; Dean et al. 2012; Kirk and Mahon 2010; Morita et al. 2005; Rousseau 2004)

An important element in any palliative sedation guideline should be the estab-lishment of clear and consistent terminology and definitions, so that end users understand what is meant by the terms they employ. Ideally the terminology should be standardized internationally; however, much work remains to be done to achieve that outcome. Agreement on what to call this practice remains varied, as previously noted reference to 'terminal sedation' has almost completely abated in the literature, however, several other terms such as: Sedation for intractable distress at the end of life; Sedation at the end-of-life; Total sedation; Palliative sedation; and, Palliative sedation therapy are all commonly used when referring to this intervention (Worthington 2005). The Canadian PST Working Group proposed a series of terms and definitions for use in policy development (see Fig. 9.3).

The inclusion of an aim statement, in the guideline, can help to inform those referring to this intervention about the exact purpose or goal of care being sought after when sedation is applied. Consensus exists in most of the literature that seda-tion is only to be used for the palliation of intractable and intolerable suffering and is not intended to shorten life. A clear aim statement serves as an articulation of the overarching intention of an intervention – which in this application, would delineate sedation as a means only to a nobler and ethically sound end.

The inclusion of a section on indicators and conditions helps the clinician to know when (or with whom) palliative sedation should be considered. As previously noted, consensus does exist that this intervention should only be used for patients with the following conditions: a terminal illness, whose symptoms are found to be refractory to alternate interventions appropriate for the condition presented, and deemed intolerable by the patient. As noted earlier in the Chapter, a lack of consen-sus does exist on the indicators for the appropriate use of sedation- however all guideline should clearly address if patient's presenting with non-physical indicators

---

Palliative Sedation Therapy (PST) (also called in the literature "Terminal Sedation", "Controlled Sedation", "Total Sedation", "Deep Sedation" and "Continuous Sedation") is the intentional lowering of a patient's level of consciousness in the last stages of life. It involves the proportional and monitored "use of specific sedative medications to relieve intolerable suffering from refractory symptoms by a reduction in patient consciousness" (de Graeff and Dean 2007).

Refractory Symptoms (also called in the literature "Intractable") are present "if all other possible treatments have failed, or it is estimated by team consensus, based on repeated and careful assessment by skilled experts, that no methods are available for alleviation within the time frame and risk/benefit ratio that the patient can tolerate"(Cherney and Portenoy 1994). Often geography and the relative availability of interventions influence the determination of refractoriness.

Suffering is "a sense of helplessness or loss in the face of a seemingly relentless and unendurable threat to quality of life or integrity of self" (Cassell 1999). Although pain, dyspnea, delirium and nausea and vomiting are frequent causes of suffering at the end of life, hopelessness, remorse, anxiety, loneliness, and loss of meaning also cause suffering. Suffering involves the whole person in physical, psychological, and spiritual ways and can also affect family, friends, and caregivers. Family members frequently feel psychological distress when they see or perceive that their loved one is suffering (de Graeff and Dean 2007).

Intolerable Suffering is determined by a patient as a symptom or state that he or she does not wish to endure (If the patient cannot communicate proxy judgment is sought).

Existential Distress' (also called in the literature "Psychic", "Psychological" or "Spiritual" distress or anguish) (Rousseau 2004; Schuman-Olivier et al. 2008) describes the experience of patients with advanced progressive illness who may or may not have physical symptoms but report distress that is unrelated to a psychiatric disorder or social isolation, but is related to one or more of: meaninglessness in present life; sense of hopelessness; perceiving oneself as a burden on others; feeling emotionally irrelevant; being dependant; feeling isolated; or grieving.

Fig. 9.3 Terminology and definitions

of suffering (i.e. existential distress) are eligible for this therapy, and also the indicated prognosis of a patient to ensure its use meets the accepted practice standards of an organization.

The criteria used for decision-making and informed consent are important process related components of the intervention that helps to ensure due process, and consideration of all factors are in place when deciding to proceed with palliative sedation. A guideline needs to consider the interdisciplinary structure of most health care environments and that clinical decisions need to consider the opinions and input from all related disciplines. A history of inappropriate use of palliative sedation- due to inexperienced clinicians, or as a result of caregiver exhaustion can be, in part, redressed by a guideline requirement asking for broad and experienced consultation prior to initiation of this therapy (Olsen et al. 2010). In addition a procedure aimed to ensure open communication with the patient and family throughout the process is very important. Similarly the skill required to appropriately assess capacity of patients at the end of life, particularly those experiencing distressing symptoms is complex and requires special attention.

A specific guideline section addressing a need for greater awareness and sensitivity to the cultural issues, inclusive of spiritual beliefs and practices, was incorporated into two of the published guidelines reviewed (de Graeff and Dean 2007; Dean et al. 2012). Literature confirms the existence of a unique institutional/health care culture, and that professional and individual health care provider beliefs and outlooks can potentially culminate into an ethnocentric bias that can be at odds with the dominant culture. In reality there exists a diversity of beliefs related towards key life events such as dying, end of life, and death. Additionally, the value a person or family associates with sentience at the end of life, and the wide range of potential meanings that can be given to human suffering requires that staff should be trained and proficient with providing culturally competent care at the end of life.

A description of the type of sedation method used will be important to guide actual practice. As noted a consensus opinion does exist, based on the published literature, recommending the use of a proportionate approach to the initiation of sedation, which would typically require the initiation of sedation at an intermittent and mild level, progressing to a continuous and potentially deep level as the situation required. In severe and rapid onset states of distress, sedation may need to be initiated in a deep and continuous manner to appropriately respond to the acuity of the presenting symptom.

A section outlining the recommended drug selection, dosing regimen and titration procedure for the induction of sedation will reflect local practices, availability of medications, and the unique experience of the clinicians involved. Common drugs typically mentioned in the literature, as drugs of choice, include: benzodiazepines (midazolam), antipsychotics (neuroleptics), barbiturates (Phenobarbital), or general anesthetics (Hauser and Walsh 2009). However, the exact choice of medication should depend of the etiology of the presenting symptom, and considerations for interaction with other medications in place. The inappropriate use of opioids for the purpose of sedation is a recommendation that has received widespread agreement (Legemaate et al. 2007).

Integral in the decision to use palliative sedation are the ancillary issues of nutrition and hydration support, and the decision related to continuance or discontinuance of concurrent medications. The concerns that not providing artificial hydration and nutrition will result in hastening the death have been at the heart of the criticism levelled against sedation therapy, resulting in it being viewed by some as a form of 'slow euthanasia' (Billings and Block 1997; Cassell and Rich 2010). Many of the new guidelines have noted the importance of making a decision related to the use (or not) of hydration and nutrition concurrent with sedation, however, the prevailing recommendation has been to make this specific decision distinct and separate from that of sedation- which would mean that any institution employing sedation therapy, should also have a policies and procedure guiding the appropriate use of artificial hydration and nutrition in the context of providing palliative care at the end of life. Similarly, a decision related to the ongoing use of concurrent medications will be specific to the patient and the underlying condition being treated. Patients receiving palliative sedation are not considered appropriate candidates for cardiopulmonary resuscitation and a guidelines should include a provision to ensure that the required conversations and decision to support this practice requirement be incorporated into the process.

The topic of palliative sedation is frequently associated with ethical concerns that should be acknowledged and discussed openly as part of any policy or guideline development. Guidelines should explore principles of intentionality and causation as it relates to the use of sedation at the end of life; provide an explanation on the differentiation between sedation and euthanasia; and the importance of clear and transparent decision-making processes. Similarly, guidelines should direct clinicians to seek appropriate consultation with the institution's ethics committee whenever ethical concerns arise from specific applications of palliative sedation.

Integral to the initiation of sedation is the need for the close monitoring and outcome assessment of this intervention with the patient. Standard protocols should exist to direct the care of patients who are sedated, either in a mild somnolent state or in a deeper non-responsive state (i.e. mouth care, skin care, management of incontinence, and bowel care, etc.). These protocols should be put into place with the use of sedation to ensure optimal patient care is provided.

In addition, a guideline should address the unique needs of both the family and staff who are caring for the patient receiving palliative sedation at the end of life to ensure both are provided with the necessary informational and emotional support.

9.8   Conclusion

The published literature to date, regarding the practice of palliative sedation continues to identify inconsistencies and practice variances with regard to its prevalence in current practice, the overall effect (outcome) of sedation on the patient, family and health care team, the practice and impact of providing (or not) hydration and nutrition on the dying process when sedation is employed, and the decision-making processes in place when this therapy is being used.

It is known that clinical tools (namely clinical protocols and pathways) derived from well established guidelines can improve the consistency and quality of care (Rotter et al. 2010). However, there is a need for more evidence-based data to inform the establishment of these protocols. Further research based on a prospective and multi-centered design, using a standardized definition of palliative sedation, and validated and reliable instruments to collect the required outcome data is needed to establish this treatment as an evidence-based practice (Claessens et al. 2008).

In the following Chapter, Dr. Scott presents a compelling and important argument for continued vigilance and concern over what he perceives to be a growing trend in the development and current focus on the creation of palliative sedation guidelines. He correctly identifies some key areas of weakness in many guidelines which remain valid points of contention related to palliative sedation. In this Chapter, I have tried to outline a need to: obtain good evidence supporting the actual impact of sedation on the timing of death; the importance of standardized clinical pathways to help in the assessment and determination of refractoriness of common symptoms associated with the end of life; and further clarification regarding the definition, diagnosis, treatment and response to existential distress that will be needed to build consensus on the appropriate role and use of palliative sedation. Without this research, palliative sedation has the potential to be used- inadvertently, as an appropriate shortcut to achieving a 'good death' for all involved in the end-of-life process. Until this research is complete, the primarily utility of guidelines, consensus statements and frameworks- aimed at providing clinical guidelines on the application of palliative sedation, can help mitigate unnecessary and inappropriate uses of this therapy.

References

Agency for Healthcare Research and Quality. 2006. *National Guideline Clearinghouse*. Available at: http://www.guideline.gov/

Alberta Health Services. 2011. *Clinical practice guidelines for palliative sedation*. Calgary Zone, Alberta, Canada. Available from http://www.docstoc.com/docs/72057199/Palliative-Sedation-Guidelines---CLINICAL-PRACTICE-GUIDELINE-FOR

Alonso-Babarro, A., M. Varela-Cerdeira, I. Torres-Vigil, R. Rodriguez-Barrientos, and E. Bruera. 2010. At-home palliative sedation for end-of-life cancer patients. *Palliative Medicine* 24(5): 486–492.

American Academy of Hospice and Palliative Medicine. 2006. *Position statement: Statement on palliative sedation*. Available at: http://www.aahpm.org/positions/default/sedation.html. Accessed 10 July 2010.

American Academy of Hospice and Palliative Medicine. 2007. Position statement on physician-assisted death. *Journal of Pain & Palliative Care Pharmacotherapy* 21(4): 55–57.

Ashby, M. 2010. Ethical issues at the end of life. In-special issue: Abstracts for the world congress of internal medicine, world congress of internal medicine in conjunction with physicians week, 20–25 March 2010, Melbourne convention & exhibition centre, Melbourne, Australia. *Internal Medicine Journal* 40(s1): 2.

Behuniak, S.M. 2003. *Physician-assisted suicide: The anatomy of a constitutional law issue*. Lanham: Rowman & Littlefield Publishers.

Billings, J.A., and S.D. Block. 1997. Opportunity to present our observations and opinions on slow euthanasia. *Journal of Palliative Care* 13(2): 55–56.

Bloche, M.G. 2006. The Supreme Court and the purposes of medicine. *The New England Journal of Medicine* 354(10): 993–995.

Broeckaert, B., P. Claessens, P. Schotsmans, and J. Menten. 2011. What's in a name? Palliative sedation in Belgium. Reply to Chambaere et al. *Journal of Pain and Symptom Management* 41(6): e2–e4.

Bulli, F., G. Miccinesi, E. Biancalani, M. Fallai, M. Mannocci, E. Paci, et al. 2007. Continuous deep sedation in home palliative care units: Case studies in the Florence area in 2000 and in 2003–2004. *Minerva Anestesiologica* 73(5): 291–298.

Cassell, E.J. 1999. Diagnosing suffering: A perspective. *Annals of Internal Medicine* 131(7): 531–534.

Cassell, E.J., and B.A. Rich. 2010. Intractable end-of-life suffering and the ethics of palliative sedation. *Pain Medicine* 11(3): 435–438.

Cellarius, V. 2008. Terminal sedation and the "imminence condition". *Journal of Medical Ethics* 34(2): 69–72.

Chater, S., R. Viola, J. Paterson, and V. Jarvis. 1998. Sedation for intractable distress in the dying–a survey of experts. *Palliative Medicine* 12(4): 255–269.

Cherny, N.I. 2006. Sedation for the care of patients with advanced cancer. *Nature Clinical Practice Oncology* 3(9): 492–500.

Cherny, N.I., and R.K. Portenoy. 1994. Sedation in the management of refractory symptoms: Guidelines for evaluation and treatment. *Journal of Palliative Care* 10(2): 31–38.

Cherny, N.I., L. Radbruch, and Board of the European Association for Palliative, Care. 2009. European Association for Palliative Care (EAPC) recommended framework for the use of sedation in palliative care. *Palliative Medicine* 23(7): 581–593.

Claessens, P., E. Genbrugge, R. Vannuffelen, B. Broeckaert, P. Schotsmans, and J. Menten. 2007. Palliative sedation and nursing: The place of palliative sedation within palliative nursing care. *Journal of Hospice and Palliative Nursing* 9(2): 100–106.

Claessens, P., J. Menten, P. Schotsmans, and B. Broeckaert. 2008. Palliative sedation: A review of the research literature. *Journal of Pain and Symptom Management* 36(3): 310–333.

Cowan, J.D., and D. Walsh. 2001. Terminal sedation in palliative medicine–definition and review of the literature. *Supportive Care in Cancer* 9(6): 403–407.

Cowan, J.D., L. Clemens, and T. Palmer. 2006. Palliative sedation in a southern Appalachian community. *The American Journal of Hospice & Palliative Care* 23(5): 360–368.

Cunningham, J. 2008. A review of sedation for intractable distress in the dying. *Irish Medical Journal* 101(3): 87–90.

de Graeff, A., and M. Dean. 2007. Palliative sedation therapy in the last weeks of life: A literature review and recommendations for standards. *Journal of Palliative Medicine* 10(1): 67–85.

Dean, M., V. Cellarius, B. Henry, D. Oneschuck, and L. Libracht. 2012. Framework for continuous palliative sedation therapy in Canada. *Journal of Palliative Medicine* 15(8): 870–879.

Devulder, J., E. Crombez, L. Ghijs, and E. Mortier. 2004. Considering palliative termination sedation. *Tijdschrift voor Geneeskunde* 60(3): 159–163.

Elsayem, A., E. Curry Iii, J. Boohene, M.F. Munsell, B. Calderon, F. Hung, et al. 2009. Use of palliative sedation for intractable symptoms in the palliative care unit of a comprehensive cancer center. *Supportive Care Cancer* 17(1): 53–59.

Enck, R.E. 1991. Drug-induced terminal sedation for symptom control. *The American Journal of Hospice & Palliative Care* 8(5): 3–5.

Engstrom, J., E. Bruno, B. Holm, and O. Hellzen. 2007. Palliative sedation at end of life – A systematic literature review. *European Journal of Oncology Nursing* 11(1): 26–35.

Fainsinger, R.L. 1998. Use of sedation by a hospital palliative care support team. *Journal of Palliative Care* 14(1): 51–54.

Fainsinger, R., M.J. Miller, E. Bruera, J. Hanson, and T. Maceachern. 1991. Symptom control during the last week of life on a palliative care unit. *Journal of Palliative Care* 7(1): 5–11.

Fainsinger, R.L., W. Landman, M. Hoskings, and E. Bruera. 1998. Sedation for uncontrolled symptoms in a South African hospice. *Journal of Pain and Symptom Management* 16(3): 145–152.

Fainsinger, R.L., D. De Moissac, I. Mancini, and D. Oneschuk. 2000a. Sedation for delirium and other symptoms in terminally ill patients in Edmonton. *Journal of Palliative Care* 16(2): 5–10.

Fainsinger, R.L., A. Waller, M. Bercovici, K. Bengtson, W. Landman, M. Hosking, et al. 2000b. A multicentre international study of sedation for uncontrolled symptoms in terminally ill patients. *Palliative Medicine* 14(4): 257–265.

Field, M.J., and K.N. Lohr (eds.). 1990. *Clinical practice guidelines: Directions for a new program.* Washington, DC: National Academy Press.

Forde, R., O.G. Aasland, E. Falkum, H. Breivik, and S. Kaasa. 2001. Palliative sedation to dying patients in Norway. *Tidsskrift for den Norske Lægeforening* 121(9): 1085–1088.

Gevers, S. 2003. Terminal sedation: A legal approach. *European Journal of Health Law* 10(4): 359–367.

Gilbert, A., F. Gomez, and E. Bruera. 2004. Global assessment of symptom control at the end of life. *Medicina Paliativa* 11(2): 79–82.

Guell, E., O. Farinas, A. Ramos, R. Solis, and A. Pascual. 2009. Cancer pain in a palliative care unit. *DOLOR* 24(1): 21–27.

Hauser, K., and D. Walsh. 2009. Palliative sedation: Welcome guidance on a controversial issue. *Palliative Medicine* 23(7): 577–579.

Jansen, L.A., and D.P. Sulmasy. 2002. Sedation, alimentation, hydration, and equivocation: Careful conversation about care at the end of life. *Annals of Internal Medicine* 136(11): 845–849.

Kawamura, A. 1998. Washington v Glucksberg and Vacco v. Quill prohibitions on assisted suicide do not violate the Fourteenth Amendment of the United States Constitution. *Journal of Contemporary Law* 24(1): 167–177.

King, P. 2000–2001. Washington v. Glucksberg: Influence of the court in care of the terminally ill and physician assisted suicide. *Journal of Law and Health* 15(2): 271–301.

Kirk, T.W., and M.M. Mahon. 2010. National Hospice and Palliative Care Organization (NHPCO) position statement and commentary on the use of palliative sedation in imminently dying terminally ill patients. *Journal of Pain and Symptom Management* 39(5): 914–923.

Latimer, E.J. 1991. Ethical decision-making in the care of the dying and its applications to clinical practice. *Journal of Pain and Symptom Management* 6(5): 329–336.

Legemaate, J., M. Verkerk, E. van Wijlick, and A. de Graeff. 2007. Palliative Sedation in the Netherlands: Starting-Points and Contents of a National Guidelines. *European Journal of Health Law* 17: 61–73.

Levisman, J.A., A.S. Abbasi, and M.L. Pearce. 1975. Posterior mitral leaflet motion in mitral stenosis. *Circulation* 51(3): 511–514.

Maltoni, M., C. Pittureri, E. Scarpi, et al. 2009. Palliative sedation therapy does not hasten death: Results from a prospective multicenter study. *Annals of Oncology* 20(7): 1163–1169.

McIver, B., D. Walsh, and K. Nelson. 1994. The use of chlorpromazine for symptom control in dying cancer patients. *Journal of Pain and Symptom Management* 9(5): 341–345.

McStay, R. 2003. Terminal sedation: Palliative care for intractable pain, post Glucksberg and Quill. *American Journal of Law and Medicine* 29(1): 45–76.

Morita, T. 2004. Palliative sedation to relieve psycho-existential suffering of terminally ill cancer patients. *Journal of Pain and Symptom Management* 28(5): 445–450.

Morita, T., S. Inoue, and S. Chihara. 1996. Sedation for symptom control in Japan: The importance of intermittent use and communication with family members. *Journal of Pain and Symptom Management* 12(1): 32–38.

Morita, T., J. Tsunoda, S. Inoue, and S. Chihara. 1999. Do hospice clinicians sedate patients intending to hasten death? *Journal of Palliative Care* 15(3): 20–23.

Morita, T., J. Tsunoda, S. Inoue, and S. Chihara. 2000. Pain and symptom management. Terminal sedation for existential distress. *American Journal of Hospice & Palliative Care* 17(3): 189–195.

Morita, T., S. Bito, Y. Kurihara, and Y. Uchitomi. 2005. Development of a clinical guideline for palliative sedation therapy using the Delphi method. *Journal of Palliative Medicine* 8(4): 716–729.

Mount, B.M. 2003. Existential suffering and the determinants of healing. *European Journal of Palliative Care* 10(2): 40–42.

Muller-Busch, H.C., I. Andres, and T. Jehser. 2003. Sedation in palliative care – A critical analysis of 7 years experience. *BMC Palliative Care* 2(1): 2.

Olsen, M.L., K.M. Swetz, and P.S. Mueller. 2010. Ethical decision making with end-of-life care: Palliative sedation and withholding or withdrawing life-sustaining treatments. *Mayo Clinic Proceedings* 85(10): 949–954.

Peruselli, C., P. Di Giulio, F. Toscani, M. Gallucci, C. Brunelli, M. Costantini, et al. 1999. Home palliative care for terminal cancer patients: A survey on the final week of life. *Palliative Medicine* 13(3): 233–241.

Porzio, G., F. Aielli, L. Verna, G. Micolucci, P. Aloisi, and C. Ficorella. 2010. Efficacy and safety of deep, continuous palliative sedation at home: A retrospective, single-institution study. *Supportive Care in Cancer* 18(1): 77–81.

Quill, T.E., and I.R. Byock. 2000. Responding to intractable terminal suffering: The role of terminal sedation and voluntary refusal of food and fluids. ACP-ASIM End-of-Life Care Consensus Panel. American College of Physicians-American Society of Internal Medicine. *Annals of Internal Medicine* 132(5): 408–414.

Quill, T.E., B. Lo, D.W. Brock, and A. Meisel. 2009. Last-resort options for palliative sedation. *Annals of Internal Medicine* 151(6): 421–424.

Rietjens, J.A., A. van der Heide, A.M. Vrakking, B.D. Onwuteaka-Philipsen, P.J. Van der Maas, and G. Van der Wal. 2005. The practice of terminal sedation in the Netherlands. *Nederlands Tijdschrift voor Geneeskunde* 149(9): 467–471.

Rietjens, J.A., et al. 2008. Continuous deep sedation for patients nearing death in the Netherlands: A descriptive study. *British Medical Journal* 336: 810–813.

Rosalki, J.R., and S.J. Karp. 1999. Guidance on the creation of evidence-linked guidelines for COIN. *Clinical Oncology (Royal College of Radiologists)* 11(1): 28–32.

Rotter, T., L. Kinsman, E. James, A. Machotta, H. Gothe, J. Willis, et al. 2010. Clinical pathways: Effects on professional practice, patient outcomes, length of stay and hospital costs. *Cochrane Database of Systematic Review* (3): CD006632.

Rousseau, P.C. 2002. Palliative sedation. *The American Journal of Hospice & Palliative Care* 19(5): 295–297.

Rousseau, P. 2003. Palliative sedation and sleeping before death: A need for clinical guidelines? *Journal of Palliative Medicine* 6(3): 425–427.

Rousseau, P.C. 2004. Palliative sedation in terminally ill patients. *Advances in Experimental Medicine and Biology* 550: 263–267.

Roy, D.J. 1990. Need they sleep before they die? *Journal of Palliative Care* 6(3): 3–4.

Roy, D.J., J.R. Williams, and B.M. Dickens (eds.). 1994. *Bioethics in Canada*. Scarborough: Prentice Hall Canada Inc.

Schuman-Olivier, Z., D.H. Brendel, M. Forstein, and B.H. Price. 2008. The use of palliative sedation for existential distress: A psychiatric perspective. *Harvard Review of Psychiatry* 16(6): 339–351.

Simon, A., M. Kar, J. Hinz, and D. Beck. 2007. Attitudes towards terminal sedation: An empirical survey among experts in the field of medical ethics. *BMC Palliative Care* 6: 4.

Sparato, R., M. Lo Re, F. Piccoli, and V. La Bella. 2010. Causes and place of death in Italian patients with amyotrophic lateral sclerosis. *Acta Neurologica Scandinavica* 122(3): 217–223.

Stiel, S., N. Krumm, O. Schroers, L. Radbruch, and F. Elsner. 2008. Indications and use of benzodiazepines in a palliative care unit. *Schmerz* 22(6): 665–671.

Stone, P., C. Phillips, O. Spruyt, and C. Waight. 1997. A comparison of the use of sedatives in a hospital support team and in a hospice. *Palliative Medicine* 11(2): 140–144.

Sykes, N., and A. Thorns. 2003a. Sedative use in the last week of life and the implications for end-of-life decision making. *Archives of Internal Medicine* 163(3): 341–344.

Sykes, N., and A. Thorns. 2003b. The use of opioids and sedatives at the end of life. *The Lancet Oncology* 4(5): 312–318.

Turner, K., R. Chye, G. Aggarwal, J. Philip, A. Skeels, and J.N. Lickiss. 1996. Dignity in dying: A preliminary study of patients in the last three days of life. *Journal of Palliative Care* 12(2): 7–13.

van der Heide, A., B.D. Onwuteaka-Philipsen, M.L. Rurup, et al. 2007. Medical decisions around the end of life in the Netherlands after the Euthanasia Act came into effect; the fourth national study. *Nederlands tijdschrift voor geneeskunde* 15129(1635): 1642.

Ventafridda, V., C. Ripamonti, F. de Conno, and M. Tamburini. 1990. Symptom prevalence and control during cancer patient's last days of life. *Journal of Palliative Care* 6(3): 7–11.

Verkerk, M., E. van Wijlick, J. Legemaate, and A. de Graeff. 2007. A national guideline for palliative sedation in the Netherlands. *Journal of Pain and Symptom Management* 34(6): 666–670.

Veterans Health Administration National Ethics Committee. 2006. The ethics of palliative sedation as a therapy of last resort. *The American Journal of Hospice & Palliative Care* 23: 483–491.

Vila Santasuana, A., N. Celorrio Jimenez, X. Sanz Salvador, J. Martinez Montauti, E. Diez-Cascon Menendez, and C. Puig Rossell. 2008. The final week of life in an acute care hospital: Review of 401 consecutive patients. *Revista Española de Geriatría y Gerontología* 43(5): 284–290.

Woolf, S. 1992. Practice guidelines, a new reality in medicine. II: Methods of developing guidelines. *Archives of Internal Medicine* 152: 946–952.

Worthington, R. (ed.). 2005. *Ethics and palliative care: A case based manual*. Abingdon: Radcliffe.

Chapter 10
The Case Against Clinical Guidelines for Palliative Sedation

John F. Scott

10.1 Introduction

This chapter will examine the arguments against the introduction of Clinical Practice Guidelines (CPG) for Palliative Sedation. The first argument will be an historical one. The pioneers of palliative care had solid reasons for avoiding the terminology of sedation and we are foolish not to heed their warning. The second argument is a clinical one. In attempting to curb abuse, CPG imposes conditions that are burdensome to both patient and clinician. Existing CPG fail to clarify several key points and therefore are prone to abuse. Most importantly, palliative sedation is clinically unnecessary since the bedside challenges of end-of-life care can be managed using the principles of clinical proportionality that are already imbedded in traditional palliative care. The third argument examines the track record of CPG as a tool to improve care. CPG were designed to disseminate new research evidence in the context of wide expert consensus. It is ill-fitted for the task of preventing abuse in an ethically-charged environment where key definitions are controversial. The power and reputation of the methodology may, inadvertently, accentuate abuse. The fourth argument examines the evidence, albeit limited, for the impact of existing CPG for palliative sedation on actual practice and extrapolates from this to the potential negative impact of widespread introduction. In conclusion, the chapter will argue there is considerable risk that dissemination of CPG on palliative sedation will have an untoward negative impact on both clinical practice and public attitudes. The concept and vocabulary of palliative sedation can and should be avoided by returning to the roots of palliative care whereby we frame our task as the control of specific symptoms. We should develop and disseminate CPG on delirium, respiratory

J.F. Scott (✉)
Division of Palliative Medicine, University of Ottawa, Ottawa, ON, Canada

Supportive and Palliative Care Program, The Ottawa Hospital,
Civic Campus, 1053 Carling Avenue, K1Y 4E9 Ottawa, ON, Canada
e-mail: joscott@toh.on.ca

P. Taboada (ed.), *Sedation at the End-of-life: An Interdisciplinary Approach*,
Philosophy and Medicine 116, DOI 10.1007/978-94-017-9106-9_10,
© Springer Science+Business Media Dordrecht 2015

distress and 'existential' distress which would incorporate medication algorithms but avoid the confusing terminology of palliative sedation.

10.2   History of Sedation in Palliative Care

Discrepancies in vocabulary form a huge part of the present controversy. The terminology in this field has never been precise and has grown increasingly ambiguous. The terms 'sedation' and 'sedative' derive from the Latin verb 'sedare' – to settle, assuage, allay, make calm or quiet. Sixteenth century medical texts advocate "sedation of payne…the circulation and the mind" using treatments that assuage an underlying disturbance, thereby allowing or facilitating sleep. The most widely used sedatives were alcohol and opium (papaver somniferum – i.e. sleep-bringing poppy). Reliable unconsciousness was not possible until the nineteenth century when the new science of anaesthesia developed chemically- induced unconsciousness in order to perform surgery. During the same century, morphine, chloral hydrate and barbiturates were developed and these remained the armentarium of sedation until the development of phenothiazines and benzodiazepines in the 1950s (Diz et al. 2002).

In recent decades, the lines between sedation, analgesia and anaesthesia have blurred. Anaesthesiology no longer relies solely on inhaled agents, often using a combination of opioids, benzodiazepines and paralytics to achieve the analgesia, unconsciousness and muscle relaxation required for surgery. Shallower forms of anaesthesia, referred to as 'conscious sedation', are used for short procedures. Critical care settings use 'sedation' to refer to varying degrees of lowered responsiveness required for intubation using a proportionate dose approach to match symptom intensity. Thus, the modern scope of the term 'sedation' is very broad, migrating towards the pole of anaesthesia/unconsciousness, while still maintaining the earlier connotations of pain relief, drowsiness and making calm. The definition of 'sedation' demands context, scope and intention.

In the early twentieth century, opioids were universally referred to as 'sedatives'. Fears of sedation, tolerance, addiction and respiratory depression led to widespread under-treatment of pain and other symptoms (Marks and Sachar 1973). Pain in advanced cancer was considered inevitable and intractable. Physicians and nurses withheld opioids until pain was severe and death imminent. Starting opioids when agonal breathing or terminal delirium was observed perpetuated the myth that they caused unconsciousness and hastened death. In the 1960s an explosion of interest in death and dying arose. In the US, this focused on issues of psychology, law and sociology, while in the UK bedside clinicians documented the burden imposed by meddlesome medicine and poor symptom relief. Cicely Saunders proposed a new framework called 'hospice care' which demonstrated a new life-affirming, energetic and optimistic approach to terminal care.

> No, it is not hopeless. Your pain is not intractable. There is much more that can be done. You matter to the last moment of your life and we will do all we can to help you not only to die peacefully, but also to live until you die. (Saunders 2006)

Pioneer hospices developed simple but innovative methods of symptom control. Chief among these was the regular 'round the clock' administration of opioids to control pain through individual fine-tuning of doses. Borrowing from the chemistry lab, this process became known as 'dose titration', the goal being to find the exact balance point where analgesia is achieved with little or no side-effects. Hospice never referred to opioids as sedatives, battling the entrenched view that symptom relief was only possible with and through somnolence. Palliative care taught that residual drowsiness after dose titration of opioids was largely due to the effects of the underlying disease. A similar approach was advocated for phenothiazines, benzodiazepines, and other psychotropics in the control of nausea, anxiety, depression, restlessness, and confusion with doses titrated to achieve symptom relief with minimum effects on alertness.

Early papers of Saunders, Twycross, and Mount (Saunders 2006; Clark 2002; Twycross and Lack 1984; Mount et al. 1976) reveal a paucity of references to sedation other than as a side effect to minimize. A few exceptions can be found which refer to the last hours or days of life in which sudden major complications such as severe bleeding, asphyxia, seizures or new severe pain were seen as demanding rapid increase in drugs in which "emphasis may have to be on sedation rather than analgesia" (Saunders 2006). Early palliative care literature reported there was no crescendo of pain and suffering in the last hours and days of life and did not designate a symptom as 'intractable' or 'refractory'. There was a steadily growing confidence in the ability of palliative care to achieve significant relief. A difficult symptom in the last hours demanded rigorous re-assessment and bold titration of drugs until distress was relieved along with non-drug measures such as nursing, spiritual, and family interventions. These early proponents accepted, and at times welcomed, the lowered level of consciousness (LOC) that developed during treatment for severe distress, but always kept their focus on symptoms.

While this palliative care approach rapidly gained acceptance internationally, there were isolated proposals in the 1980s for deep continuous sedation to unconsciousness for the terminally ill (Scott 1989; Greene and Davis 1991). They were criticized by mainstream palliative care as arising from a lack of skill in using palliative care techniques and/or a disguised form of euthanasia. The looming threat of legislated euthanasia gave urgency to early hospice work. This ethical backdrop was a pivotal reason for the avoidance and rejection of the concept and terminology of sedation. The hospice pioneers considered it essential to maintain life-affirming, symptom-directed methods of care that could never be construed as hastening death or putting patients to sleep. It is interesting that the threat of euthanasia in the 1990s may have led some palliative care leaders to the opposite strategy i.e. by incorporating sedation as a therapy, palliative care could present itself as being capable of handling all distress without resorting to euthanasia. The first generation of palliative care would have resisted this temptation to claim complete relief and would have rejected the vocabulary and conceptual framework of palliative sedation.

The 1990 publication of Ventafridda was a watershed event (Ventafridda et al. 1990). Clinicians trained in the UK or Canadian palliative care models were shocked by the finding that 52.5 % of patients in this study had unendurable symptoms controllable only with sedation-induced sleep. Mount immediately challenged the authors (Mount 1990) and the report was generally dismissed by palliative care leaders as issuing from a relatively new program without strong ties to the original hospice philosophy and methodology. Poor standards of palliative care were suspected and/or a misuse of the term 'sedation'. Palliative medicine reacted by publishing data to show that the crescendo of symptoms described by Ventafridda does not occur (Lichter and Hunt 1990; Fainsinger et al. 1991). Although significant levels of dyspnea and respiratory secretions were present, there was no evidence of a generalized crescendo of suffering as death approached – a crescendo that might justify sedation as a 'last resort' measure.

In 1991, Enck picked up on Ventafridda's paper, coining the label "terminal sedation" (Enck 1991). For the first time, palliative medicine began to examine the concept of purposeful sedation for the dying when symptoms are intractable. Ethicists asked "Need they sleep before they die?" (Roy 1990) In the mid 1990s, Chater polled palliative care experts on their sedation beliefs and practices (Chater et al. 1998). The study revealed continuing confusion over the bedside meaning of 'sedation for intractable distress'. While many clinicians described a set of practices consistent with historical hospice philosophy, some were re-framing how they perceived this issue, discussing cases in which symptoms were so severe that the drugs used were knowingly sedating the patients. There was a strong consensus in those who used 'sedation for intractable distress' that this was a rare, last-resort measure. Many centres began to publish data on the prevalence of sedation in a variety of palliative care settings. Blair, in Chap. 9, presents a summary of the discrepancies in prevalence rates (8–65 %) across countries and settings. It remains unclear how much of this variation reflects differences in practice, populations, or definition of sedation.

The term 'palliative sedation' was first introduced in 2000 and quickly replaced earlier vocabulary (Rousseau 2000). The 2000–2010 decade was a period of rapid acceptance and guideline development. While there continued to be voices of caution (Battin 2008; Von Roenn and von Gunten 2009), mainstream palliative medicine seemed increasingly ready to accept the basic tenet that 'sometimes' sedation to unconsciousness is the only means to relieve severe suffering that is refractory to standard palliative care.

In summary, early palliative care faced a pervading culture of fear and pessimism not unlike our own. They recognized that linking sedation with symptom control enhances fear in patient, family, clinician and public and thereby becomes an obstacle to symptom relief. Equally, these pioneers understood that sedation-talk ('putting patients to sleep') could be misconstrued as euthanasia and therefore act as a further obstacle to care. We would be wise to follow their lead in avoiding this vocabulary.

10.3   Clinical Critique of the Guideline Framework

Throughout a 40 year career in palliative care, I have never ordered 'palliative sedation' or used the vocabulary of 'terminal' or 'palliative sedation'. The very concept or framework encompassed by the term 'palliative sedation' fails to capture my clinical reasoning. I do not manage delirium, shortness of breath and pain with standard treatments and then designate a symptom 'intractable', turning to a 'last-resort' therapy for severe cases. I do not shift my clinical goal from symptom relief to 'sedation', nor do I pre-determine that unconsciousness is the only means by which symptoms can be relieved.

While I agree with Blair (Chap. 9) that there has been growing acceptance of palliative sedation over the last decade within mainstream palliative medicine, I would argue it is a tenuous consensus. Some continue to oppose sedation protocols and others are ambivalent, failing to use CPG in their own institutions even while supporting CPG at an international level. The sedation framework of The European Association of Palliative Care (EAPC) reflects a series of uneasy compromises and seems to accept CPG almost reluctantly, more as a harm reduction strategy than as optimal practice (Cherny and Radbruch 2009). Concerns over practice in Netherlands and Belgium lie behind this framework yet are not tackled head-on. In this section it will be argued that CPG for palliative sedation are clinically confusing, burdensome and ultimately unnecessary.

(a) *Proportionality and the goal of therapy*

Clinical proportionality has been proposed as the key criterion for well-boundaried palliative sedation (Canadian Society of Palliative Care Physicians Task Force: Dean MM et al. 2012). Evidence supports that benefit is maximized and harm minimized when treatments and drug dosages are 'just enough' i.e. proportionate to the underlying problem. Yet the literature on palliative sedation fails to clarify what is the immediate goal of therapy. For some clinicians, it remains the relief of delirium, breathlessness, pain or other symptom. For others the goal is the achievement of a comatose state. This leads to two very different ways to judge proportionality; just enough to control distress or just enough to maintain deep unconsciousness? Most CPG fail to clarify this point and I suspect the ambiguity has been purposeful in order to achieve consensus. Proportionality has been a cornerstone of palliative medicine which taught us the art and science of dose titration for opioids and other drugs of symptom relief. Handling difficult cases which require high doses or bold increases in dose are core to our specialty. We can continue to anchor our care of these patients in the proportionality of symptom relief already imbedded in palliative medicine without resorting to a label of palliative sedation. Continuously, we adjust therapy to achieve relief and in rare cases this will mean using combinations of drugs at doses that may well affect level of consciousness (LOC). But this need not involve an abrupt shift in goals of care but a gradual, flexible transition in response to changes in the patient's condition. Framing our clinical reasoning and practice as symptom relief is the best way to ensure proportionality in end-of-life care.

(b) *Level of consciousness*

There is grave danger in taking our attention away from symptom distress and focusing instead on level of consciousness (LOC). The published literature on palliative sedation fails to acknowledge the complexity, variation and uncertainty in our understanding of LOC. The measurement tools for LOC remain imprecise, focussing on responsiveness to certain stimuli while other issues of sensation, awareness, cognition, and memory are not addressed. For example, a patient can be deeply unconscious, by LOC scales, and yet show signs of pain or respiratory distress that will require titration of opioids and other drugs. The absence of communication does not mean that suffering is not present. In general, LOC decreases in the dying regardless of medication. In early hospice studies, 23 % were unresponsive during the last day of life, 67 % were semi-conscious (asleep but rousable) and 10 % were alert (Saunders 1989). In the majority of cases, decreased LOC is due to the underlying illness and not to the medications. We observe a huge variability in LOC with frequent fluctuations over short periods, often without clear correlation to medication levels. In the dying process, a low LOC is the norm. However, unrelieved symptoms of pain, dyspnea and delirium can cause the patient to arouse to the point of expressing distress. Once these symptoms are better controlled, the low basal level of consciousness caused by impending death is re-established. Treatment to relieve symptoms in this context may be inappropriately labelled 'sedation'.

Even when aiming at deep continuous sedation, the ability to achieve unconsciousness without distress is incomplete. Here again, we observe oversimplification and false sense of control. Starting a sedative infusion will not eradicate all suffering. In pain control we have come to learn the importance of careful titration. When increasing doses of opioids, side effects and toxicity may occur, including delirium, hallucinations, twitching of muscles, increased pain sensitivity and even seizures. In a similar way, benzodiazepines, psychotropics and barbiturates can be associated with disturbing side effects or paradoxical worsening of delirium. Rapid tolerance can occur with loss of initial positive benefit and only partial relief achieved despite rapid dose escalation. By using medication doses proportionate to symptom intensity we minimize the chance of untoward effects. Purposefully increasing medication levels in an attempt to achieve a deep unconsciousness may fail in some cases and cause other forms of distress. In those who aim to achieve 'deep continuous sedation', the failure rate to achieve unconsciousness without symptom distress may be as high as 17 % (Davis 2009).

(c) *Lack of specificity*

Palliative sedation is proposed as a 'one size fits all' solution to every form of intractable distress. This is a red flag for clinicians. Traditional palliative care assesses each patient's unique constellation of symptoms, seeking to understand the physiological mechanism of each symptom and designing treatments to match. Individualized therapy continues right until death. For example, the treatments, drugs and dosages used to manage severe breathlessness will often be different than those for delirium. This personalized, symptom-specific approach is often lost in discussions of palliative sedation.

(d) *Intractability and false dichotomies*

The concept of intractability is pivotal to palliative sedation. The framework is built on the premise that symptoms or sources of distress have become 'intractable' – i.e. out of control. I contend that this is based on a false dichotomy in which an arbitrary, ill-defined line is drawn in what is a complex, ever-changing process of dying – a line that shifts depending on the skills, fears and philosophy of the clinician. Palliative sedation creates a false ethical dilemma, a choice between suffering and unconsciousness which does not match with bedside reality. The literature too often employs a series of dichotomies: tractable/intractable, conscious/unconscious, dying/not dying, symptom relief/sedation, suffering/no suffering. Such forms of black and white thinking are not helpful at the bedside. In the real world of medicine we face ambiguity, uncertainty and partially achieved goals. The art of medicine demands subtlety, titration, persistence, waiting, innovation and humility.

CPG propose palliative sedation be reserved for situations that combine intractability and imminent death. Evidence points to a shift in the pattern of symptoms in the last days of life with delirium and respiratory symptoms increasing while pain and other symptoms diminish. No generalized crescendo of suffering occurs and there is no evidence that the last days of life are associated with more 'intractability'. Patients are increasingly unable to report symptoms, forcing clinicians to assess signs of distress (grimacing, muscle tension, moaning, restlessness, secretions in airway, increased work of breathing, changes in vital signs). An experienced nurse or physician who has access to the typical drugs of palliative care handles the symptoms through frequent reassessment, titration of drugs and nursing measures (positioning, mouth care etc.). Intractability imposes a radically new decision into palliative care. Is there nothing more that can be done? Palliative care philosophy was built on the premise that there is always more to be done; a new combination of drugs, tweaking of doses, a pillow to be adjusted or a hand to be held. Widespread 'marketing' of palliative sedation for intractable symptoms may undermine what has been achieved in palliative medicine over the last four decades. Instead of searching for new strategies and seeking expert advice, sedation may appear to be an easier solution for the distressed clinician. The 2008 study by Rietjens revealed that only 9 % of this sample of Dutch patients receiving palliative sedation had been assessed by palliative care in the month prior to death (Rietjens et al. 2008). When de Graeff studied 113 palliative care consultations for palliative sedation in a Dutch cancer hospital, 47 cases (41 %) were deemed not to have refractory symptoms (de Graeff 2008).

(e) *Prognosis*

CPG restrict palliative sedation to those close to death but many extend this to a prognosis of weeks. Does this criterion form an effective barrier to abuse? In the palliative care setting, there are a series of changes in vital signs (LOC, circulation, respiration) that can give us some sense that a patient may be imminently dying in hours to days. However, when vital signs are stable, predicting time of death in terms of weeks is prone to significant error. Therefore, prognostication of death cannot form an effective boundary to abuse. If a clinician wants to use palliative sedation, it will not be difficult to justify a short prognosis. Clinicians with little experience in palliative care may be faced with what they consider to be intractable symptoms at much earlier points in disease. They will be tempted to turn to palliative sedation even when death is not imminent, especially since CPG do not give a convincing rationale for the prognostic boundary. Ethicists may argue that relief of suffering trumps the prognostic limit. Once the framework of palliative sedation is established as normative, I see no way it can be restricted to the imminently dying.

(f) *Burden of Consent*

CPG consent requirements may be burdensome for patient, family and clinician. Responding to Dutch surveys on deep continuous sedation initiated without consent, guidelines mandate consent by the patient or the substitute decision-maker. However, this formalized consent process may be an onerous and unnecessary burden for patient and family. Certainly ethical practice demands informed participation by patients in all aspects of care. The goal of symptom-focused palliative care and the concept of titrating medications to match symptom intensity should be explained and agreed upon. The suffering of the last days of life calls for a continuation and extension of this symptom-directed approach. If aiming at symptom relief and not deep unconsciousness, consent can be obtained without burden. "Your shortness of breath is not well-controlled today. I think we can do better. You received a few doses of a drug last night that seems to have given you relief for a short period. If you agree, I am planning to start a slow infusion of that drug today at a low dose. You may feel drowsier for longer periods but I think much of your sleepiness is because of your illness and not because of drugs."

The formal consent outlined in all CPG will be misconstrued by many patients and family. Consent to change goals of care to 'palliative sedation' or 'putting you to sleep' will be viewed as a euphemism for hastened death, despite assurances. This adds a further burden of distress at a time of great vulnerability.

(g) *Existential Suffering*

Herein lies the exception that betrays the weakness and danger of the whole framework. Some CPG express discomfort with 'existential distress or suffering' and label it as a 'controversial' indication for palliative sedation (Cherny and Radbruch 2009). Yet most include this ill-defined term even in the complete absence of any physical symptoms.

In a Dutch study comparing sedation before and after introduction of a national guideline, 'existential distress', as an indication for palliative sedation, increased from 18.2 to 25.8 %, and 'perceived loss of dignity' rose from 20.1 to 27.0 %. The prevalence of continuous sedation without presence of any physical symptoms remained high- 11.3 vs. 9.4 % (Hasselaar et al. 2009). This absence of concomitant physical symptoms is problematic.

Some of the cases in the literature do appear to have occurred in the last days of life. However, when a crescendo of mental/emotional/spiritual distress occurs so close to death, it almost always has physiological roots. Multi-organ failure impacts on cognition and emotion, causing voiced and/or behavioural distress. Physiologically-driven anxiety and subtle forms of delirium may be misunderstood as psychological or existential distress. This requires bold treatment with medications for anxiety and delirium with doses titrated to relief.

On the other hand, I suspect many of the cases in the literature occur at earlier points in the illness, well before the last days. A significant majority of patients maintain a positive, life-affirming outlook in the face of death. A small proportion feels overwhelmed and actively seeks death or unconsciousness. Loss of dignity, loss of control, sense of burden and other psychosocial constructs appear to be more critical than physical symptoms. Anxiety and depression are often present but difficult to diagnose since somatic criteria are not applicable. Frequently this desire for death or unconsciousness peaks well before the last days of life and the fear of the future is more prominent than present distress. Four decades of palliative medicine has accumulated a significant reservoir of skill to assist with this crisis of fear and anguish. While medication for the anxiety, insomnia and depression components of this suffering is important, much of the response will be non-pharmacological. Chochinov's 'dignity therapy' (Chochinov et al. 2005) and Brietbart's 'meaning therapy' (Brietbart et al. 2009) give us promising new possibilities of assisting these forms of suffering. Many in our society suffer from mental and spiritual anguish that are not terminally ill but nonetheless feel their lives are meaningless and unbearable. Just as we persist in seeking more effective ways to ease their distress and to protect and comfort them while they search for relief, so too, for those with terminal illness. The failure of CPG to exclude the vague concept of existential distress is a fatal flaw that leaves it vulnerable to abuse. Its inclusion may lead to a paradigm shift from intractable symptom to 'unbearable anguish' or even 'intolerable life'. Once it becomes available for those who no longer feel able to bear with life, we are on a very slippery slope that will reach far beyond the terminally ill.

(h) *Absence of Clinical Necessity*

Ultimately, there is no evidence that the framework of palliative sedation is necessary in order to achieve symptom relief in the last days of life. Proportionate increases in the medications already used in palliative care for delirium, respiratory distress and pain can achieve the relief called for in CPG without resorting to the label 'palliative sedation' or to the process of designating a symptom 'intractable'.

10.4 Limitations of Guidelines as a Tool for Changing Practice

Clinical Practice Guidelines (CPG) are "systematically developed statements to assist practitioner and patient decisions about appropriate health care for specific clinical circumstances" (Field and Lohr 1990) but now more widely defined to include clinical, policy-related and system-related decisions (Brouwers et al. 2010).

In the last two decades, we have seen exponential growth in CPG development with directories and clearing-houses established in order to track the thousands of such guidelines and their revisions. Despite the wide promulgation, the evidence for efficacy and effectiveness remains weak. When combined with enthusiastic multi-modal implementation strategies, CPG have been associated with measurable improvements in patient outcomes. However, development and publication of the guideline alone appears to have limited effect on physician behaviour (Francke et al. 2008). There is substantial literature on rates of physician adherence to CPG (often in 30–60 % ranges) and on the barriers to physician uptake of recommendations. These barriers include lack of awareness of CPG existence, lack of familiarity with its content, lack of agreement either with guidelines in general or the specifics of this guideline, lack of confidence to perform the recommended change, lack of outcome expectancy, inertia of previous practice and external barriers such as financial disincentives, lack of time or staff. Some characteristics of the guideline itself encourage implementation – simplicity, specificity of purpose, ease of use and trialability (ability to experiment with CPG on a limited basis) with elimination of an established behaviour being more difficult to achieve than adding a new behaviour (Cabana et al. 1999).

Understanding the popularity of CPG is complex. Managing the explosive growth of research evidence in medicine is a critical pre-requisite. The rise of evidence based medicine and clinical epidemiology provided tools to judge the quality of evidence and facilitated exponential growth in RCT and other studies. The subsequent urgency to transfer best evidence to best practice led to CPG as one tool of implementing change (Grol and Grimshaw 2003).

Even more importantly, governments and third party payers look to CPG as a quality management tool to contain rising costs. They act as a standard and boundary-making method to decrease utilization of expensive services. Whenever there is variation in service delivery among practitioners, hospitals or regions, governments perceive an opportunity to 'rationalize' care, enhance efficiency and improve the public image of the system. Thus, CPG can become management algorithms and auditing tools, a purpose not envisioned by the professionals who developed them (Woolf et al. 1999). With a large proportion of health care costs spent in the last 6 months of life, governments are keenly interested in guidelines that might decrease these costs.

A third set of motives arise from within the internal politics of medicine, an arena of particular risk for palliative sedation and other ethically charged end-of-life decisions. In some cases, specialities have engaged in 'turf wars' using CPG to gain ownership over specific treatments and procedures or to ensure that primary care looks to them for leadership in this area. Pharmaceutical companies may influence this process by sponsoring symposia aimed at developing CPG consensus with the hope their drug will be included. Woolf et al. (1999) provides an interesting discussion of the potential benefits, limitations and harms of CPG which are particularly relevant to palliative sedation. The benefit to patients incurs from decreasing inconsistency and speeding the implementation of new research evidence to the bedside. Potential harm is heightened when the scientific evidence is lacking or misleading. In fact, literature reviews of palliative sedation reveal that a high proportion of this literature consists of expert opinion and ethical debate, as opposed to research (De Graeff and Dean 2007). Whenever recommendations are based on opinions of experts, there remains a danger that economic, political, and special interest factors will influence the guideline development group composition and skew the recommendations.

Guidelines can lead to clinical rigidity, reduction of individualised care and impairment of access to a fuller menu of options that may be best for some patients. "Algorithms that reduce patient care into a sequence of binary (yes/no) decisions often do injustice to the complexity of medicine." (Woolf et al. 1999)

CPG, as a tool, was not designed to address a topic like palliative sedation. Far from curbing ethical abuses, it may increase harm by escalating prevalence and by using the aura of international approval to mask poor practice.

10.5   Evidence for the Impact of Palliative Sedation Guidelines

From earliest days, the potential dangers of terminal or palliative sedation has led to calls for clinical practice guidelines (CPG) as a means to prevent abuse (Cherny and Portenoy 1994).

To date, sparse data exists on adherence, efficacy and impact of these guidelines but some data from Netherlands and Belgium may help. Soon after the Dutch guidelines were published, a survey of 793 physicians demonstrated that 35 % were aware of the existence of practice guidelines on palliative sedation. Of those aware, 83 % had read them and 52 % had used them in patient care. Of those who used guidelines, 94 % felt they were 'supportive' providing a 'clear procedure' and 'confirmation/support of decision'. The authors conclude that "practice guidelines on medical end-of-life decisions can give physicians advice on how to proceed and can also reassure them about the appropriateness of their actions" (Hesselink et al. 2010). Retrospective questionnaires confirm a significant increase in prevalence of palliative sedation (defined as continuous deep sedation to death) in the Netherlands. In the period 2001–2005, palliative sedation cases rose from 8,500 (5.6 % of deaths) to 9,700 (7.1 %) while euthanasia fell from 3,500 (2.6 % of deaths) to 2,325 (1.7 %) (Rietjens et al. 2008). The recent survey for the year 2010 reveals that continuous deep sedation has risen rapidly to 12.3 % of all deaths while euthanasia has increased to 2.8 % (Onwuteaka-Philipsen et al. 2012). This dramatic increase was one of the factors leading to the development of a national guideline on palliative sedation released December 2005 (revised 2009) by the Royal Dutch Medical Association. Critics of Dutch practice interpreted the data as indicating Dutch physicians were turning to palliative sedation as an alternative or replacement for euthanasia (van der Heide et al. 2007; Hasselaar et al. 2007). Hasselaar and colleagues conducted a 2003–2005 retrospective questionnaire of 492 Dutch physicians (Hasselaar et al. 2008) and repeated the data collection with 341 physicians in 2007, 2 years after a national guideline was published (Hasselaar et al. 2009). The proportion of physicians who followed the guideline for continuous sedation, sometimes or always, increased from 52.9 to 89.5 %, a level much higher than in most studies of physician adherence to CPG. The authors believe there may be evidence of improved outcomes as a result of the guideline. The use of benzodiazepines increased from 69.9 to 90.4 % and the use of opioids alone for sedation decreased from 23.1 to 8.8 % -a shift in drug utilization advocated by the guideline. Secondly, patients were more frequently involved in the decision to start sedation (from 72.3 to 82.2 %) -again a requirement of the Dutch national guideline. However, the increased use of benzo-diazepines and the increase in patient participation could have been unrelated to guideline development since the same trends occurred where no national guidelines exists (Bulli et al. 2007).

Furthermore, Hasselaar points to some disturbing trends in Dutch practice that appear to be more in a direction opposite to that of the guidelines. There is a trend towards deeper levels of sedation (78.8 % in 2007 versus 56.3 %) and explicit deci-sions not to give artificial hydration during sedation (in 2007 34.2 % of physicians were convinced that sedation shortened life because of dehydration). In an earlier Dutch study, hastening death was one of the intentions of the physician in 47 % of cases and the explicit intention in 17 % (Rietjens et al. 2004). The 2007 survey showed physicians remained reluctant to use opioids for pain and dyspnea – "it seems that palliative sedation and symptom directed treatments are often regarded as opposites rather than supplements" (Hasselaar et al. 2009). A substantial segment of physicians continued to believe the sedation was not symptom control (29.8–25.4 %) despite the strong advocacy of the national guideline on this point. There was a significant rise in both 'existential distress' and 'exhaustion' as indications for sedation. There was no significant decrease in sedation for non-physical distress (without concomitant physical symptoms) (11.3–9.4 %) despite the attempt of the national guideline to limit this indication.

A steady increase in the prevalence of palliative sedation has been noted in the United Kingdom, Belgium and Netherlands (Seale 2009; Chambaere et al. 2010; Rietjens et al. 2008; Onwuteaka-Philipsen et al. 2012). In Belgium, a retrospective study of physicians in 2001, repeated in 2007, revealed a rapid and significant rise in continuous deep sedation ("continuously and deeply sedated until death by the use of one or more drugs") from 8.2 % of deaths to 14.5 %. This rise occurred during the same time period as the dissemination of multiple guidelines. Are these guidelines limiting the use of palliative sedation, having no impact or inadvertently encouraging their use?

10.6 Potential Dangers of Guidelines

Janssens, in his 2012 ethical critique of the Royal Dutch Medical Association Guideline on Palliative Sedation, proposes that sedation is "less normal" than depicted (Janssens et al. 2012). The paper tries to demonstrate evidence of bias caused by the pre-existing agenda of the CPG developers. Dutch physicians, for political and logistic reasons, wanted to sharply distinguish euthanasia (requiring specific and time-consuming societal control mechanisms) from palliative sedation (requiring no controls since it was "normal medical practice"). This focus on nor-malizing sedation leads to pushing morally problematic aspects under the surface. I would argue that the same criticism can be levelled at CPG for conservative proportionate forms of sedation. Here an equally strong intention is to portray sedation as a part of 'normal' palliative care and completely distinct from euthanasia. This political agenda can lead to a minimization of deficiencies. Certainly the 2009 EAPC framework on sedation does acknowledge the clinical and ethical dangers of palliative sedation (Cherny and Radbruch 2009). It defines abuse as sedation to purposefully hasten death, whether openly or covertly, when symptoms are not truly refractory or when the doses used far exceed the requirements of symptom control. The framework also attempted to exclude "injudicious use" of sedation including the overlooking of reversible causes of distress, the failure to ask advice, the demand for sedation coming from the needs of the family instead of the patient and sedation that springs from physician frustration or fatigue when faced with complex symptoms. While no quantification of abuse has been attempted in the literature, the rapid increase in prevalence of sedation may hint at its scope.

CPG are generally used to introduce new therapies or change practice patterns to match new research evidence. Yet in the case of palliative sedation, the rationale of international palliative care was to tighten boundaries, prevent abuse and distance palliative care from any suggestion of hastening death. Will guidelines limit abuse? Some clinicians who are wary of the concept of palliative sedation accept the importance of CPG as a harm reduction strategy. There is Dutch evidence that CPG may change practice in terms of drug choice and consent procedures, but little else to guide our speculation on the impact of guidelines. The need to standardize definitions and indications and to set other boundaries (prognosis, intractability, proportionality etc.) has wide agreement. However, an analysis of the resulting guidelines continues to show wide disparities and ambiguities.

There are reasons to believe that CPG will not reduce harm. The publication of guidelines with the imprimatur of national and international bodies may increase prevalence, stifle debate and imbed the practice. CPG may even mask abuse. The failure of most guidelines to distinguish proportional symptom relief from extreme Dutch and Belgian practices and the continued use of 'palliative sedation' to cover all forms of sedation, may allow extreme practices to 'hide' from scrutiny under the umbrella of international approval. The potential for abuse may even be higher than other end-of-life options. Euthanasia and assisted suicide are monitored, to some degree, by the jurisdictions authorizing them. In contrast, there is no legal obligation for reporting or auditing sedation. The only evidence collected to date comes from voluntary retrospective surveys.

Introduction of palliative sedation CPG in an institution or country could lead to fear, distrust or misunderstanding of palliative care and thus act as a deterrent to optimal symptom relief. It might even lead to decreasing levels of public and institutional support for palliative care. The promotion of palliative sedation protocols in the present cultural and historical context has a high potential to cause misunderstanding. Palliative sedation reinforces the public fear that pain may become refractory and that relief requires sedation. The request for permission to sedate will be easily misinterpreted as a euphemism for euthanasia. In an era of media attention to the right to die, a protocol to put patients to sleep is guaranteed to create a public perception that palliative care is associated with the hastening of death.

A protocol on sedation at the end of life that is well boundaried and proportionate can be morally acceptable. Blair (Chap. 9) provides us with strong arguments in favour of CPG and one can point to examples of clinically and ethically responsible guidelines for sedation at the end of life (Sykes and Thorns 2003a, b). Nonetheless, there is a significant risk that protocols, indirectly, may lead us further towards euthanasia. Guidelines may be used to 'market' a euthanasia mentality which claims that suffering can be avoided by choosing how and when to die. No longer a symptom control therapy, palliative sedation becomes an exit strategy. As we have seen in euthanasia and assisted suicide, guidelines give a false illusion of safeguards and controls (Pereira 2011).

Because CPG for palliative sedation focuses on preventing abuse through boundaries, one can foresee a gradual pushing or extending of these boundaries. There is already evidence for a 'slippery slope' in guideline development. Initial discussions of palliative sedation spoke of clinical proportionality with titration of drug doses to match symptom intensity. Progressively, we encounter guidelines that focus entirely on achieving deep unconsciousness without reference to symptoms (Miccinesi et al. 2006). As for prognosis, we see widening of prerequisites from days to weeks. Berger advocates the lifting of requirements for a short survival or even the necessity of refractory symptoms (Berger 2010). Similarly, Cellarius concludes "if no robust justification for the imminence condition is forth-coming, we should reject the imminence condition and accept that cases of ETS (early terminal sedation) will occur and will foreseeably and considerably hasten death" (Cellarius 2008). In terms of indications, the presence of intractable symptoms has gradually given way to a broader concept of unbearable distress. The failure of most CPG to draw clear lines on the issue of existential suffering is the pivotal weakness. By failing to restrict palliative sedation to symptom relief, guidelines facilitate a shift of sedation into another option for hastened or designed death. While proportionate palliative sedation is radically different from euthanasia, they may share the same 'zeitgeist', issuing from the controlling pole of medicine where fear of death, failure and impotence drives physicians to either futile life-prolongation or abruptly turning to unconsciousness or death as the way to maintain control. In sharp contrast, palliative medicine recognizes the inability to eradicate all suffering – in our living and in our dying- but is inspired by the sixteenth century aphorism "we cure sometimes, relieve often, comfort always".

10.7 Conclusion: Returning to a Symptom Focus

Language and the fears of dying remain the pivotal dynamics in the sedation debate. Despite the intention of proponents, the concept and language of palliative sedation will increase fear in patients, professionals and the public. And fear spirals into poor care and bad law. The CPG strategy relies on boundaries to curb abuse, while, in fact, the critical issue is the vocabulary itself. The word 'sedation' has a powerful impact on our cultural psyche, evoking an instinctual fear of being put to sleep which is really a proxy for our fear of death. When one combines historical connotations and clinical ambiguities attached to the term 'sedation' with the media focus on Dutch-style practice, we will not win this rhetorical battle. Regardless of strict CPG criteria, any therapy whose title contains the word 'sedation' will create fear and misunderstanding.

I contend that the optimal method for minimizing fear is to ensure our vocabulary and clinical focus remains fixed on symptom relief. We need to engage professionals, empowering them with knowledge and specialized back-up for challenging cases, so that we can return to the symptom focus that revolutionized end-of-life care in the 1970s. We need to promote guidelines for 'Symptom Relief in the Last Days of Life' which incorporates medication algorithms for delirium, respiratory distress and pain. We must equip professionals to manage the demoralization and psycho-spiritual anguish that leads to cries for death and unconsciousness.

We must also engage our culture, recognizing that talk of putting people to sleep is not reassuring but fear-provoking. We need to decrease fear by telling stories of pain relief and good care, stories of the human spirit overcoming fear and despair, of living until we die.

The palliative care community sought in CPG a method to rein in the abuse of jurisdictions that use palliative sedation, not for symptom relief, but as an exit strategy. From my bedside perspective, harm reduction through CPG development has largely failed. The only effective way to distance ourselves from these abuses is to abandon the vocabulary of sedation and return to the language and clinical reasoning of symptom relief.

References

Battin, M.P. 2008. Terminal sedation: Pulling the sheet over our eyes. *Hastings Center Report* 38(5): 27–30.

Berger, J.T. 2010. Rethinking guidelines for the use of palliative sedation. *Hastings Center Report* 40(3): 32–38.

Brietbart, W., B. Rosenfeld, C. Gibson, H. Pessin, S. Poppito, C. Nelson, et al. 2009. Meaning-centred group psychotherapy for patients with advanced cancer: A pilot randomized controlled trial. *Psycho-Oncology* 19(1): 21–28.

Brouwers, M., M.E. Kho, G.P. Browman, J.S. Burgers, F. Cluzeau, G. Feder, et al. 2010. AGREE II: Advancing guideline development, reporting and evaluation in health care. *Canadian Medical Association Journal* 182(18): E839–E842.

Bulli, F., G. Miccinesi, E. Biancalini, et al. 2007. Continuous deep sedation in home palliative care units: Case studies in the Florence area in 2000 and in 2003–4. *Minerva Anestesiologica* 73(5): 291–298.

Cabana, M.D., C.S. Rand, N.R. Powe, A.W. Wu, M.H. Wilson, and P.C. Abboud. 1999. Why don't physicians follow clinical practice guidelines? A framework for improvement. *JAMA* 282(15): 1458–1465.

Canadian Society of Palliative Care Physicians Task Force: Dean, M.M., Cellarius, V., Henry, B., Oneschuk, D., and Librach, S.L. 2012. Framework for Continuous Palliative Sedation Therapy (CPST) in Canada. *Journal of Palliative Medicine* 15(8): 1–10.

Cellarius, V. 2008. Terminal sedation and the imminence condition. *Journal of Medical Ethics* 34: 69–72.

Chambaere, K., J. Bilsen, J. Cohen, J.A. Rietjens, B.D. Onwuteaka-Philipsen, F. Mortier, et al. 2010. Continuous deep sedation until death in Belgium: A nationwide survey. *Archives of Internal Medicine* 170(5): 490–493.

Chater, S., R. Viola, J. Paterson, and J. Jarvis. 1998. Sedation for intractable distress in the dying – A survey of experts. *Palliative Medicine* 12: 255–269.

Cherny, N.I., and R.K. Portenoy. 1994. Sedation in the management of refractory symptoms: Guidelines for evaluation and treatment. *Journal of Palliative Care* 10(2): 31–38.

Cherny, N.I., and L. Radbruch. 2009. The board of the European Association for Palliative Care. European Association for Palliative Care (EAPC) recommended framework for the use of sedation in palliative care. *Palliative Medicine* 23(7): 581–593.

Chochinov, H., T. Hack, T. Hassard, L.J. Kristjanson, S. McClemont, and M. Harlos. 2005. Dignity therapy: A novel psychotherapeutic intervention for patients near the end of life. *Journal of Clinical Oncology* 23(24): 5520–5525.

Clark, D. 2002. *Cicely Saunders, founder of the hospice movement, selected letters 1959–1999.* Oxford: Oxford University Press.

Davis, M.P. 2009. Does palliative sedation always relieve symptoms? *Journal of Palliative Medicine* 12(10): 875–877.

de Graeff, A. 2008. De rol van consultatie bij palliatieve sedatie in de region Midden-Nederland. *Nederlands Tijdschrift Voor Geneeskunde* 152: 2346–2350.

De Graeff, A.D., and M. Dean. 2007. Palliative sedation therapy in the last weeks of life: A literature review and recommendations for standards. *Journal of Palliative Medicine* 10(1): 67–85.

Diz, J.C., A. Franco, D.R. Bacon, J. Rupreht, and J. Alvarez (eds.). 2002. *The history of anesthesia*, Excerpta medica international congress series, vol. 1242. Amsterdam: Elsevier.

Enck, R.E. 1991. Drug-induced terminal sedation for symptom control. *The American Journal of Hospice Care* 8: 3–5.

Fainsinger, R., M.J. Miller, E. Bruera, and T. Maceachern. 1991. Symptom control during the last week of life on a palliative care unit. *Journal of Palliative Care* 7(1): 5–11.

Field, M.J., and M.J. Lohr (eds.). 1990. *Clinical practice guidelines: Directions for a new program.* Washington, DC: National Academy Press.

Francke, A.L., Smit, M.C., de Veer, A.J.E., and Mistiaen, P. 2008. Factors influencing the implementation of clinical guidelines for health care professionals: a systematic meta-review. *BMC Medical Informatics and Decision Making* 8(38). doi:10.1186/1472-6947-8-38.

Greene, W.R., and W.H. Davis. 1991. Titrated intravenous barbiturates in the control of symptoms in patients with terminal cancer. *Southern Medical Journal* 84: 332–337.

Grol, R., and J. Grimshaw. 2003. From best evidence to best practice: Effective implementation of change in patients' care. *Lancet* 362: 1225–1230.

Hasselaar, J.G.J., R.P.B. Reuzel, S.C.A.H.V.M. Verhagen, A. de Graeff, K.C.P. Vissers, and B.J.P. Crul. 2007. Improving prescription in palliative sedation, compliance with Dutch guidelines. *Archives of Internal Medicine* 167(11): 1166–1171.

Hasselaar, J.G.J., R.P.B. Reuzel, M.E. van den Muijsenbergh, R.T. Koopmans, C.J. Leget, B.J. Crul, et al. 2008. Dealing with delicate issues in continuous deep sedation. *Archives of Internal Medicine* 168(5): 537–543.

Hasselaar, J.G., S.C. Verhagen, A.P. Wolff, Y.E. Engels, B.J. Crul, and K.C. Vissers. 2009. Changed patterns in Dutch palliative sedation practices after the introduction of a national guideline. *Archives of Internal Medicine* 169(5): 430–437.

Hesselink, B.A.M., H.R.W. Pasman, G. van der Wal, P. van der Maas, A. van der Heide, and B.D. Onwuteaka-Philipsen. 2010. Awareness and use of practice guidelines on medical end-of-life decisions in Dutch hospitals. *Patient Education and Counseling* 80: 21–28.

Janssens, R., J.J.M. van Delden, and G.A.M. Widdershoven. 2012. Palliative sedation: Not just normal medical practice. Ethical reflections on the Royal Dutch Medical Association's guideline on palliative sedation. *Journal of Medical Ethics* 0: 1–5. doi:10.1136/medethics-2011-100353.

Lichter, I., and E. Hunt. 1990. The last 48 hours. *Journal of Palliative Care* 6(4): 7–15.

Marks, R.M., and E.J. Sachar. 1973. Undertreatment of medical patients with narcotic analgesics. *Annals of Internal Medicine* 78(2): 173–181.

Miccinesi, G., J.A.C. Rietjens, L. Deliens, E. Paci, G. Bosshard, T. Nilstun, et al. 2006. Continuous deep sedation: Physicians' experiences in six European countries. *Journal of Pain and Symptom Management* 31: 122–129.

Mount, B. 1990. A final crescendo of pain? *Journal of Palliative Care* 6(3): 5–6.

Mount, B.M., I. Ajemian, and J.F. Scott. 1976. Use of the Brompton mixture in treating the chronic pain of malignant disease. *CMAJ* 115: 122–124.

Onwuteaka-Philipsen, B.D., Brinkman-Stoppelenburg, A., Penning, C., de Jong-Krul, G.J.F., van Delden, J.J.M., and van der Heide, A. 2012. Trends in end-of-life practices before and after the enactment of the euthanasia law in the Netherlands from 1990 to 2010: A repeated cross-sectional survey. *Lancet*. http://dx.doi.org/10.1016/S0140-6736(12)61034-4.

Pereira, J. 2011. Legalizing euthanasia or assisted suicide: The illusion of safeguards and controls. *Current Oncology* 18(2): e38–e45.

Rietjens, J.A.C., A. van der Heide, A.M. Vrakking, B.D. Onwuteaka-Philipsen, P.J. van der Maas, and G. van der Wal. 2004. Physician reports of terminal sedation without hydration or nutrition for patients nearing death in the Netherlands. *Annals of Internal Medicine* 141: 178–185.

Rietjens, J., van Delden, J., Onwuteaka-Philipsen, B., Buiting, H., van der Maas, P., and van der Heide, A. 2008. Continuous deep sedation for patients nearing death in the Netherlands: A descriptive study. *BMJ*. doi:10.1136/bmj.39504.531505.25.

Rousseau, P. 2000. The ethical validity and clinical experience of palliative sedation. *Mayo Clinic Proceedings* 75: 1064–1069.

Roy, D.J. 1990. Need they sleep before they die? *Journal of Palliative Care* 6(3): 3–4.

Saunders, C. 1989. Pain and impending death. In *Textbook of pain*, 2nd ed, ed. P.D. Wall and R. Melzack, 624–631. Edinburgh: Churchill-Livingstone.

Saunders, C. 2006. *Cicely Saunders: Selected writings 1958–2004*. Oxford: Oxford University Press.

Scott, J.F. 1989. Twilight sedation: Analgesia or euthanasia? *Pain Management Digest and Dialogue* 5(1): 4.

Seale, C. 2009. End-of-life decisions in the UK involving medical practitioners. *Palliative Medicine* 23: 198–204.

Sykes, N., and A. Thorns. 2003a. Sedative use in the last week of life and the implications for end-of-life decision making. *Archives of Internal Medicine* 163: 341–344.

Sykes, N., and A. Thorns. 2003b. The use of opioids and sedatives at the end of life. *The Lancet Oncology* 4: 312–318.

Twycross, R.G., and S.A. Lack. 1984. *Symptom control in far advanced cancer: Pain relief.* London: Pitman.

van der Heide, A., B.D. Onwuteaka-Philpsen, M.L. Rurup, et al. 2007. End-of-life practices in the Netherlands under the Euthanasia Act. *The New England Journal of Medicine* 356(19): 1957–1965.

Ventafridda, V., C. Ripamonti, F. DeConno, M. Tambarini, and B.R. Cassileth. 1990. Symptom prevalence and control during cancer patients' last days of life. *Journal of Palliative Care* 6(3): 7–11.

Von Roenn, J.H., and C.F. von Gunten. 2009. Are we putting the cart before the horse? *Archives of Internal Medicine* 169(5): 429.

Woolf, S.H., R. Grol, A. Hutchinson, M. Eccles, and J. Grimshaw. 1999. Potential benefits, limitations and harms of clinical guidelines. *BMJ* 318: 527–530.

Epilogue

The '*Leitmotiv*' of this book is a number of ethical questions that arise from the use of sedation at the end-of-life. Among these questions are the following (Table 1):

1. Whether there is an ethically sound difference between palliative sedation (PS) and euthanasia and physician-assisted-suicide;
2. Whether the principle of double effect can be appropriately applied to justify the use of sedation in some cases at the end-of-life.
3. Whether PS might be ethically acceptable in the case of patients that are not imminently dying (agony);
4. Whether decisions to limit medically assisted nutrition and hydration are essentially linked to PS or whether they should be regarded as independent issues;
5. Whether sedation is an adequate response to 'existential suffering';
6. Whether sedation could ever be used in the case of patients who are not able to give their informed consent (e.g. patients with cognitive impairment of diverse origins, etc.).

Facing these questions, the need for the identification of the anthropological foundations of the right goals of care at the end-of-life was highlighted and some ethical criteria which facilitate decision-making in health professionals, patients and their families regarding the adequate use of sedation at the end-of-life were identified (Taboada 2006, 2012; Cherny and Radbruch 2009; Hauser and Walsh 2009; National Ethics Committee Veterans Health Administration 2006; Boyle 2004a; Tulsky 2006; Onwuteaka-Philipsen et al. 2003). In each of the chapters of this book, different authors have made important contributions to the analysis of the ethical-anthropological foundations of PS. At the conclusion of this book, it seems adequate to offer a synthesis of the main contributions related to each of these ethical questions. Undoubtedly, the reflections proposed here do not intend to encompass all the complexity and depth of the ethical-anthropological contributions offered in the different chapters of this book. The objective of these closing reflec-

P. Taboada (ed.), *Sedation at the End-of-life: An Interdisciplinary Approach*, 161
Philosophy and Medicine 116, DOI 10.1007/978-94-017-9106-9,
© Springer Science+Business Media Dordrecht 2015

Table 1 Ethically relevant questions related to the use of PS

1. Are there ethically relevant differences between PS and euthanasia?
2. Is the application of the principle of double effect necessary for the moral justification of PS?
3. Is PS ethically appropriate for patients that are not in a stage of imminent death (agony)?
4. Are decisions to limit medically-assisted nutrition and hydration a necessary condition to indicate PS?
5. Is sedation an appropriate answer for the management of psycho-spiritual symptoms, including 'existential suffering'?
6. Can PS be used in incompetent patients, that is, in the case of patients who are unable to give an informed consent (e.g. due to cognitive impairment of diverse origin)?

tions is – rather – to motivate a personal reflection and the study of a sensitive topic which still needs some answers.

I shall summarize the main contributions made for each of the six above mentioned questions:

1 Are There Ethically Relevant Differences Between PS and Euthanasia?

A reflection on the ethical-anthropological foundations which guide medical practice suggests that the distinction between appropriate and inappropriate uses of sedation at the end-of-life is clarified when the focus of the ethical discussion is centred on the goals of care at the end-of-life. In this context, it becomes evident that the ethically appropriate use of sedatives must share certain common characteristics with the goals of care of Palliative Medicine in general (Cherny and Portenoy 1994). According to the WHO definition, what characterizes Palliative Medicine is – among others – that it "affirms life and regards dying as a normal process; intends neither to hasten nor postpone death; provides relief from pain and other distressing symptoms" (World Health Organization 1990). We can therefore say that Palliative Medicine's own objectives specifically exclude the intentional acceleration of death.

Thus, from a clinical and anthropological point of view, to arrive at an ethically appropriate use of sedation at the end-of-life, it is indispensable to clearly formulate the 'therapeutic objective' which defines this medical action (Taboada 2012; Cherny and Radbruch 2009; Hauser and Walsh 2009; Cherny 2006; Krakauer 2009; Claessens et al. 2008). According to the *lex artis,* the therapeutic objective of palliative sedation is "to reduce the consciousness of a terminal patient as much as necessary to adequately relieve one or more refractory symptoms" (Claessens et al. 2008, p. 329). This goal of care is completely in agreement with the principles of Palliative Medicine which seek to respect life and the dignity of dying patients, providing them with all the necessary care to alleviate 'total pain' during the last stages of life (Cherny and Portenoy 1994; World Health Organization 1990).

On the other hand, the different moral and legal status attributed to PS and euthanasia in most of contemporary societies is based on the concept of respect for the 'inviolability of human life' (Keown 2012; Finnis 2011; Vivanco 2006). Therefore to judge an action with possible negative consequences – as the eventual hastening of death caused by the use of sedatives at the end-of-life – from an ethical and legal perspective a distinction is usually drawn between the 'direct intention' and the 'oblique intention' of the acting person, rejecting any action which seeks *directly* to hasten death in a patient (Keown 2012; Finnis 2011; Vivanco 2006). This distinction coincides with the difference between 'intended effects' and 'foreseeable effects' established by the ethical principle of double effect, a principle whose applicability to the justification of PS has been accurately analized in this book.

Thus, in spite of the undeniable importance of respect for 'autonomy', both for patients and also for health professionals, respect for autonomy should always be subordinated to the respect we owe to the 'basic human goods' of which the first and most important one is life itself (Gómez-Lobo 2006). In fact, life is a necessary condition, albeit not sufficient, for the exercise of autonomy and of all the other basic human goods (Keown 2012; Finnis 2011; Vivanco 2006; Gómez-Lobo 2006).

Consequently, the relevant ethical and legal differences between PS and euthanasia should be sought, basically, at the level of: (a) the 'therapeutic objective' (to alleviate severe and refractory symptoms vs. to intentionally cause death); (b) the content of the 'direct intention' and of the 'oblique intention' of the acting person; and (c) the character 'intended' or 'tolerated' of the eventual negative effects (application of the principle of double effect). Hence, it can be concluded that it is possible to establish an important and solid distinction between PS and euthanasia, both from the ethical and the legal perspective.

2 Is the Application of the Principle of Double Effect Necessary for the Moral Justification of PS?

The use of medications which alter a patient's state of consciousness – like sedatives and/or opioids – may give rise to ethical doubts in health care professionals and/or the patients and their relatives (Cherny and Radbruch 2009; Hauser and Walsh 2009; National Ethics Committee Veterans Health Administration 2006; Boyle 2004a; Tulsky 2006; Taboada 2006; Onwuteaka-Philipsen et al. 2003). It is feared that the adverse effects associated with the use of this type of drugs – like hypotension, respiratory depression, impairment in the use of mental properties, etc. - could represent a form of euthanasia (Cherny and Radbruch 2009; Hauser and Walsh 2009; National Ethics Committee Veterans Health Administration 2006; Boyle 2004a; Tulsky 2006; Taboada 2006; Onwuteaka-Philipsen et al. 2003). In fact, in contemporary bioethics some authors have used the expression 'indirect euthanasia' to refer to the use of drugs to alleviate pain and other symptoms, when those interventions include the risk of indirectly accelerating death (Tulsky 2006). Even though the use of the term 'indirect euthanasia' to indicate these kind of actions seems inadequate from the conceptual point of view, it cannot be ignored that the fear of committing euthanasia could be one of the reasons that explains the under-utilization of opioids and sedatives, which some authors have reported specially in Latin American countries (Eisenschlas 2007).

With regards to this concern it is worth recalling that when opiods and sedatives are used in a clinically appropriate way, the empirical evidence shows that they do not produce an acceleration of death (Cherny and Radbruch 2009; Claessens et al. 2008; Regnard et al. 2011). Nevertheless, even if in some particular case it could be foreseen that some undesirable effects may occur – including the unintentional acceleration of death – the ethical tradition affirms that the use of these therapies might be morally correct. Indeed, their ethical legitimacy is usually justified through the application of the ethical principle of 'double effect' (PDE) (Anscombe 2001; Boyle 1980, 2004b; Cassell and Rich 2010; Jansen 2010; Jansen and Sulmasy 2002; Fohr 1998). According to this principle, an action that has simultaneous and inseparable good and bad effects is morally permitted only if the following conditions are simultaneously fulfilled:

– the action itself must be morally permitted;
– the good effect, which is the object of the agent's intention, must not be obtained through the bad effect;
– the bad effect, which is foreseeable and inevitable, is not the direct object of the agent's intention (i.e. the bad effect could be foreseeable, foretold or tolerated, but should not be intended as the purpose of the action);
– there must be a proportion between the good and bad effects (Gómez-Lobo 2006, p. 107–8).

There are authors who add a fifth condition: that there is no other way of achieving the good effect, without having the bad effect (Anscombe 2001; Boyle 1980, 2004b). On the other hand, some ethicists affirm that the above stated conditions could be summarized in two: (1) that the damages (or adverse effects) are not voluntarily intended (but arise as unwanted collateral effects); and (2) that there are sufficiently serious moral reasons to bring about these damages (Anscombe 2001; Boyle 1980, 2004b).

Nevertheless, some authors question the validity and/or the foundations of the PDE (Veatch 2003; Quill et al. 1997a; Donagan 1988, 1991; Quinn 1989, 1991). Among the main criticisms formulated against this ethical principle are the difficulties of: (1) accepting the existence of causes that could produce effects that are independent from one another; (2) distinguishing between 'intended' and 'foreseeable' effects and accepting the fact that foreseeable bad effects could be only indirectly tolerated (and are not necessarily included in the intention of the acting person); (3) applying the conditions required by the PDE to certain concrete situations; (4) admitting the existence of absolute moral norms (i.e. norms which do not admit any exception).

A critical analysis of these and other objections to the PDE shows that the PDE has been frequently misunderstood or incorrectly applied, especially in the context of caring for patients at the end-of-life. Indeed, Miranda emphasizes that the field of application of the PDE is more limited than what is sometimes thought (Miranda 2008).

Therefore, in order to analyse whether the administration of drugs that have the effect of depriving someone of consciousness is an action that could (or should) be justified by the application of the PDE, it is necessary to first establish which is the proper field of application of this principle. We must remember that the PDE is not applicable to all effects that can be called bad/evil. In fact, this ethical principle is only applied to justify those effects that would never be legitimate to intend, not even as means to a good end.

Therefore, when asking if the use of sedatives at the end-of-life belongs to the field of application of the PDE, it is necessary to identify the negative effects whose occurrence requires an ethical justification. It is known that the main negative effects which give rise to ethical questions in relation to sedation are: (1) the deprivation of consciousness at such a significant time in the life of a patient and, (2) the possible acceleration of the patient's death.

The deprivation of consciousness – considered by itself – is not an effect that requires an ethical foundation through the application of the PDE, because it can be provoked intentionally if it were necessary in order to achieve a good end, as is the case in surgical interventions, or in the relief of severe and refractory symptoms of a terminally ill patient. Thus, a deprivation of consciousness does not need to be, in itself, justified by the PDE. The ethical principle that justifies this kind of medical actions is the existence of a proportionally serious reason (principle of therapeutic proportionality or parsimony).

However, when it is possible to foresee that the use of sedatives will produce an acceleration of the patient's death, or that the patient, after being sedated, will not recover consciousness and/or the sedation will impede him/her from carrying out other ethical, legal and/or religious obligations before dying, then the PDE will indeed gain relevance. This is so because, both the death of the patient and the permanent suppression of consciousness that impede the fulfilment of important duties are effects that it would never be legitimate to procure intentionally. However, they might be accepted as collateral effects of actions that are necessary to achieve proportionally important goods, as could be the control of severe symptoms at the end-of-life, which have not responded to other forms of therapy (Miranda 2008). Thus, the ethical justification for the use of sedatives in these cases would indeed require the application of the PDE, because it would draw the distinction between the acceleration of death sought as the aim of the action (euthanasia) or tolerated only as a collateral effect of the use of sedatives.

3   Is PS Ethically Appropriate for Patients That Are Not in a Stage of Imminent Death (Agony)?

Most of the existing clinical guidelines for the use of PS propose to restrict this intervention exclusively to patients in a stage of agony (that is to say, during the last hours or days of life), especially in the case of the so-called 'deep continuous sedation'

(Cherny and Radbruch 2009; Hauser and Walsh 2009; National Ethics Committee Veterans Health Administration 2006; Claessens et al. 2008). For example, the Dutch clinical guidelines establish that: "besides the presence of medical indications, a precondition for the use of continuous sedation is the expectation that death will occur in the reasonably near future, that is, within one or two weeks" (Royal Dutch Medical Association Committee on National Guideline for Palliative Sedation 2009, p. 6). The reasons are eminently pragmatic in character and can be grouped in two categories: (a) that the eventual risk of accelerating death, as an undesirable effect of the use of sedatives, does not have any relevance in the agony stage, neither from the ethical nor the legal point of view; and (b) that the idea of keeping a patient under sedation for longer periods of time (weeks or months) would be counter-intuitive, because it would approximate to a 'social death.'

However, not all authors agree that the imminence of death should be considered as an indispensable requirement for the ethical and legal justification of sedation at the end-of-life (Keown 2012; Miranda 2008). In fact, from a clinical perspective, there could be situations in which patients who are not in a stage of agony could show severe and refractory symptoms, the management of which would require the use of PS as a last resource (Cherny and Radbruch 2009; Hauser and Walsh 2009; Cherny 2006; Krakauer 2009; Claessens et al. 2008). It is not clear why the use of PS should be proscribed in these situations. In this context, the ethical principle of proportionality in therapies should be enough to justify the recourse to sedation. On the other hand, the distinction between 'direct' and 'oblique' effects (mentioned before) suggests that – when there is a proportionally serious reason – the use of sedatives can be ethically and legally permitted, even at the risk of accelerating death and/or permanently depriving the patient of consciousness, provided always that these effects are tolerated as collateral effects of legal and necessary actions to bring about a benefit of proportionate importance (application of PDE).

In this context, it may be necessary to mention that 'proportionality,' as an ethical foundation for PS, has been criticized for its possible arbitrariness (Cherny and Radbruch 2009). In fact, the degree of 'severity' of a symptom tends to be classified according to the subjective assessment that the patient makes of it. On the other hand, the refractoriness of a symptom has also diverse interpretations depending on the experience of clinical personnel, and/or the therapeutic resources available. Thus, a bad application of the 'proportionality' criterion could lead to the use of PS in a way that does not comply with the international standards of 'good clinical practices,' a risk that could be even higher in economically deprived sectors of society, such as the developing countries (Eisenschlas 2007).

Therefore, when analysing if the imminence of death is a necessary requirement to justify the recourse to PS from the ethical and legal points of view, it is relevant to reflect on the ethical-anthropological implications of the eventual subjectivity of the 'refractoriety' and 'severity' criteria of the symptoms, as well as the 'proportionality' criterion in the therapies, depending on the clinical experience and the socio-economic context in which they are applied. So, even though – in principle – there seem not to be sufficient reasons to restrict the use of palliative sedation to situations of inminent death, there are prudential arguments that suggest the need to be especially strict in verifying the compliance with clinical and ethical criteria when using PS in a context other than agony.

4   Are Decisions to Limit Medically-Assisted Nutrition and Hydration a Necessary Condition to Indicate PS?

Some authors have proposed that to discontinuing hydration and nutrition would be a 'typical' or 'essential' component of the sedation technique at the end-of-life (Quill and Byock 2000; Quill et al. 1997b; Orentlicher and Caplan 1999; Rietjens et al. 2004; Verkerk et al. 2007). Rietjens, for example, introduces this aspect in the very definition of 'terminal sedation,' which for this author is the administration of drugs to keep the patient in deep sedation or coma until death, without giving artificial nutrition or hydration" (Rietjens et al. 2008, p. 179). Even though this proposition does not have wide acceptance among specialists, it leads to a reflection on its clinical and ethical foundations.

From a clinical perspective, it is expected that a patient who receives PS for the management of severe and refractory symptoms at the end-of-life will lose the capacity to spontaneously hydrate and nourish him/herself. This will occur to a different extend depending on the level of sedation that is required. In those cases in which deep sedation is used, the inevitable clinical and ethical questions arise whether to initiate or maintain artificial hydration or medically-assisted nutrition. During the last decades, the foundations of the prescriptions of artificial hydration and medically-assisted nutrition in terminal patients have been intensively debated (Taboada et al. 2010; Palma et al. 2011). Among the controversial points are not only questions related to the eventual clinical benefits and risks associated with these practices, but also questions regarding the ethical principles and values that are involved. For example, it has been discussed whether artificial hydration in terminal patients can: (a) be a means to alleviate frequent symptoms, like thirst, or to reverse neurological alterations, like delirium; (b) artificially prolong life (or whether its omission could shorten life); (c) provoke unnecessary suffering and risks; etc. It is obvious that these questions have ethical implications because they are directly related to some relevant moral principles and values in the care of terminal patients, like: (1) respect for life and the dignity of the dying; (2) the moral obligation of implementing proportional medical care; (3) respect for the symbolic value attributed to hydration and nutrition, as a manifestation of the duties of care and companionship towards the most vulnerable; (4) the duty not to harm; (5) the obligation to encourage the responsible exercise of patients' freedom (autonomy), especially in the final stages of life; etc (Taboada et al. 2010; Palma et al. 2011).

The majority of palliative care specialists coincide in stating that invasive forms of medically assisted nutrition are not part of the usual care required by patients who have lost the ability to feed themselves spontaneously in the final stages of life (Cherny and Radbruch 2009; Taboada et al. 2010; Palma et al. 2011). However, there seems to be also a certain agreement among specialists on the need to provide a minimum degree of artificial hydration to those patients whose estimated time of survival is greater than one or two weeks, because otherwise their normal loss of liquid could cause death by dehydration (Cherny and Radbruch 2009; Jansen and Sulmasy 2002; Cassell and Rich 2010; Jansen 2010). This suggests that – in principle – there should be a moral obligation to assure a minimum of hydration to those patients who require to be sedated and whose estimated life expectancy is more than one or two weeks. If this were not carried out, those cases in which an early death occurs as a consequence of dehydration and not as a consequence of the natural evolution of the disease could correspond to acts of euthanasia by omission.

Therefore, the European Association for Palliative Care (EAPC) proposes that prescriptions of PS and indications regarding artificial hydration and medically-assisted nutrition should be considered as independent decisions, because they correspond – in fact – to separate clinical problems and, are – therefore – based on different clinical and ethical criteria (Cherny and Radbruch 2009).

5   Is Sedation an Appropriate Answer for the Management of Psycho-Spiritual Symptoms, Including 'Existential Suffering'?

Some of the existing clinical guidelines suggest the use of PS both for the management of physical symptoms as well as psycho-spiritual symptoms, including the so called 'existential suffering.' The latter has been defined as "the feeling that one's own existence is empty or meaningless" (Royal Dutch Medical Association Committee on National Guideline for Palliative Sedation 2009, p. 6). This subjective perception of the 'meaninglessness' of one's own existence, particularly when death is expected to occur within a few days or weeks, may cause intense anxiety or unbearable suffering to dying patients. Under these circumstances, a patient could request sedation as a means to no longer feel this insupportable anxiety. Among the ethical principles that have been called upon to justify sedation in these cases is the respect due to the autonomous decisions of patients (Cherny and Radbruch 2009; Bolmsjo 2000; Roy 1990; Breitbart et al. 1998, 2000; Morita et al. 2000; Cherny 1998; Rousseau 2001).

As should be expected, at present there is no consensus among specialists on the medical and ethical justification for the indication of PS in these cases. In fact, the management of psycho-spiritual symptoms and 'existential suffering' through sedation is one of the most controversial indications of this clinical practice. Some palliative care specialists ask themselves if the aims of medicine should include the alleviation of all forms of human suffering. The majority seems to agree that the relief of psycho-spiritual suffering goes beyond the limits of medicine (Cherny and Radbruch 2009; Jansen and Sulmasy 2002; Cassell and Rich 2010; Jansen 2010; Bolmsjo 2000; Breitbart et al. 1998, 2000; Morita et al. 2000; Cherny 1998; Rousseau 2001). We know that human suffering – in its different forms – is an integral part of human existence and it could never be completely eliminated by medicine (Cherny and Radbruch 2009; Jansen and Sulmasy 2002; Cassell and Rich 2010; Jansen 2010).

Thus, some authors sustain that the management of these kinds of situations requires special considerations, which go beyond the strict respect for autonomy (Cherny and Radbruch 2009; Keown 2012; McCall Smith 1997; O'Neill 2002). The reasons adduced for that are fundamentally the following:

– The nature of these symptoms makes it very difficult to establish criteria to determine their true 'refractoriness;'
– The severity of the distress caused by these symptoms could be very dynamic and idiosyncratic and the appearance of adaptation mechanisms is frequent;
– The normal interventions for the relief of this kind of symptoms (e.g. psychotherapy, spiritual accompaniment, alternatives therapies, etc.) usually are very cost-effective.
– The presence of these symptoms does not necessarily indicate progress towards psychological deterioration.

All these reasons tend to support the need for an integral and periodical clinical assessment of terminal patients with psycho-spiritual symptoms and reinforce also the need for a multi-professional team-work which includes psychiatrists, psychologists, chaplains, therapists, ethicists, etc. Such a team could explore the multifactorial causes that are often hidden behind intense psycho-spiritual symptoms. Similarly, the intrinsic dynamism and the idiosyncrasy of the answers demonstrate the need to give enough time to the different therapeutic strategies implemented, without the premature recourse to the wiping out of consciousness.

Thus, the validity of 'existential suffering' as a criterion to prescribe PS is undermined by the ambiguity of its definition, as well as by the practical difficulties that the assessment of this symptom and the determination of its refractoriness entail. In fact, a review of the literature shows that this term has been used in a way that includes virtually all types of psychological symptoms. On the other hand, the proposition of limiting its use to symptoms related to the *distress* caused by one's mortality itself has not helped to improve its specificity, because practically all the preoccupations at the end-of-life are strongly coloured by the context of mortality.

Accordingly, it seems suitable to consider 'existential suffering' not only as a symptom emerging from 'inside' the patient, but also as coming from the exterior: from the patient's 'social context'. From this consideration a very concrete therapeutic proposition is derived, namely, to mobilize all the patient's family and other significant people and all the members of the medical team who could have an important role in the relief and prevention of 'existential suffering' at the end-of-life. In fact, the occurrence of unbearable existential anguish at the end-of-life could be secondary to a failure to implement the appropriate interventions during the early stages of the development of the disease. Indeed, several useful therapeutic tools have been described for the management of this type of symptoms, coming from psychiatry, psychology and spiritual support. They have demonstrated clinical success in the alleviation of psycho-spiritual symptoms, including 'existential suffering.' In fact, these interventions help to prevent or deal with existential suffering and foster the psychological and spiritual growth of patients at the end-of-life, enabling them to face that moment in peace.

Not withstanding the foregoing, a thorough analysis has to be made as to whether, in exceptional and well qualified cases, the need for the recourse to an intermittent sedation could be established, with the objective of offering 'respite' periods to over-distressed patients, thus gaining time so that the psychological processes of bereavement and the adaptation mechanisms can come into play. In other words, the possibility of using PS for the alleviation of psycho-spiritual symptoms at the en-of-life cannot be totally excluded. But the need to use it in this setting could reflect a lack of the timely application of other support tools that are available today.

This has important ethical-anthropological implications, because inducing a permanent loss of consciousness at such a crucial life moment could represent a form of 'social euthanasia', especially if the clinical criteria of severity and the lack of response to other types of interventions has not been duly verified. Consequently, the eventual ethical justification of PS for the alleviation of 'existential suffering' at the end-of-life is conditioned to a clarification of the definition of the symptom and of the criteria for refractoriness and intolerability. It would be desirable to have an early referral to specialists in mental health or spiritual accompaniment, so that an adequate assessment and a timely management of 'existential anguish' can be done, avoiding the use of sedation.

6 Can PS Be Used in Incompetent Patients, that is, in the Case of Patients Who Are Unable to Give an Informed Consent (e.g. due to Cognitive Impairment of Diverse Origin)?

The respect for the right of competent and informed patients to actively participate in medical decision-making is an ethical principle that is widely accepted today (autonomy). In fact, among the ethical criteria that are frequently invoked to justify the recourse to PS is that its prescription responds to an express request from the patient and/or that there is an informed consent signed by the patient or a valid surrogate (Veatch 2003; Finnis 2009; Keown and Gormally 1999).

That is why some clinical guidelines propose that an 'ethical requirement' for the prescription of PS is to obtain a valid informed consent and do not permit its use in those cases in which the patient is not able to give the due consent and/or does not have someone that could represent him/her in decision-making (Royal Dutch Medical Association Committee on National Guideline for Palliative Sedation 2009). Besides safeguarding the principle of autonomy, another reason underlying this requirement is the possible misuse of sedation in the case of incompetent patients, that is to say, in the case of patients with cognitive impairment of diverse origin, for example when they show socially inadequate behaviour and/or their conduct could be disturbing to others. The potential risk of abusing the recourse to sedation in such cases could be exacerbated in those health centres with shortage of staff, as often happens in the most exposed socio-economic sectors in Latin-American countries (Eisenschlas 2007).

However, it cannot be ignored that there are some patients with cognitive impairment of different origin – who, by definition, are incompetent – who could experience severe and refractory symptoms at the end-of-life, as any other patient. Moreover, with this kind of patients it is not infrequent to have difficulties to find a valid legal representative, especially in low socio-economical settings (Eisenschlas 2007). The fact that in these situations it is not possible to obtain a valid informed consent should not necessarily imply that the recourse to sedation should be totally excluded for these patients, as they may need this therapeutic tool as any other patient with severe, refractory symptoms. Hence, the danger of abusing sedation in incompetent patient should not become an argument to discriminate them by not allowing them the access to a therapeutic tool that might be clinically justified.

Although incompetent patients correspond, by definition, to a vulnerable group, in which the exercise of autonomy must be usually subrogated (Finnis 2009; Keown and Gormally 1999), for an adequate decision-taking in relation to the use of sedation at the end-of-life it is not enough to identify a legally valid representative. We must also make sure that the decision is really oriented to the 'best interest' of the individual patient. In this context, it is important to point out that autonomy must be subordinated to the principle of inviolability of human life and that the concept of 'best interest' (welfare) has always a double component, 'objective' and 'subjective' (Keown 2012; Vivanco 2006).

Consequently, the ethical criterion that requires the informed consent of the patient (or a legally valid representative) in order to prescribe PS at the end-of-life needs to be refined. Without ignoring the importance of the respect due to the responsible exercise of freedom (principle of autonomy), a complement to this important ethical principle could be proposed in the light of other ethical-anthropological criteria, that are perhaps equally relevant, such as the 'best interest', solidarity and justice, especially with the most vulnerable. A complement of this kind would help to do justice to the different clinical scenarios described above.

To conclude these reflections, we want to stress that the variety of ethical and anthropological questions that arise at present from the recourse to sedation at the end-of-life bear witness to the need to identify criteria which could guide health professionals, patients and their relatives in clinical decision-making. Despite the fact that PS is considered today as a helpful therapeutic tool for the management of severe and refractory symptoms at the end-of-life, the possible adverse effects and eventual risks associated with the use of sedatives demands a prudent and well founded use of this tool, especially in the case of terminal patients.

Among the values and ethical principles that guide an adequate use of PS, the following can be mentioned (Table 2): (1) The inviolability of human life; (2) The

Table 2 Some ethical principles/values relevant to the use of sedation at the-end-of-life

1. Inviolability of human life
2. Respect for the dignity of the dying
3. Therapeutic principle and proportionality in care
4. Principle of double effect
5. Respect for the responsible exercise of freedom (autonomy)
6. Justice and solidarity

respect due to the dignity of the dying; (3) The therapeutic principle and the proportionality in care; (4) The principle of double effect; (5) The respect for the responsible exercise of freedom (autonomy); (6) Solidarity and justice.

Dying people correspond – undoubtedly- to one of the most vulnerable groups of people in our society (Taboada 2006, 2012; Cherny and Radbruch 2009; Hauser and Walsh 2009; National Ethics Committee Veterans Health Administration 2006; Boyle 2004a; Tulsky 2006; Onwuteaka-Philipsen et al. 2003). Consequently, their life and dignity deserve our special respect and attention. If we accept the premise that an individual's *moral quality* is expressed – in an eminent manner – by the way in which that individual cares for the most vulnerable in society, we could assume that future generations could judge the *moral quality* of contemporary societies by the way in which we treat the most vulnerable groups, among which are certainly the dying. It is precisely here where our respect for human life and dignity, as well as the meaning we attribute to the value of belonging to the human family is put to the test.

Palliative Medicine understands the 'right to die with dignity' as the right of each person to receive competent, holistic and compassionate assistance at the end-of-life. This form of accompaniment to the 'good death' implies a number of *ethical requirements* for health professionals and for society in general. These requirements take the shape of a duty to provide medical assistance of technical and humane quality, which encompasses all dimensions of the person, that is to say, the moral obligation to alleviate not only physical symptoms, but also the different sources of psychological, spiritual and social suffering that usually accompany the dying process: the so called 'total pain.' Hence, the access to palliative medicine of excellence – both technical and humane – should be considered as a right derived from the most fundamental human rights.

Santiago, Chile

Paulina Taboada

References

Anscombe, E. 2001. Medalist's address: Action, intention and double effect. In *The doctrine of double effect*, ed. P.A. Woodward. Notre Dame: University of Notre Dame Press.

Bolmsjo, I. 2000. Existential issues in palliative care – Interviews with cancer patients. *Journal of Palliative Care* 16: 20–24.

Boyle, J. 1980. Toward understanding double effect. *Ethics* 90: 527–538.

Boyle, J. 2004a. Medical ethics and double effect; a case of terminal sedation. *Theoretical Medicine and Bioethics* 25: 52–60.

Boyle, J. 2004b. Medical ethics and double effect. The case of terminal sedation. *Theoretical Medicine and Bioethics* 25: 53–54.

Breitbart, W., H.M. Chochinov, and S.D. Passik. 1998. Psychiatric aspects of palliative care. In *Oxford textbook of palliative medicine*, 2nd ed, ed. D. Doyle, G. Hanks, and N. MacDonald, 933–954. Oxford: Oxford University Press.

Breitbart, W., B. Rosenfeld, H. Pessin, et al. 2000. Depression, hopelessness, and desire for hastened death in terminally ill patients with cancer. *Journal of the American Medical Association* 284: 2907–2911.

Cassell, E.J., and B.A. Rich. 2010. Intractable end-of-life suffering and the ethics of palliative sedation. *Pain Medicine* 11: 435–438.

Cherny, N.I. 1998. Commentary: Sedation in response to refractory existential distress: Walking the fine line. *Journal of Pain and Symptom Management* 16: 404–406.

Cherny, N. 2006. Palliative sedation. In *Textbook of palliative medicine*, ed. E. Bruera, I. Higginson, C. Ripamonti, and C. von Gunten, 976–987. London: Hodder Arnold.

Cherny, N.I., and R.K. Portenoy. 1994. Sedation in the management of refractory symptoms: Guidelines for evaluation and treatment. *Journal of Palliative Care* 10: 31–38.

Cherny, N., and L. Radbruch. 2009. European Association for Palliative Care (EAPC) recommended framework for the use of sedation in palliative care. *Palliative Medicine* 23(7): 581–593.

Claessens, P., J. Menten, P. Schotsmans, and B. Broeckaert. 2008. Palliative sedation: A review of the research literature. *Journal of Pain and Symptom Management* 36: 310–333.

Donagan, A. 1988. *The theory of morality*. Chicago: Chicago University Press.

Donagan, A. 1991. Moral absolutism and the double effect exception: Reflections on Josef Boyle's "Who is entitled to double effect?". *The Journal of medicine and philosophy* 16: 571–585.

Eisenschlas, J.H. 2007. Palliative sedation. *Current Opinion in Supportive and Palliative Care* 1: 207–212.

Finnis, J. 2009. The Mental Capacity Act 2005: Some ethical and legal issues. In *Incapacity and care*, ed. H. Watt. London: The Linacre Centre.

Finnis, J. 2011. *Intention and identity*. Oxford: Oxford University Press (Part Three).

Fohr, S. 1998. The double effect of pain medication: Separating myth from reality. *Journal of Palliative Medicine* 1: 315–328.

Gómez-Lobo, A. 2006. *Los bienes humanos. Ética de la ley natural* [The human goods. Ethics of natural law]. Santiago de Chile: Ed. Mediterráneo.

Hauser, K., and D. Walsh. 2009. Palliative sedation: Welcome guidance on a controversial issue. *Palliative Medicine* 23(7): 577–579.

Jansen, L.A. 2010. Intractable end-of-life suffering and the ethics of palliative sedation: A commentary on Cassell and Rich. *Pain Medicine* 11: 440–441.

Jansen, L.A., and D.P. Sulmasy. 2002. Sedation, alimentation; Hydration, and equivocation: Careful conversation about care at the end of life. *Annals of Internal Medicine* 136: 845–849.

Keown, J. 2012. *The law and ethics of medicine: Essays on the inviolability of human life*. Oxford: Oxford University Press.

Keown, J., and L. Gormally. 1999. Human dignity, autonomy and mentally-incapacitated patients: A critique of who decides?. *Web Journal of Current Legal Issues*. Available at: http://www.wjcli.ncl.ac.uk

Krakauer, E.L. 2009. Sedation in palliative medicine. In *Oxford textbook of palliative medicine*, 4th ed, ed. G. Hanks, N. Cherny, N.A. Christakis, M. Fallon, S. Kaasa, and R.K. Portenoy. Oxford: Oxford University Press.

McCall Smith, A. 1997. Beyond Autonomy. *Journal of Contemporary Health Law and Policy* 14: 23.

Miranda, A. 2008. El principio del doble efecto y su relevancia en el razonamiento jurídico [The double effect principle and its relevance in legal reasoning]. *Revista Chilena de Derecho* [Chilean Law Magazine] 35(3): 485–519.

Morita, T., J. Tsunoda, S. Inoue, and S. Chihara. 2000. Terminal sedation for existential distress. *The American Journal of Hospice & Palliative Care* 17: 189–195.

National Ethics Committee Veterans Health Administration. 2006. The ethics of palliative sedation as a therapy of last resort. *The American Journal of Hospice & Palliative Care* 23: 483–491.

O'Neill, O. 2002. *Autonomy and trust in bioethics*. Cambridge: Cambridge University Press.

Onwuteaka-Philipsen, B., Van der Heide, A., Koper, D., Keij-Deerenberg, I., Rietiens, J., et al. Euthanasia and other end-of-life decisions in The Netherlands. *The Lancet*, online 17 June, 2003.

Orentlicher, D., and A. Caplan. 1999. The Pain Relief Promotion Act of 1999: A serious threat to palliative care. *The Journal of the American Academy of Psychiatry and the Law* 27: 527–539.

Palma, A., J.C. Said, and P. Taboada. 2011. ¿Es necesario hidratar artificialmente a los pacientes terminales? [Should we artificially hydrate terminally ill patients]. *Revista médica de Chile* 139: 1229–1234.

Quill, T.E., and I.R. Byock. 2000. Responding to intractable terminal suffering: the role of terminal sedation and voluntary refusal of food and fluids. ACP-ASIM End-of-Life Care Consensus Panel. American College of Physicians-American Society of Internal Medicine. *Annals of Internal Medicine* 123: 408–414.

Quill, T.E., R. Dresser, and D.W. Broca. 1997a. The rule of double effect – A critique of its role in end-of-life decision making. *The New England Journal of Medicine* 337: 1768–1771.

Quill, T.E., B. Lo, and D.W. Broca. 1997b. Palliative options of last resort: A comparison of voluntary stopping eating and drinking, terminal sedation, physician assisted suicide, and voluntary active euthanasia. *Journal of American Medical Association* 278: 2099–2104.

Quinn, W. 1989. Actions, intentions, and consequences: The doctrine of double effect. *Philosophy and Public Affairs* 18: 334–351.

Quinn, W. 1991. Reply to Boyle's "Who is entitled to double effect?". *The Journal of medicine and philosophy* 16: 511–514.

Regnard, C., R. George, E. Grogan, T. Harlow, S. Hutchison, J. Keen, S. McGettrick, C. Manson, S.A. Murray, V. Robinson, P. Stone, and C. Tallon. 2011. So, farewell then, doctrine of double effect. *British Medical Journal* 343: d4512. doi:10.1136/bmj.d4512.

Rietjens, J.A., A. van der Heide, A.M. Vrakking, B.D. Onwuteaka-Philipsen, P.J. van der Maas, and G. van der Wal. 2004. Physician reports of terminal sedation without hydration or nutrition for patients nearing death in the Netherlands. *Annals of Internal Medicine* 141: 178–185.

Rietjens, J.A., L. van Zuylen, H. van Veluw, L. van der Wijk, A. van der Heide, and C.C. van der Rijt. 2008. Palliative sedation in a specialized unit for acute palliative care in a cancer hospital: Comparing patients dying with and without palliative sedation. *Journal of Pain and Symptom Management* 36: 228–234.

Rousseau, P. 2001. Existential suffering and palliative sedation: A brief commentary with a proposal for clinical guidelines. *The American Journal of Hospice & Palliative Care* 18: 151–153.

Roy, D.J. 1990. Need they sleep before they die? *Journal of Palliative Care* 6: 3–4.

Royal Dutch Medical Association Committee on National Guideline for Palliative Sedation. 2009. *Guideline for palliative sedation 2009*. Utrecht: Royal Dutch Medical Association (KNMG).

Taboada, P. 2006. Principles of bioethics in palliative care. In *Textbook of palliative medicine*, ed. E. Bruera, I. Higginson, C. Ripamonti, and C. von Gunten, 85–91. London: Hodder Arnold.

Taboada, P. 2012. Sedación Paliativa (Parte I). Controversias sobre términos, definiciones y aplicaciones clínicas. [Controversies over terms, definitions and clinical applications]. *Acta Bioethica* 18(2): 155–162.

Taboada, P., A. Palma, B. Shand, et al. 2010. Ethics and medically assisted nutrition and hydration. In *Nutrition and the cancer patient*, ed. E. Del Fabbro, E. Bruera, W. Demark-Wahnefried, and V. Baracos, 295–318. Oxford: Oxford University.

Tulsky, J. 2006. Ethics in the practice of palliative care. In *Textbook of palliative medicine*, ed. E. Bruera, I. Higginson, C. Ripamonti, and C. von Gunten, 92–99. London: Hodder Arnold.

Veatch, R. 2003. *The basis of bioethics*, 2nd ed. Upper Saddle River: Prentice Hall.

Verkerk, M., E. van Wijick, J. Legemaele, and A. de Graeff. 2007. A National Guideline for Palliative Sedation in The Netherlands. *Journal of Pain and Symptom Management* 34(6): 666–670.

Vivanco, A. 2006. La Eutanasia ante el Derecho: Definición y penalización de la conducta eutanásica [Euthanasia within the Law: definition and sanctioning of euthanasic conduct]. *Ars Médica* 12: 53–92.

World Health Organization. 1990. *Alivio del dolor y tratamiento paliativo en cáncer. Informe de un Comité de expertos* [WHO expert committee on cancer pain relief and active supportive care], Technical report series 804, 11–12. Geneva: WHO.

Printed by Printforce, the Netherlands